ECCLESIASTES

❀

❀

EDITED BY Peter B. Steese

The Pennsylvania State University

ALLYN AND BACON, INC. • BOSTON, 1966

ALLYN AND BACON CASEBOOK SERIES

GENERAL EDITOR • LEONARD F. DEAN

PREFACE

The writer of Ecclesiastes approaches the problems of life from a perspective which appeals to contemporary readers. He does not assume a moralizing tone or offer his opinions in a didactic manner. No future utopia is promised nor is a solution given to the riddle of existence. The author instead speaks to men in their questionings, refusing to offer assurances or false hopes. His conclusions are based on personal experiences from a full life "under the sun" and he does not attempt to fabricate a systematic philosophy where he can find none.

Ecclesiastes almost was not included in the Old Testament. The Jewish Synod of Jamnia (about 100 A.D.) questioned the book, along with Esther and the Song of Solomon, because of its skeptical tone. It was finally received into the canon because the allusion in the opening verse to the Preacher as "the son of David, king in Jerusalem" suggested that Solomon was the author. The concluding verses also stressed a more orthodox obedience to the commandments of God and were felt to counteract the previous skeptical portions of the book. Although readers have commented for over two thousand years on the literary beauty of the book, many have been disturbed by the absence of an absolute value system. As recently as the beginning of this century, William Forbush could write: "The book of Ecclesiastes is not popular. It has furnished few texts for the clergy. As for the laity, they do not read it and are rather suspicious of it." [1] This certainly is no longer true. Far from being suspicious of the book, modern readers are attracted to Ecclesiastes because the author does not offer patent solutions to the frustrating problems of life. Instead he presents both the possibilities and limitations of life without illusion. The book today is accepted for precisely the reasons that caused previous generations to reject it.

The Biblical text in this casebook is that of the King James Version.

The related writings of Part Two range from the Egyptian "A Song of the Harper" to Paul Tillich's sermon, "The Right Time" and contain ideas relevant to the major themes of Ecclesiastes. Some of these relationships are mentioned in the introductory essay to Part Two; others are discussed in the questions at the end of the section. The

[1] *Ecclesiastes in the Metre of Omar* (Boston: Houghton Mifflin and Co., 1906), p. 3.

perceptive reader will discover many more common ideas for himself. To support this thematic relationship, the critical essays of Part Three help the reader to establish the historical setting of Ecclesiastes and enable him to trace some of the prevailing critical interpretations of the book. The first group of general questions shows how some of the topics of the three parts of the casebook are interrelated; the second group explores similarities between the theme of Ecclesiastes and several longer works not included in this text, such as *Siddhartha* by Hermann Hesse. It is my hope that this casebook will enable the reader to discover for himself how relevant the ideas expressed by the writer of Ecclesiastes are to the problems of contemporary life.

Peter B. Steese

CONTENTS

PART THREE: CRITICAL ESSAYS

PART ONE

✻

✻

ECCLESIASTES

INTRODUCTION

Ecclesiastes is a Greek term for "Preacher," the subtitle of the book which is repeated in the first verse. The original Hebrew word is *Koheleth*, meaning one who conducts a group or assembly, and because of the connotations surrounding the word preacher most contemporary writers prefer to use the Hebrew word.[1] It is true that the author of Ecclesiastes is anything but a preacher in the narrow sense of the term. No other book in the Old Testament attacks a broader subject than this one. In a manner as relentless and devastating as that of Voltaire in *Candide*, Koheleth systematically sets out to test his society. He first tries the path of social reform, only to discover that "that which is crooked cannot be made straight" (1:15). Material possessions are only vanity (etymologically the Hebrew word means breath or vapor), bringing "vexation of spirit" (2:11). Nature brings nothing new in its recurring cycles and man's life seems to share the meaninglessness of the endless routine of the seasons.

The pessimism of the book increases, for Koheleth is preoccupied not only with the senseless routine of life but also with death which comes alike to the wise man and the fool. The picture is not completely black, for man does have life. In vivid words Koheleth concludes that "a living dog is better than a dead lion." And knowledge of life and death itself gives man something inevitable to which he can attach meaning: "For the living know that they shall die: but the dead know not anything" (9:5). How similar this statement is to the reaction of Meursault to the priest in Albert Camus' *The Stranger*: "Actually, I was sure of myself, sure about everything, far surer than he; sure of my present life and of the death that was coming. That, no doubt, was all I had; but at least the certainty was something I could get my teeth into—just as it had got its teeth into me."[2]

Skeptical passages in Ecclesiastes have led some to believe that the writer was an agnostic. But the very existence of the world is proof to Koheleth of the existence of God. While the writer does not see the glory of God in nature observed by the Psalmist ("The heavens declare the glory of God; and the firmament showeth his handiwork."—Ps. 19:1), he does observe a pattern in the recurring seasons described in chapter 1 and the ordered affairs of mankind seen in chapter 3. But it is presumptuous for a mortal to think that he can understand God or even discern the meaning of His works, whether in nature or society:

[1] Throughout this casebook I have used Koheleth when referring to the author and Ecclesiastes when referring to the book.

[2] Trans. Stuart Gilbert (New York: Albert A. Knopf, Inc., 1946), p. 151.

"As thou knowest not what is the way of the spirit, nor how the bones do grow in the womb of her that is with child: even so thou knowest not the works of God who maketh all" (11:5). Man should work, enjoy the bounty of life and maintain a healthy humility before God, always remembering that He "is in heaven, and thou upon earth: therefore let thy words be few" (5:2).

In the past many who studied Ecclesiastes thought that it could be fully appreciated only by readers beyond the prime of life. St. Jerome believed it was intended for the middle-aged; Schopenhauer said that no one could really understand Ecclesiastes until he was seventy. Probably one reason for this conclusion is the maturity of Koheleth who writes from a lifetime of experience in seeking the meaning of existence. Another reason is that the interpreters of the allegorical picture of old age (12:1–7), always one of the favorite passages in the book, have overlooked the fact that this description is directed to the young man, opening "Remember now thy Creator in the days of thy youth." Perhaps we have aged earlier in the twentieth century. Life now moves at a far more rapid pace than in the world of Koheleth, St. Jerome, or even Schopenhauer. The *weltschmerz* felt by Koheleth was a very real emotion to the young, war-weary generation of Ernest Hemingway's *The Sun Also Rises*. The very title is taken from Ecclesiastes 1:5, part of the passage which describes the continual repetition of nature; and the lives of Hemingway's disillusioned expatriates reflect the meaninglessness of this cycle, the impossibility of finding real satisfaction in life.

The ideas expressed in Ecclesiastes seem more contemporary to the twentieth-century reader than those of any other book in the Bible. Man today distrusts systems of philosophy, and Ecclesiastes speaks to modern man in his questionings rather than attempting to provide answers to his problems. Koheleth in his skeptical attitude towards the institutions and philosophies of his society is similar in many respects to some existentialists who question the adequacy of human reason to explain the universe. In a sermon based on Ecclesiastes 3:1–8 entitled *The Right Time*, Paul Tillich emphasizes this similarity: "The spirit of the Preacher is strong today in our minds. His mood fills our philosophy and poetry. The vanity of human existence is described powerfully by those who call themselves philosophers or poets of existence. They are all the children of the Preacher, this great existentialist of his period." [3] For Koheleth, like modern man, the earthen vessels of material wealth, reputation and even wisdom itself have been shattered. Undergoing a mental turmoil comparable to that of Job, he rejects the conclusions of his forefathers and attempts to find a meaningful philosophy of life based on his own experience.

[3] *The New Being* (New York: Charles Scribner's Sons, 1955), p. 168.

ECCLESIASTES OR THE PREACHER

ALL IS VANITY

1 The words of the Preacher, the son of David, king in Jerusalem. ² Vanity of vanities, saith the Preacher, vanity of vanities; all is vanity. ³ What profit hath a man of all his labor which he taketh under the sun? ⁴ One generation passeth away, and another generation cometh: but the earth abideth for ever. ⁵ The sun also ariseth, and the sun goeth down, and hasteth to his place where he arose. ⁶ The wind goeth toward the south, and turneth about unto the north; it whirleth about continually, and the wind returneth again according to his circuits. ⁷ All the rivers run into the sea; yet the sea is not full: unto the place from whence the rivers come, thither they return again. ⁸ All things are full of labor; man cannot utter it: the eye is not satisfied with seeing, nor the ear filled with hearing. ⁹ The thing that hath been, it is that which shall be; and that which is done is that which shall be done: and there is no new thing under the sun. ¹⁰ Is there any thing whereof it may be said, See, this is new? it hath been already of old time, which was before us. ¹¹ There is no remembrance of former things; neither shall there be any remembrance of things that are to come with those that shall come after.

THE EXPERIENCE OF THE PREACHER

12 I the Preacher was king over Israel in Jerusalem. ¹³ And I gave my heart to seek and search out by wisdom concerning all things that are done under heaven: this sore travail hath God given to the sons of man to be exercised therewith. ¹⁴ I have seen all the works that are done under the sun; and, behold, all is vanity and vexation of spirit. ¹⁵ That which is crooked cannot be made straight: and that which is wanting cannot be numbered.

16 I communed with mine own heart, saying, Lo, I am come to great estate, and have gotten more wisdom than all they that have been before me in Jerusalem: yea, my heart had great experience of wisdom and knowledge. ¹⁷ And I gave my heart to know wisdom, and to know madness and folly: I perceived that this also is vexation of spirit. ¹⁸ For in much wisdom is much grief: and he that increaseth knowledge increaseth sorrow.

2 I said in mine heart, Go to now, I will prove thee with mirth; there-fore enjoy pleasure: and, behold, this also is vanity. [2] I said of laughter, It is mad: and of mirth, What doeth it? [3] I sought in mine heart to give myself unto wine, yet acquainting mine heart with wisdom; and to lay hold on folly, till I might see what was that good for the sons of men, which they should do under the heaven all the days of their life. [4] I made me great works; I builded me houses; I planted me vine-yards: [5] I made me gardens and orchards, and I planted trees in them of all kinds of fruits: [6] I made me pools of water, to water therewith the wood that bringeth forth trees: [7] I got me servants and maidens, and had servants born in my house; also I had great possessions of great and small cattle above all that were in Jerusalem before me: [8] I gathered me also silver and gold, and the peculiar treasure of kings and of the provinces: I got me men singers and women singers, and the delights of the sons of men, as musical instruments, and that of all sorts.

9 So I was great, and increased more than all that were before me in Jerusalem: also my wisdom remained with me. [10] And whatsoever mine eyes desired I kept not from them, I withheld not my heart from any joy; for my heart rejoiced in all my labor: and this was my portion of all my labor. [11] Then I looked on all the works that my hands had wrought, and on the labor that I had labored to do: and, behold, all was vanity and vexation of spirit, and there was no profit under the sun.

12 And I turned myself to behold wisdom, and madness, and folly: for what can the man do that cometh after the king? even that which hath been already done. [13] Then I saw that wisdom excelleth folly, as far as light excelleth darkness. [14] The wise man's eyes are in his head; but the fool walketh in darkness: and I myself perceived also that one event happeneth to them all. [15] Then said I in my heart, As it happeneth to the fool, so it happeneth even to me; and why was I then more wise? Then I said in my heart, that this also is vanity. [16] For there is no re-membrance of the wise more than of the fool for ever; seeing that which now is the days to come shall all be forgotten. And how dieth the wise man? as the fool. [17] Therefore I hated life; because the work that is wrought under the sun is grievous unto me: for all is vanity and vexation of spirit.

18 Yea, I hated all my labor which I had taken under the sun: because I should leave it unto the man that shall be after me. [19] And who knoweth whether he shall be a wise man or a fool? yet shall he have rule over all my labor wherein I have labored, and wherein I have showed myself wise under the sun. This is also vanity. [20] Therefore I went about to cause my heart to despair of all the labor which I took under the sun. [21] For there is a man whose labor is in wisdom, and in knowledge, and in equity; yet to a man that hath not labored therein shall he leave it for his portion. This also is vanity and a great evil. [22] For what hath man of all his labor, and of the vexation of his heart, wherein

he hath labored under the sun? [23] For all his days are sorrows, and his travail grief; yea, his heart taketh not rest in the night. This is also vanity.

24 There is nothing better for a man, than that he should eat and drink, and that he should make his soul enjoy good in his labor. This also I saw, that it was from the hand of God. [25] For who can eat, or who else can hasten hereunto, more than I? [26] For God giveth to a man that is good in his sight, wisdom, and knowledge, and joy: but to the sinner he giveth travail, to gather and to heap up, that he may give to him that is good before God. This also is vanity and vexation of spirit.

A TIME FOR EVERYTHING

3 To every thing there is a season, and a time to every purpose under the heaven:

2 a time to be born, and a time to die;
a time to plant, and a time to pluck up that which
is planted;

3 a time to kill, and a time to heal;
a time to break down, and a time to build up;

4 a time to weep, and a time to laugh;
a time to mourn, and a time to dance;

5 a time to cast away stones, and a time to gather
stones together;
a time to embrace, and a time to refrain from
embracing;

6 a time to get, and a time to lose;
a time to keep, and a time to cast away;

7 a time to rend, and a time to sew;
a time to keep silence, and a time to speak

8 a time to love, and a time to hate;
a time of war, and a time of peace.

9 What profit hath he that worketh in that wherein he laboreth?

10 I have seen the travail, which God hath given to the sons of men to be exercised in it. [11] He hath made every thing beautiful in his time: also he hath set the world in their heart, so that no man can find out the work that God maketh from the beginning to the end. [12] I know that there is no good in them, but for a man to rejoice, and to do good in his life. [13] And also that every man should eat and drink, and enjoy the good of all his labor, it is the gift of God. [14] I know that, whatsoever God doeth, it shall be for ever: nothing can be put to it, nor any thing taken from it: and God doeth it, that men should fear before him. [15] That which hath been is now; and that which is to be hath already been; and God requireth that which is past.

THE INJUSTICE OF LIFE

16 And moreover I saw under the sun the place of judgment, that wickedness was there; and the place of righteousness, that iniquity was there. ¹⁷ I said in mine heart, God shall judge the righteous and the wicked: for there is a time there for every purpose and for every work. ¹⁸ I said in mine heart concerning the estate of the sons of men, that God might manifest them, and that they might see that they themselves are beasts. ¹⁹ For that which befalleth the sons of men befalleth beasts; even one thing befalleth them: as the one dieth, so dieth the other; yea, they have all one breath; so that a man hath no pre-eminence above a beast: for all is vanity. ²⁰ All go unto one place; all are of the dust, and all turn to dust again. ²¹ Who knoweth the spirit of man that goeth upward, and the spirit of the beast that goeth downward to the earth? ²² Wherefore I perceive that there is nothing better, than that a man should rejoice in his own works; for that is his portion: for who shall bring him to see what shall be after him?

4 So I returned, and considered all the oppressions that are done under the sun: and behold the tears of such as were oppressed, and they had no comforter; and on the side of their oppressors there was power; but they had no comforter. ² Wherefore I praised the dead which are already dead, more than the living which are yet alive. ³ Yea, better is he than both they, which hath not yet been, who hath not seen the evil work that is done under the sun.

4 Again, I considered all travail, and every right work, that for this a man is envied of his neighbor. This is also vanity and vexation of spirit.

5 The fool foldeth his hands together, and eateth his own flesh.

6 Better is a handful with quietness, than both the hands full with travail and vexation of spirit.

7 Then I returned, and I saw vanity under the sun. ⁸ There is one alone, and there is not a second; yea, he hath neither child nor brother: yet is there no end of all his labor; neither is his eye satisfied with riches; neither saith he, For whom do I labor, and bereave my soul of good ? This is also vanity, yea, it is a sore travail.

9 Two are better than one; because they have a good reward for their labor. ¹⁰ For if they fall, the one will lift up his fellow: but woe to him that is alone when he falleth; for he hath not another to help him up. ¹¹ Again, if two lie together, then they have heat: but how can one be warm alone? ¹² And if one prevail against him, two shall withstand him; and a threefold cord is not quickly broken.

13 Better is a poor and a wise child, than an old and foolish king, who will no more be admonished. ¹⁴ For out of prison he cometh to reign; whereas also he that is born in his kingdom becometh poor. ¹⁵ I considered all the living which walk under the sun, with the second

child that shall stand up in his stead. ¹⁶ There is no end of all the people, even of all that have been before them: they also that come after shall not rejoice in him. Surely this also is vanity and vexation of spirit.

THE FOLLY OF RASH VOWS

5 Keep thy foot when thou goest to the house of God, and be more ready to hear, than to give the sacrifice of fools: for they consider not that they do evil. ² Be not rash with thy mouth, and let not thine heart be hasty to utter any thing before God: for God is in heaven, and thou upon earth: therefore let thy words be few.

3 For a dream cometh through the multitude of business; and a fool's voice is known by multitude of words.

4 When thou vowest a vow unto God, defer not to pay it; for he hath no pleasure in fools: pay that which thou hast vowed. ⁵ Better is it that thou shouldest not vow, than that thou shouldest vow and not pay. ⁶ Suffer not thy mouth to cause thy flesh to sin; neither say thou before the angel, that it was an error: wherefore should God be angry at thy voice, and destroy the work of thine hands?

7 For in the multitude of dreams and many words there are also divers vanities: but fear thou God.

THE VANITY OF LIFE

8 If thou seest the oppression of the poor, and violent perverting of judgment and justice in a province, marvel not at the matter: for he that is higher than the highest regardeth; and there be higher than they. ⁹ Moreover the profit of the earth is for all: the king himself is served by the field.

10 He that loveth silver shall not be satisfied with silver; nor he that loveth abundance with increase: this is also vanity.

11 When goods increase, they are increased that eat them: and what good is there to the owners thereof, saving the beholding of them with their eyes?

12 The sleep of a laboring man is sweet, whether he eat little or much: but the abundance of the rich will not suffer him to sleep.

13 There is a sore evil which I have seen under the sun, namely, riches kept for the owners thereof to their hurt. ¹⁴ But those riches perish by evil travail: and he begetteth a son, and there is nothing in his hand. ¹⁵ As he came forth of his mother's womb, naked shall he return to go as he came, and shall take nothing of his labor, which he may carry away in his hand. ¹⁶ And this also is a sore evil, that in all points as he came, so shall he go: and what profit hath he that hath labored for the wind? ¹⁷ All his days also he eateth in darkness, and he hath much sorrow and wrath with his sickness.

18 Behold that which I have seen: it is good and comely for one to eat and to drink, and to enjoy the good of all his labor that he taketh under the sun all the days of his life, which God giveth him: for it is his portion. ¹⁹ Every man also to whom God hath given riches and wealth, and hath given him power to eat thereof, and to take his portion, and to rejoice in his labor; this is the gift of God. ²⁰ For he shall not much remember the days of his life; because God answereth him in the joy of his heart.

6 There is an evil which I have seen under the sun, and it is common among men: ² a man to whom God hath given riches, wealth, and honor, so that he wanteth nothing for his soul of all that he desireth, yet God giveth him not power to eat thereof, but a stranger eateth it: this is vanity, and it is an evil disease. ³ If a man beget a hundred children, and live many years, so that the days of his years be many, and his soul be not filled with good, and also that he have no burial; I say, that an untimely birth is better than he. ⁴ For he cometh in with vanity, and departeth in darkness, and his name shall be covered with darkness. ⁵ Moreover he hath not seen the sun, nor known any thing: this hath more rest than the other. ⁶ Yea, though he live a thousand years twice told, yet hath he seen no good: do not all go to one place?

7 All the labor of man is for his mouth, and yet the appetite is not filled. ⁸ For what hath the wise more than the fool? what hath the poor, that knoweth to walk before the living? ⁹ Better is the sight of the eyes than the wandering of the desire: this is also vanity and vexation of spirit.

10 That which hath been is named already, and it is known that it is man: neither may he contend with him that is mightier than he. ¹¹ Seeing there be many things that increase vanity, what is man the better? ¹² For who knoweth what is good for man in this life, all the days of his vain life which he spendeth as a shadow? for who can tell a man what shall be after him under the sun?

WISDOM AND FOLLY COMPARED

7 A good name is better than precious ointment; and the day of death than the day of one's birth. ² It is better to go to the house of mourning, than to go to the house of feasting: for that is the end of all men; and the living will lay it to his heart. ³ Sorrow is better than laughter: for by the sadness of the countenance the heart is made better. ⁴ The heart of the wise is in the house of mourning; but the heart of fools is in the house of mirth. ⁵ It is better to hear the rebuke of the wise, than for a man to hear the song of fools. ⁶ For as the crackling of thorns under a pot, so is the laughter of the fool: this also is vanity. ⁷ Surely oppression maketh a wise man mad; and a gift

destroyeth the heart. [8] Better is the end of a thing than the beginning thereof: and the patient in spirit is better than the proud in spirit. [9] Be not hasty in thy spirit to be angry: for anger resteth in the bosom of fools. [10] Say not thou, What is the cause that the former days were better than these? for thou dost not inquire wisely concerning this. [11] Wisdom is good with an inheritance: and by it there is profit to them that see the sun. [12] For wisdom is a defense, and money is a defense: but the excellency of knowledge is, that wisdom giveth life to them that have it. [13] Consider the work of God: for who can make that straight, which he hath made crooked?

14 In the day of prosperity be joyful, but in the day of adversity consider: God also hath set the one over against the other, to the end that man should find nothing after him.

15 All things have I seen in the days of my vanity: there is a just man that perisheth in his righteousness, and there is a wicked man that prolongeth his life in his wickedness. [16] Be not righteous over much, neither make thyself over wise: why shouldest thou destroy thyself? [17] Be not over much wicked, neither be thou foolish: why shouldest thou die before thy time? [18] It is good that thou shouldest take hold of this; yea, also from this withdraw not thine hand: for he that feareth God shall come forth of them all.

19 Wisdom strengtheneth the wise more than ten mighty men which are in the city.

20 For there is not a just man upon earth, that doeth good, and sinneth not.

21 Also take no heed unto all words that are spoken; lest thou hear thy servant curse thee: [22] for oftentimes also thine own heart knoweth that thou thyself likewise hast cursed others.

23 All this have I proved by wisdom: I said, I will be wise; but it was far from me. [24] That which is far off, and exceeding deep, who can find it out? [25] I applied mine heart to know, and to search, and to seek out wisdom, and the reason of things, and to know the wickedness of folly, even of foolishness and madness: [26] and I find more bitter than death the woman, whose heart is snares and nets, and her hands as bands: whoso pleaseth God shall escape from her; but the sinner shall be taken by her. [27] Behold, this have I found, saith the Preacher, counting one by one, to find out the account; [28] which yet my soul seeketh, but I find not: one man among a thousand have I found; but a woman among all those have I not found. [29] Lo, this only have I found, that God hath made man upright; but they have sought out many inventions.

8 Who is as the wise man? and who knoweth the interpretation of a thing? a man's wisdom maketh his face to shine, and the boldness of his face shall be changed.

2 I counsel thee to keep the king's commandment, and that in regard of the oath of God. [3] Be not hasty to go out of his sight: stand not in

an evil thing; for he doeth whatsoever pleaseth him. ⁴ Where the word of a king is, there is power: and who may say unto him, What doest thou? ⁵ Whoso keepeth the commandment shall feel no evil thing: and a wise man's heart discerneth both time and judgment. ⁶ Because to every purpose there is time and judgment, therefore the misery of man is great upon him. ⁷ For he knoweth not that which shall be: for who can tell him when it shall be? ⁸ There is no man that hath power over the spirit to retain the spirit; neither hath he power in the day of death: and there is no discharge in that war; neither shall wickedness deliver those that are given to it. ⁹ All this have I seen, and applied my heart unto every work that is done under the sun: there is a time wherein one man ruleth over another to his own hurt.

THE INEQUALITIES OF LIFE

10 And so I saw the wicked buried, who had come and gone from the place of the holy, and they were forgotten in the city where they had so done: this is also vanity. ¹¹ Because sentence against an evil work is not executed speedily, therefore the heart of the sons of men is fully set in them to do evil. ¹² Though a sinner do evil a hundred times, and his days be prolonged, yet surely I know that it shall be well with them that fear God, which fear before him: ¹³ but it shall not be well with the wicked, neither shall he prolong his days, which are as a shadow; because he feareth not before God.

14 There is a vanity which is done upon the earth; that there be just men, unto whom it happeneth according to the work of the wicked; again, there be wicked men, to whom it happeneth according to the work of the righteous: I said that this also is vanity. ¹⁵ Then I commended mirth, because a man hath no better thing under the sun, than to eat, and to drink, and to be merry: for that shall abide with him of his labor the days of his life, which God giveth him under the sun.

16 When I applied mine heart to know wisdom, and to see the business that is done upon the earth: (for also there is that neither day nor night seeth sleep with his eyes:) ¹⁷ then I beheld all the work of God, that a man cannot find out the work that is done under the sun: because though a man labor to seek it out, yet he shall not find it; yea further; though a wise man think to know it, yet shall he not be able to find it.

9 For all this I considered in my heart even to declare all this, that the righteous, and the wise, and their works, are in the hand of God: no man knoweth either love or hatred by all that is before them. ² All things come alike to all: there is one event to the righteous, and to the wicked; to the good and to the clean, and to the unclean; to him that sacrificeth, and to him that sacrificeth not: as is the good, so is the sinner; and he that sweareth, as he that feareth an oath. ³ This is an evil among all things that are done under the sun, that there is one event unto all: yea, also the heart of the sons of men is full of evil, and madness is in their heart while they live, and after that they go to the dead. ⁴ For to him that is joined to all the living there is hope: for a living dog is better than a dead lion. ⁵ For the living know that they shall die: but the dead know not any thing, neither have they any more a reward; for the memory of them is forgotten. ⁶ Also their love, and their hatred, and their envy, is now perished; neither have they any more a portion for ever in any thing that is done under the sun.

7 Go thy way, eat thy bread with joy, and drink thy wine with a merry heart; for God now accepteth thy works.

8 Let thy garments be always white; and let thy head lack no ointment.

9 Live joyfully with the wife whom thou lovest all the days of the life of thy vanity, which he hath given thee under the sun, all the days of thy vanity: for that is thy portion in this life, and in thy labor which thou takest under the sun. ¹⁰ Whatsoever thy hand findeth to do, do it with thy might; for there is no work, nor device, nor knowledge, nor wisdom, in the grave, whither thou goest.

11 I returned, and saw under the sun, that the race is not to the swift, nor the battle to the strong, neither yet bread to the wise, nor yet riches to men of understanding, nor yet favor to men of skill; but time and chance happeneth to them all. ¹² For man also knoweth not his time: as the fishes that are taken in an evil net, and as the birds that are caught in the snare; so are the sons of men snared in an evil time, when it falleth suddenly upon them.

13 This wisdom have I seen also under the sun, and it seemed great unto me: ¹⁴ there was a little city, and few men within it; and there came a great king against it, and besieged it, and built great bulwarks against it. ¹⁵ Now there was found in it a poor wise man, and he by his wisdom delivered the city; yet no man remembered that same poor man. ¹⁶ Then said I, Wisdom is better than strength: nevertheless the poor man's wisdom is despised, and his words are not heard.

17 The words of wise men are heard in quiet more than the cry of him that ruleth among fools. ¹⁸ Wisdom is better than weapons of war: but one sinner destroyeth much good.

THE EXCELLENCE OF WISDOM

10 Dead flies cause the ointment of the apothecary to send forth a stinking savor: so doth a little folly him that is in reputation for wisdom and honor. ² A wise man's heart is at his right hand; but a fool's heart at his left. ³ Yea also, when he that is a fool walketh by the

way, his wisdom faileth him, and he saith to every one that he is a fool. ⁴ If the spirit of the ruler rise up against thee, leave not thy place; for yielding pacifieth great offenses.

5 There is an evil which I have seen under the sun, as an error which proceedeth from the ruler: ⁶ folly is set in great dignity, and the rich sit in low place. ⁷ I have seen servants upon horses, and princes walking as servants upon the earth. ⁸ He that diggeth a pit shall fall into it; and whoso breaketh a hedge, a serpent shall bite him. ⁹ Whoso removeth stones shall be hurt therewith; and he that cleaveth wood shall be endangered thereby. ¹⁰ If the iron be blunt, and he do not whet the edge, then must he put to more strength: but wisdom is profitable to direct. ¹¹ Surely the serpent will bite without enchantment; and a babbler is no better.

12 The words of a wise man's mouth are gracious; but the lips of a fool will swallow up himself. ¹³ The beginning of the words of his mouth is foolishness: and the end of his talk is mischievous madness. ¹⁴ A fool also is full of words: a man cannot tell what shall be; and what shall be after him, who can tell him? ¹⁵ The labor of the foolish wearieth every one of them, because he knoweth not how to go to the city.

16 Woe to thee, O land, when thy king is a child, and thy princes eat in the morning! ¹⁷ Blessed art thou, O land, when thy king is the son of nobles, and thy princes eat in due season, for strength, and not for drunkenness! ¹⁸ By much slothfulness the building decayeth; and through idleness of the hands the house droppeth through. ¹⁹ A feast is made for laughter, and wine maketh merry: but money answereth all things. ²⁰ Curse not the king, no not in thy thought; and curse not the rich in thy bedchamber: for a bird of the air shall carry the voice, and that which hath wings shall tell the matter.

11 Cast thy bread upon the waters: for thou shalt find it after many days. ² Give a portion to seven, and also to eight; for thou knowest not what evil shall be upon the earth. ³ If the clouds be full of rain, they empty themselves upon the earth: and if the tree fall toward the south, or toward the north, in the place where the tree falleth, there it shall be. ⁴ He that observeth the wind shall not sow; and he that regardeth the clouds shall not reap. ⁵ As thou knowest not what is the way of the spirit, nor how the bones do grow in the womb of her that is with child: even so thou knowest not the works of God who maketh all. ⁶ In the morning sow thy seed, and in the evening withhold not thine hand: for thou knowest not whether shall prosper, either this or that, or whether they both shall be alike good.

7 Truly the light is sweet, and a pleasant thing it is for the eyes to behold the sun: ⁸ but if a man live many years, and rejoice in them all; yet let him remember the days of darkness; for they shall be many. All that cometh is vanity.

ADVICE TO THE YOUNG

9 Rejoice, O young man, in thy youth; and let thy heart cheer thee in the days of thy youth, and walk in the ways of thine heart, and in the sight of thine eyes: but know thou, that for all these things God will bring thee into judgment. [10] Therefore remove sorrow from thy heart, and put away evil from thy flesh: for childhood and youth are vanity.

12 Remember now thy Creator in the days of thy youth, while the evil days come not, nor the years draw nigh, when thou shalt say, I have no pleasure in them; [2] while the sun, or the light, or the moon, or the stars, be not darkened, nor the clouds return after the rain: [3] in the day when the keepers of the house shall tremble, and the strong men shall bow themselves, and the grinders cease because they are few, and those that look out of the windows be darkened, [4] and the doors shall be shut in the streets, when the sound of the grinding is low, and he shall rise up at the voice of the bird, and all the daughters of music shall be brought low; [5] also when they shall be afraid of that which is high, and fears shall be in the way, and the almond tree shall flourish, and the grasshopper shall be a burden, and desire shall fail: because man goeth to his long home, and the mourners go about the streets: [6] or ever the silver cord be loosed, or the golden bowl be broken, or the pitcher be broken at the fountain, or the wheel broken at the cistern. [7] Then shall the dust return to the earth as it was: and the spirit shall return unto God who gave it. [8] Vanity of vanities, saith the Preacher; all is vanity.

THE WHOLE DUTY OF MAN

9 And moreover, because the Preacher was wise, he still taught the people knowledge; yea, he gave good heed, and sought out, and set in order many proverbs. [10] The Preacher sought to find out acceptable words: and that which was written was upright, even words of truth.

11 The words of the wise are as goads, and as nails fastened by the masters of assemblies, which are given from one shepherd. [12] And further, by these, my son, be admonished: of making many books there is no end; and much study is a weariness of the flesh.

13 Let us hear the conclusion of the whole matter: Fear God, and keep his commandments: for this is the whole duty of man. [14] For God shall bring every work into judgment, with every secret thing, whether it be good, or whether it be evil.

CONSIDERATIONS AND QUESTIONS
FOR DISCUSSION

1. In what ways does Koheleth try to find meaning in life in chapters 1 and 2? Does he cover all possibilities? Why isn't wisdom the answer to man's problems? Notice that Koheleth explores madness and folly in this search. Can one understand wisdom without a knowledge of folly any more than one can understand goodness without an awareness of evil?

2. In his search for pleasure in chapter 2, Koheleth states: "For my heart rejoiced in all my labor," implying that the race is often more enjoyable than the victory. Find other passages in the book which support this position.

3. Chapter 3 describes an ordered existence. Does this pattern give meaning to man's life? What statements are made about man's relationship to God in this chapter? The portion of verse 11 which reads "He hath set the world in their heart" is translated in the Revised Standard Version "He has put infinity in man's mind." Is this a description of man's desire to go beyond human limitations, to search for forbidden knowledge like Dr. Faustus? Can we see this desire in Koheleth's search to find meaning for his own life?

4. Chapter 7 contains maxims similar in form to those found in the book of Proverbs and the other wisdom writings of the Old Testament. However, Koheleth uses this traditional vocabulary to express his own concepts. For example, Proverbs 22:1 states: "A good name is rather to be chosen than great riches, and loving favour rather than silver and gold." The second half of the proverb reinforces the ideas expressed in the first part. Notice how Koheleth takes this proverb and gives it a pessimistic conclusion in 7:1. Relate the other proverbs in this chapter to the opinions expressed in the rest of Ecclesiastes.

5. Ecclesiastes 8:15 commends the *carpe diem* philosophy as an answer to the injustices of life. Man must seize the pleasures of the day and enjoy each moment. But unlike some Epicureans, Koheleth does not stop here. What one event is a constant threat to man's existence? Can the man who centers his life on the proverb "Eat, drink and be merry" ever completely forget the other half of the sentence?

6. Koheleth says that "time and chance happeneth to . . . all" (9.11). But men react to time in different ways. Some feel that time can be compared to a flowing river which carries all men relentlessly towards death. Others, in the words of Henry Thoreau, conclude that "time is but the stream I go a-fishing in," implying that man must use and enjoy

time rather than fear it. Which of these two positions would Koheleth be likely to accept? Why?

7. Ecclesiastes has been called "the most unecclesiastical book in the Bible." What evidence in the book supports this statement? In what ways does Koheleth avoid making the doctrinaire statements we would expect of a preacher?

8. The word "vanity" is repeated frequently throughout the book and helps set the prevailing tone. What does the word mean in this context? What connotations are suggested by the etymological meaning of the Hebrew word for vanity: breath or vapor? Notice how the word accumulates meaning as it is used throughout the book. Not only do all attempts to find meaning in life lead to vanity, but even the statements Koheleth makes about his experience are described as "vanity and vexation of spirit."

9. Another phrase which is often repeated is "under the sun." What is its meaning? Does this limit the context of Koheleth's statements and leave room for the fear of God mentioned in 12:13?

10. Is Koheleth a detached observer rather than an active participant in life's trials? When he argues that the "crooked cannot be made straight," that man cannot change the world, is he writing from observation or experience? Can one contend that his picture of the world is static in contrast to the dynamic world of the Old Testament prophets such as Amos, Isaiah or Jeremiah?

11. Ecclesiastes has often been called a pessimistic or a negative book. But is this really "the conclusion of the whole matter"? What two things can man know? Can man construct his life around these realities?

12. Compare Koheleth's attitude with that of modern existentialist writers who feel that human reason cannot explain the enigma of the universe. Is this stance similar to Koheleth's rejection of wisdom? Some existentialists would go on to say that man, sensing this meaninglessness, arrives at a feeling of anxiety and loneliness. Can Koheleth's repeated use of the word "vanity" be seen as an expression of this meaninglessness? Sartre and other existentialists would argue that when man becomes aware of the meaninglessness of his situation, he can move to give his life meaning through action. Find passages in Ecclesiastes which would substantiate this conclusion.

13. Some commentators have felt that the Biblical book of Job illustrates a nobler skepticism than that of Ecclesiastes because Job moves through the shadows of doubt to faith while Koheleth never gets beyond the doubts. Which type of skepticism do you feel is nobler? Which type seems more closely related to your own experiences? Can questioning and honest doubting lead to a firmer faith?

14. Compare the Revised Standard Version of Ecclesiastes to the King James Version. Find phrases which are more easily understood, such as "striving after wind" instead of the older "vexation of spirit." Notice that the word "vanity" has been retained in the Revised Standard Version even though in other sections of this version words like empti-

ness (Job 7:3), breath (Psalm 93:11), and worthlessness (Jer 2:5) have been substituted. Why do you think the word "vanity" is retained in Ecclesiastes? In what other ways has the Revised Standard Version attempted to preserve the literary flavor of the King James Version? Make similar comparisons using other translations such as the Jewish Publication Society of America edition of the Masoretic Text, the Catholic Confraternity Version or the Monsignor Ronald A. Knox translation.

PART TWO

❀

❀

RELATED WRITINGS

INTRODUCTION

The major ideas of Ecclesiastes have found varied expression in literature, for throughout history men have searched to find the meaning of life and have tried to reconcile themselves to the inevitable fact of death. The hero of the Babylonian epic *Gilgamesh*, written about 2000 B.C., fears death and desires to find the secret of immortality. But Shamash tells him: "Gilgamesh, whither rovest thou? The life thou pursuest thou shalt not find." Gilgamesh must enjoy the pleasures of this life, advice similar to that given by Koheleth in Ecclesiastes 8:15. The finality of death is vividly described in *A Song of the Harper* written by an Egyptian poet a thousand years before Ecclesiastes. Although the harper does not feel that death is the end, his skeptical attitude about knowledge of the future life is unusual in a culture which was based on the certainty of an afterlife, a certainty seen in the elaborate preparations of the pharaohs in building their pyramids.

One of the central problems of Koheleth is foreshadowed in earlier Old Testament writings in which one can trace the development of the Hebrew concept of divine reward and punishment. Psalm 1 clearly differentiates between the earthly rewards which the righteous man may expect and the punishment which will be meted out to the wicked. The maxims found in Proverbs elaborate this doctrine of the two ways. Koheleth attacks this teaching vigorously. The position of the wisdom writers represented in Proverbs is questioned and even contradicted by Koheleth who boasts, "I have communed with mine own heart . . . and have gotten more wisdom than all they that have been before me in Jerusalem" (1:16). In his experience, the righteous have often been punished and the evil rewarded. Life cannot be explained by the ready-made aphorisms of the earlier wisdom schools. Man must accept the fact that he cannot understand the way in which God works. Perhaps this conclusion raises more questions than it answers; perhaps it does not bring the comfort of the earlier wisdom writings. But Koheleth refuses to propound a solution which cannot be proved in practical life.

Some critics have felt that the Wisdom of Solomon (dated between 40 B.C. and 40 A.D.) was written to answer some of the problems unresolved in Ecclesiastes. The book shows the influence of Hellenistic thought, particularly in the introduction of the Greek concept of an afterlife. This offers an escape from the dilemma which had confronted Koheleth. The justice which appears to be denied to the good man on earth is really given in heaven: "But the righteous live for evermore;

their reward is with the Lord, and the care of them is with the most High. Therefore shall they receive a glorious kingdom, and a beautiful crown from the Lord's hand" (Wisdom: 5:15, 16).

Koheleth recognized that there are actually two types of wisdom. The first is the wisdom of man which is vanity; the second is the wisdom of God which man cannot discover. In I Corinthians 1:13–2:17 too, the lower "wisdom of this world" is contrasted to the higher wisdom of God. But man can discover this higher wisdom, for God has revealed it to him through Christ. The passage closes with the ringing affirmation "But we have the mind of Christ;" and the influence of this higher wisdom can be seen in the selected writings of John Donne, Blaise Pascal, Samuel Johnson, T. S. Eliot and Paul Tillich.

Marcus Aurelius in *Meditations* (c. 180 A.D.) approaches the problems of life and the question of death in a manner comparable to the opening of Ecclesiastes. Even though they treat similar themes, however, Aurelius is more the detached observer than Koheleth and is able to keep from becoming emotionally involved. He can stoically conclude that one who desires "posthumous fame does not consider that every one of those who remember him will himself also die very soon" (Sec. 19), while Koheleth is obviously greatly disturbed that "there is no remembrance of the wise more than of the fool for ever; seeing that which now is in the days to come shall all be forgotten" (2:16).

St. Augustine in *The City of God* feels that the writer of Ecclesiastes vividly described the vanity of life in the earthly city of men. Yet Koheleth must have recognized the heavenly city of God for he "devoted this whole book to a full exposure of this vanity, evidently with no other object than that we might long for that life in which there is no vanity under the sun, but verity under Him who made the sun." John Donne's *Sermon XIX* from Ecclesiastes 12:1 ("Remember now thy creator in the dayes of thy youth.") is a Christian interpretation of the text. Donne follows the passage word by word, defining each from other Biblical passages and writings from the church fathers. Blaise Pascal, also writing from the Christian perspective, vividly portrays the dilemma of man —a dilemma which easily leads to skepticism: "But, wretched as we are, and more so than if there were no greatness in our condition, we have an idea of happiness, and cannot reach it. We perceive an image of truth, and possess only a lie." Man has at the same time too little knowledge and too much. In the words of Koheleth, the Creator "has put eternity into man's mind, yet so that he cannot find out what God has done from the beginning to the end" (Revised Standard Version, 3:11).

Samuel Johnson in *The Vanity of Human Wishes* formally sets out to "survey mankind" and its pretensions. In the poem the word "vanity" sometimes means pride, but frequently it has the connotations of breath or vapor found in Ecclesiastes. Johnson describes how man "betrayed by venturous pride . . . Shuns fancied ills, or chases airy good," only to discover like Koheleth that "all is vanity." The pretensions of man are also portrayed in Nathaniel Hawthorne's short story, *The Ambitious Guest*. The young stranger who feels that he has a great destiny infects the other members of the New England family group. Caught in a landslide, he and his dream of earthly immortality are destroyed, "his death and his existence equally a doubt!"

The vanity of life and the meaninglessness of death sometimes turn men to pleasure. Koheleth himself counsels pleasure in moderation: "It is good and comely for one to eat and to drink, and to enjoy the good of all his labor that he taketh under the sun all the days of his life, which God giveth him: for it is his portion" (5:18). Omar Khayyám in the Persian *Rubáiyát* also advises man to "fill the Cup, and in the fir of Spring/Your Winter-garment of Repentance fling" (25–26).

T. S. Eliot is preoccupied with time in the opening sections of *East Coker*, using phrases and ideas which are reminiscent of Ecclesiastes 3:

> Houses live and die: there is a time for building
> And a time for living and for generation
> And a time for the wind to break the loosened pane
> And to shake the wainscot where the field-mouse trots
> And to shake the tattered arras woven with a silent motto.

Paul Tillich bases his sermon, *The Right Time*, on the same portion, asserting that man is timed whereas God is beyond time. Time is affirmed by eternity for "through our timing [God] elevates the time of vanity into the time of fulfillment." Both Eliot and Tillich use Ecclesiastes as a foundation which gives the message of Christ real meaning. Both find in the book a picture of the "old reality" which anticipates the "new reality" of Christ.

THE EPIC OF GILGAMESH*

Tablet X

This tablet, which traces further the successive stages in Gilgamesh's quest of immortality, happens to be represented by as many as four separate versions. Two of these, however, the Hittite and Hurrian, are extant only in fragments that are too slight for connected translation. Substantial portions are available, on the other hand, in the Old Babylonian and Assyrian recensions.

Old Babylonian Version

(i)

(top broken away)

"[. . .] . . .
With their skins [he clothes himself], as he eats flesh.
[.] . . , O Gilgamesh, which has not happened
As long as my wind drives the waters."
Shamash was distraught, as he betook himself to him;
He says to Gilgamesh:
"Gilgamesh, whither rovest thou?
The life thou pursuest thou shalt not find."
Gilgamesh says to him, to valiant Shamash:
"After marching (and) roving over the steppe,   (10)
Must I lay my head in the heart of the earth
That I may sleep through all the years?
Let mine eyes behold the sun
    That I may have my fill of the light!
Darkness withdraws when there is enough light.
May one who indeed is dead behold yet the radiance
    of the sun!"

(ii)

(Beginning lost. Gilgamesh is addressing Siduri, the ale-wife:)

"He who with me underwent all hard[ships]—
Enkidu, whom I loved dearly,

* Reprinted from *The Ancient Near East: An Anthology of Texts and Pictures*, edited by James B. Pritchard, by permission of Princeton University Press. Copyright 1958 by Princeton University Press.

Who with me underwent all hardships—
Has now gone to the fate of mankind!
Day and night I have wept over him.
I would not give him up for burial—
In case my friend should rise at my plaint—
Seven days and seven nights,
Until a worm fell out of his nose.
Since his passing I have not found life,   (10)
I have roamed like a hunter in the midst of the steppe.
O ale-wife, now that I have seen thy face,
Let me not see the death which I ever dread."

The ale-wife said to him, to Gilgamesh:

(iii)

"Gilgamesh, whither rovest thou?
The life thou pursuest thou shalt not find.
When the gods created mankind,
Death for mankind they set aside,
Life in their own hands retaining.
Thou, Gilgamesh, let full be thy belly,
Eccles. 5:18   Make thou merry by day and by night.
Of each day make thou a feast of rejoicing,
Eccles. 8:15   Day and night dance thou and play!
Eccles. 9:8–9   Let thy garments be sparkling fresh,   (10)
Thy head be washed; bathe thou in water.
Pay heed to the little one that holds on to thy hand,
Let thy spouse delight in thy bosom!
For this is the task of [mankind]!"

(remainder of the column broken away)

(iv)

In his wrath he shatters them.[1]
When he returned, he goes up to him.[2]
Sursunabu[3] his eyes behold.
Sursunabu says to him, to Gilgamesh:
"Tell me, thou, what is thy name?
I am Sursunabu, (he) of Utanapishtim[4] the Faraway."
Gilgamesh said to him, to Sursunabu:
"As for me, Gilgamesh is my name,
Who have come from Uruk-Eanna,

---

[1] Apparently the mysterious "Stone Things."
[2] To the boatman.
[3] The Urshanabi of the Assyrian Version.
[4] Assyrian Utnapishtim.

Who have traversed the mountains,   (10)
A distant journey, as the sun *rises*.
O Sursunabu, now that I have seen thy face,
Show me Utanapishtim the Faraway."
Sursunabu [says] to him, to Gilgamesh.

(remainder broken away)

(The Assyrian Version of Tablet X gives the episodes of the meetings with Siduri and with Sursunabu [Urshanabi in the Assyrian Version] and an account of the crossing of the Waters of Death to the abode of Utnapishtim. The concluding part of Tablet X follows:)

(v)

Gilgamesh also said to him, to Utnapishtim: (23)
"That now I might come and behold Utnapishtim,
    Whom they call the Faraway,
I ranged and wandered over all the lands,
I traversed difficult mountains,
I crossed all the seas!
My face was not sated with sweet sleep,
I fretted myself with wakefulness;
    I filled my joints with misery.
I had not reached the ale-wife's house,
    When my clothing was used up.   (30)
[I sl]ew bear, hyena, lion, panther,
    Tiger, stag, (and) ibex—
    The wild beasts and creeping things of the steppe.
Their [flesh] I ate and their skins I wr[apped about me]."

(The remainder of this column is too mutilated for translation. The beginning of the last column is broken away, except for the conclusion of the sage observations of Utnapishtim:)

(vi)

"Do we build a house for ever?   (26)
    Do we seal (contracts) for ever?
Eccles. 9:6 Do brothers divide shares for ever?
    Does hatred persist for ever in [the land]?
    Does the river for ever raise up (and) bring on floods?
    The dragon-fly [leaves] (its) shell   (30)
    That its face might (but) glance at the face of the sun.
Eccles. 1:11; 1:4; Since the days of yore there has been no [permanence];
2:16; 9:5; 3:19 The resting and the dead, how alike [they are]!

Do they not compose a picture of death,
The commoner and the noble,
  Once they are near to [their fate]?
The Anunnaki, the great gods, foregather;
Mammetum, maker of fate, with them the fate decrees:
Death and life they determine.
(But) of death, its days are not revealed."

A SONG OF THE HARPER*

The song which is in the House of King Intef, the triumphant, and which is before the singer with the harp.

> Prosperous is he, this good prince,
> Even though good fortune may suffer harm![1]
> Generations pass away, and others remain
> Since the time of the ancestors.[2]
> The gods who lived formerly rest in their pyramids,
> The beatified dead also, buried in their pyramids.[3]   (5)
> And they who built houses—their places are not.
> See what has been made of them!
> I have heard the words of Ii-em-hotep and Hor-dedef,
> With whose discourses men speak so much.[4]
> What are their places (now)?
> Their walls are broken apart, and their places are not—
> As though they had never been!
> There is none who comes back from (over) there,
> That he may tell their state,
> That he may tell their needs,
> That he may still our hearts,
> Until we (too) may travel to the place where they have
>   gone.
> Let thy desire flourish,
> In order to let thy heart forget the beatifications for
>   thee.[5]

* Reprinted from *Ancient Near Eastern Texts Relating to the Old Testament*, edited by James B. Pritchard, by permission of Princeton University Press. Copyright 1950 by Princeton University Press.

[1] The fate of death may not be happy, but this prince need not fear. The version in the tomb of Nefer-hotep, "How weary is this righteous prince; the goodly fortune has come to pass," makes death a kindly release.

[2] The Nefer-hotep version, "Generations pass away since the time of the god, (but) young people come in their place," shows that the meaning is the transition from one generation to another.

[3] The dead kings and nobles of older times.

[4] Ii-em-hotep, the famous vizier of Djoser, and Hor-dedef, the son of Khufu, were traditional sages of Egypt.

[5] An important part of the funerary services was "beatification" or "making (the deceased) an effective personality."

Follow thy desire, as long as thou shalt live.
Put myrrh upon thy head and clothing of fine linen upon
thee,   (10)
Being anointed with genuine marvels of the god's
property.
Set an increase to thy good things;
Let not thy heart flag.
Follow thy desire and thy good.
Fulfill thy needs upon earth, after the command of thy
heart,
Until there come for thee that day of mourning.
The Weary [of Heart] hears not their [mourn]ing,[6]
And wailing saves not the heart of a man from the
underworld.

REFRAIN: Make holiday, and weary not therein!
Behold, it is not given to a man to take his property
with him.
Behold, there is not one who departs who comes back
again!

---

[6] Osiris, the god of the dead, is not concerned with the earthly mourning
for the dead.

1 Blessed is the man that walketh not in the counsel of the ungodly,
    nor standeth in the way of sinners,
    nor sitteth in the seat of the scornful.
2 But his delight is in the law of the Lord;
    and in his law doth he meditate day and night.
3 And he shall be like a tree planted by the rivers of water,
    that bringeth forth his fruit in his season;
    his leaf also shall not wither;
    and whatsoever he doeth shall prosper.
4 The ungodly are not so:
    but are like the chaff which the wind driveth away.
5 Therefore the ungodly shall not stand in the judgment,
    nor sinners in the congregation of the righteous.
6 For the Lord knoweth the way of the righteous:
    but the way of the ungodly shall perish.

THE PROVERBS

THE VALUE OF PROVERBS

1 The Proverbs of Solomon the son of David, king of Israel:
2 To know wisdom and instruction;
to perceive the words of understanding;
3 to receive the instruction of wisdom,
justice, and judgment, and equity;
4 to give subtilty to the simple,
to the young man knowledge and discretion.
5 A wise man will hear, and will increase learning;
and a man of understanding shall attain unto wise counsels:
6 to understand a proverb, and the interpretation;
the words of the wise, and their dark sayings.
7 The fear of the Lord is the beginning of knowledge:
but fools despise wisdom and instruction.

WISDOM'S WARNING

8 My son, hear the instruction of thy father,
and forsake not the law of thy mother:
9 for they shall be an ornament of grace unto thy head,
and chains about thy neck.
10 My son, if sinners entice thee,
consent thou not.
11 If they say, Come with us, let us lay wait for blood,
let us lurk privily for the innocent without cause:
12 let us swallow them up alive as the grave;
and whole, as those that go down into the pit:
13 we shall find all precious substance,
we shall fill our houses with spoil:
14 cast in thy lot among us;
let us all have one purse:
15 my son, walk not thou in the way with them;
refrain thy foot from their path:
16 for their feet run to evil,
and make haste to shed blood.
17 Surely in vain the net is spread
in the sight of any bird.

18 And they lay wait for their own blood;
   they lurk privily for their own lives.
19 So are the ways of every one that is greedy of gain;
   which taketh away the life of the owners thereof.
20 Wisdom crieth without;
   she uttereth her voice in the streets:
21 she crieth in the chief place of concourse,
   in the openings of the gates:
   in the city she uttereth her words, saying,
22 How long, ye simple ones, will ye love simplicity?
   and the scorners delight in their scorning,
   and fools hate knowledge?
23 Turn you at my reproof:
   behold, I will pour out my spirit unto you,
   I will make known my words unto you.
24 Because I have called, and ye refused;
   I have stretched out my hand, and no man regarded;
25 but ye have set at nought all my counsel,
   and would none of my reproof:
26 I also will laugh at your calamity;
   I will mock when your fear cometh;
27 when your fear cometh as desolation,
   and your destruction cometh as a whirlwind;
   when distress and anguish cometh upon you.
28 Then shall they call upon me,
   but I will not answer;
   they shall seek me early,
   but they shall not find me:
29 for that they hated knowledge,
   and did not choose the fear of the Lord:
30 they would none of my counsel:
   they despised all my reproof.
31 Therefore shall they eat of the fruit of their own way,
   and be filled with their own devices.
32 For the turning away of the simple shall slay them,
   and the prosperity of fools shall destroy them.
33 But whoso hearkeneth unto me shall dwell safely,
   and shall be quiet from fear of evil.

THE REWARD OF SEEKING WISDOM

2 My son, if thou wilt receive my words,
   and hide my commandments with thee;
2 so that thou incline thine ear unto wisdom,
   and apply thine heart to understanding;

3 yea, if thou criest after knowledge,
and liftest up thy voice for understanding;

4 if thou seekest her as silver,
and searchest for her as for hid treasures;

5 then shalt thou understand the fear of the Lord,
and find the knowledge of God.

6 For the Lord giveth wisdom:
out of his mouth cometh knowledge and understanding.

7 He layeth up sound wisdom for the righteous:
he is a buckler to them that walk uprightly.

8 He keepeth the paths of judgment,
and preserveth the way of his saints.

9 Then shalt thou understand righteousness,
and judgment, and equity;
yea, every good path.

10 When wisdom entereth into thine heart,
and knowledge is pleasant unto thy soul;

11 discretion shall preserve thee,
understanding shall keep thee:

12 to deliver thee from the way of the evil man,
from the man that speaketh froward things;

13 who leave the paths of uprightness,
to walk in the ways of darkness;

14 who rejoice to do evil,
and delight in the frowardness of the wicked;

15 whose ways are crooked,
and they froward in their paths:

16 to deliver thee from the strange woman,
even from the stranger which flattereth with her words;

17 which forsaketh the guide of her youth,
and forgetteth the covenant of her God.

18 For her house inclineth unto death,
and her paths unto the dead.

19 None that go unto her return again,
neither take they hold of the paths of life.

20 That thou mayest walk in the way of good men,
and keep the paths of the righteous.

21 For the upright shall dwell in the land,
and the perfect shall remain in it.

22 But the wicked shall be cut off from the earth,
and the transgressors shall be rooted out of it.

EXHORTATIONS TO OBEDIENCE

3 My son, forget not my law;
but let thine heart keep my commandments:

2 for length of days, and long life,
   and peace, shall they add to thee.
3 Let not mercy and truth forsake thee:
   bind them about thy neck;
   write them upon the table of thine heart:
4 so shalt thou find favor and good understanding
   in the sight of God and man.
5 Trust in the Lord with all thine heart;
   and lean not unto thine own understanding.
6 In all thy ways acknowledge him,
   and he shall direct thy paths.
7 Be not wise in thine own eyes:
   fear the Lord, and depart from evil.
8 It shall be health to thy navel,
   and marrow to thy bones.
9 Honor the Lord with thy substance,
   and with the firstfruits of all thine increase:
10 so shall thy barns be filled with plenty,
   and thy presses shall burst out with new wine.
11 My son, despise not the chastening of the Lord;
   neither be weary of his correction:
12 for whom the Lord loveth he correcteth;
   even as a father the son in whom he delighteth.
13 Happy is the man that findeth wisdom,
   and the man that getteth understanding:
14 for the merchandise of it is better than the merchandise of silver,
   and the gain thereof than fine gold.
15 She is more precious than rubies:
   and all the things thou canst desire are not to be compared unto her.
16 Length of days is in her right hand;
   and in her left hand riches and honor.
17 Her ways are ways of pleasantness,
   and all her paths are peace.
18 She is a tree of life to them that lay hold upon her:
   and happy is every one that retaineth her.
19 The Lord by wisdom hath founded the earth;
   by understanding hath he established the heavens.
20 By his knowledge the depths are broken up,
   and the clouds drop down the dew.
21 My son, let not them depart from thine eyes:
   keep sound wisdom and discretion:
22 so shall they be life unto thy soul,
   and grace to thy neck.
23 Then shalt thou walk in thy way safely,
   and thy foot shall not stumble.

24 When thou liest down, thou shalt not be afraid:
   yea, thou shalt lie down, and thy sleep shall be sweet.
25 Be not afraid of sudden fear,
   neither of the desolation of the wicked, when it cometh.
26 For the Lord shall be thy confidence,
   and shall keep thy foot from being taken.
27 Withhold not good from them to whom it is due,
   when it is in the power of thine hand to do it.
28 Say not unto thy neighbor,
   Go, and come again, and tomorrow I will give;
   when thou hast it by thee.
29 Devise not evil against thy neighbor,
   seeing he dwelleth securely by thee.
30 Strive not with a man without cause,
   if he have done thee no harm.
31 Envy thou not the oppressor,
   and choose none of his ways.
32 For the froward is abomination to the Lord:
   but his secret is with the righteous.
33 The curse of the Lord is in the house of the wicked:
   but he blesseth the habitation of the just.
34 Surely he scorneth the scorners:
   but he giveth grace unto the lowly.
35 The wise shall inherit glory:
   but shame shall be the promotion of fools.

THE BENEFICENCE OF WISDOM

4 Hear, ye children, the instruction of a father,
   and attend to know understanding.
2 For I give you good doctrine,
   forsake ye not my law.
3 For I was my father's son,
   tender and only beloved in the sight of my mother.
4 He taught me also, and said unto me,
   Let thine heart retain my words:
   keep my commandments, and live.
5 Get wisdom, get understanding:
   forget it not; neither decline from the words of my mouth.
6 Forsake her not, and she shall preserve thee:
   love her, and she shall keep thee.
7 Wisdom is the principal thing;
   therefore get wisdom:
   and with all thy getting get understanding.

8 Exalt her, and she shall promote thee:
   she shall bring thee to honor, when thou dost embrace her.
9 She shall give to thine head an ornament of grace:
   a crown of glory shall she deliver to thee.
10 Hear, O my son, and receive my sayings;
   and the years of thy life shall be many.
11 I have taught thee in the way of wisdom;
   I have led thee in right paths.
12 When thou goest, thy steps shall not be straitened;
   and when thou runnest, thou shalt not stumble.
13 Take fast hold of instruction;
   let her not go:
   keep her; for she is thy life.
14 Enter not into the path of the wicked,
   and go not in the way of evil men.
15 Avoid it, pass not by it,
   turn from it, and pass away.
16 For they sleep not, except they have done mischief;
   and their sleep is taken away, unless they cause some to fall.
17 For they eat the bread of wickedness,
   and drink the wine of violence.
18 But the path of the just is as the shining light,
   that shineth more and more unto the perfect day.
19 The way of the wicked is as darkness:
   they know not at what they stumble.
20 My son, attend to my words;
   incline thine ear unto my sayings.
21 Let them not depart from thine eyes;
   keep them in the midst of thine heart.
22 For they are life unto those that find them,
   and health to all their flesh.
23 Keep thy heart with all diligence;
   for out of it are the issues of life.
24 Put away from thee a froward mouth,
   and perverse lips put far from thee.
25 Let thine eyes look right on,
   and let thine eyelids look straight before thee.
26 Ponder the path of thy feet,
   and let all thy ways be established.
27 Turn not to the right hand nor to the left:
   remove thy foot from evil.

THE EXCELLENCE AND ETERNITY OF WISDOM

8 Doth not wisdom cry?
   and understanding put forth her voice?

2 She standeth in the top of high places,
by the way in the places of the paths.

3 She crieth at the gates,
at the entry of the city,
at the coming in at the doors:

4 Unto you, O men, I call;
and my voice is to the sons of man.

5 O ye simple, understand wisdom:
and, ye fools, be ye of an understanding heart.

6 Hear; for I will speak of excellent things;
and the opening of my lips shall be right things.

7 For my mouth shall speak truth;
and wickedness is an abomination to my lips.

8 All the words of my mouth are in righteousness;
there is nothing froward or perverse in them.

9 They are all plain to him that understandeth,
and right to them that find knowledge.

10 Receive my instruction, and not silver;
and knowledge rather than choice gold.

11 For wisdom is better than rubies;
and all things that may be desired are not to be compared to it.

12 I wisdom dwell with prudence,
and find out knowledge of witty inventions.

13 The fear of the Lord is to hate evil:
pride, and arrogancy, and the evil way,
and the froward mouth, do I hate.

14 Counsel is mine, and sound wisdom:
I am understanding; I have strength.

15 By me kings reign,
and princes decree justice.

16 By me princes rule, and nobles,
even all the judges of the earth.

17 I love them that love me;
and those that seek me early shall find me.

18 Riches and honor are with me;
yea, durable riches and righteousness.

19 My fruit is better than gold, yea, than fine gold;
and my revenue than choice silver.

20 I lead in the way of righteousness,
in the midst of the paths of judgment:

21 that I may cause those that love me to inherit substance;
and I will fill their treasures.

22 The Lord possessed me in the beginning of his way,
before his works of old.

23 I was set up from everlasting,
from the beginning,

or ever the earth was.

24 When there were no depths, I was brought forth;
when there were no fountains abounding with water.

25 Before the mountains were settled,
before the hills was I brought forth:

26 while as yet he had not made the earth, nor the fields,
nor the highest part of the dust of the world.

27 When he prepared the heavens, I was there:
when he set a compass upon the face of the depth:

28 when he established the clouds above:
when he strengthened the fountains of the deep:

29 when he gave to the sea his decree,
that the waters should not pass his commandment:
when he appointed the foundations of the earth:

30 then I was by him,
as one brought up with him:
and I was daily his delight,
rejoicing always before him;

31 rejoicing in the habitable part of his earth;
and my delights were with the sons of men.

32 Now therefore hearken unto me, O ye children:
for blessed are they that keep my ways.

33 Hear instruction, and be wise,
and refuse it not.

34 Blessed is the man that heareth me,
watching daily at my gates,
waiting at the posts of my doors.

35 For whoso findeth me findeth life,
and shall obtain favor of the Lord.

36 But he that sinneth against me wrongeth his own soul:
all they that hate me love death.

13 A wise son heareth his father's instruction:
but a scorner heareth not rebuke.

2 A man shall eat good by the fruit of his mouth:
but the soul of the transgressors shall eat violence.

3 He that keepeth his mouth keepeth his life:
but he that openeth wide his lips shall have destruction.

4 The soul of the sluggard desireth, and hath nothing:
but the soul of the diligent shall be made fat.

5 A righteous man hateth lying:
but a wicked man is loathsome, and cometh to shame.

6 Righteousness keepeth him that is upright in the way:
but wickedness overthroweth the sinner.

7 There is that maketh himself rich, yet hath nothing:
there is that maketh himself poor, yet hath great riches.

8 The ransom of a man's life are his riches:
but the poor heareth not rebuke.
9 The light of the righteous rejoiceth:
but the lamp of the wicked shall be put out.
10 Only by pride cometh contention:
but with the well advised is wisdom.
11 Wealth gotten by vanity shall be diminished:
but he that gathereth by labor shall increase.
12 Hope deferred maketh the heart sick:
but when the desire cometh, it is a tree of life.
13 Whoso despiseth the word shall be destroyed:
but he that feareth the commandment shall be rewarded.
14 The law of the wise is a fountain of life,
to depart from the snares of death.
15 Good understanding giveth favor:
but the way of transgressors is hard.
16 Every prudent man dealeth with knowledge:
but a fool layeth open his folly.
17 A wicked messenger falleth into mischief:
but a faithful ambassador is health.
18 Poverty and shame shall be to him that refuseth instruction:
but he that regardeth reproof shall be honored.
19 The desire accomplished is sweet to the soul:
but it is abomination to fools to depart from evil.
20 He that walketh with wise men shall be wise:
but a companion of fools shall be destroyed.
21 Evil pursueth sinners:
but to the righteous good shall be repaid.
22 A good man leaveth an inheritance to his children's children:
and the wealth of the sinner is laid up for the just.
23 Much food is in the tillage of the poor:
but there is that is destroyed for want of judgment.
24 He that spareth his rod hateth his son:
but he that loveth him chasteneth him betimes.
25 The righteous eateth to the satisfying of his soul:
but the belly of the wicked shall want.

14 Every wise woman buildeth her house:
but the foolish plucketh it down with her hands.
2 He that walketh in his uprightness feareth the Lord:
but he that is perverse in his ways despiseth him.
3 In the mouth of the foolish is a rod of pride:
but the lips of the wise shall preserve them.
4 Where no oxen are, the crib is clean:
but much increase is by the strength of the ox.
5 A faithful witness will not lie:

but a false witness will utter lies.

6 A scorner seeketh wisdom, and findeth it not:
but knowledge is easy unto him that understandeth.

7 Go from the presence of a foolish man,
when thou perceivest not in him the lips of knowledge.

8 The wisdom of the prudent is to understand his way:
but the folly of fools is deceit.

9 Fools make a mock at sin:
but among the righteous there is favor.

10 The heart knoweth his own bitterness;
and a stranger doth not intermeddle with his joy.

11 The house of the wicked shall be overthrown:
but the tabernacle of the upright shall flourish.

12 There is a way which seemeth right unto a man;
but the end thereof are the ways of death.

13 Even in laughter the heart is sorrowful;
and the end of that mirth is heaviness.

14 The backslider in heart shall be filled with his own ways:
and a good man shall be satisfied from himself.

15 The simple believeth every word:
but the prudent man looketh well to his going.

16 A wise man feareth, and departeth from evil:
but the fool rageth, and is confident.

17 He that is soon angry dealeth foolishly:
and a man of wicked devices is hated.

18 The simple inherit folly:
but the prudent are crowned with knowledge.

19 The evil bow before the good;
and the wicked at the gates of the righteous.

20 The poor is hated even of his own neighbor:
but the rich hath many friends.

21 He that despiseth his neighbor sinneth:
but he that hath mercy on the poor, happy is he.

22 Do they not err that devise evil?
But mercy and truth shall be to them that devise good.

23 In all labor there is profit:
but the talk of the lips tendeth only to penury.

24 The crown of the wise is their riches:
but the foolishness of fools is folly.

25 A true witness delivereth souls:
but a deceitful witness speaketh lies.

26 In the fear of the Lord is strong confidence:
and his children shall have a place of refuge.

27 The fear of the Lord is a fountain of life,
to depart from the snares of death.

28 In the multitude of people is the king's honor:
but in the want of people is the destruction of the prince.
29 He that is slow to wrath is of great understanding:
but he that is hasty of spirit exalteth folly.
30 A sound heart is the life of the flesh:
but envy the rottenness of the bones.
31 He that oppresseth the poor reproacheth his Maker:
but he that honoreth him hath mercy on the poor.
32 The wicked is driven away in his wickedness:
but the righteous hath hope in his death.
33 Wisdom resteth in the heart of him that hath understanding:
but that which is in the midst of fools is made known.
34 Righteousness exalteth a nation:
but sin is a reproach to any people.
35 The king's favor is toward a wise servant:
but his wrath is against him that causeth shame.

15 A soft answer turneth away wrath:
but grievous words stir up anger.
2 The tongue of the wise useth knowledge aright:
but the mouth of fools poureth out foolishness.
3 The eyes of the Lord are in every place,
beholding the evil and the good.
4 A wholesome tongue is a tree of life:
but perverseness therein is a breach in the spirit.
5 A fool despiseth his father's instruction:
but he that regardeth reproof is prudent.
6 In the house of the righteous is much treasure:
but in the revenues of the wicked is trouble.
7 The lips of the wise disperse knowledge:
but the heart of the foolish doeth not so.
8 The sacrifice of the wicked is an abomination to the Lord:
but the prayer of the upright is his delight.
9 The way of the wicked is an abomination unto the Lord:
but he loveth him that followeth after righteousness.
10 Correction is grievous unto him that forsaketh the way:
and he that hateth reproof shall die.
11 Hell and destruction are before the Lord:
how much more then the hearts of the children of men?
12 A scorner loveth not one that reproveth him:
neither will he go unto the wise.
13 A merry heart maketh a cheerful countenance:
but by sorrow of the heart the spirit is broken.
14 The heart of him that hath understanding seeketh knowledge:
but the mouth of fools feedeth on foolishness.
15 All the days of the afflicted are evil:

but he that is of a merry heart hath a continual feast.
16 Better is little with the fear of the Lord,
than great treasure and trouble therewith.
17 Better is a dinner of herbs where love is,
than a stalled ox and hatred therewith.
18 A wrathful man stirreth up strife:
but he that is slow to anger appeaseth strife.
19 The way of the slothful man is as a hedge of thorns:
but the way of the righteous is made plain.
20 A wise son maketh a glad father:
but a foolish man despiseth his mother.
21 Folly is joy to him that is destitute of wisdom:
but a man of understanding walketh uprightly.
22 Without counsel purposes are disappointed:
but in the multitude of counselors they are established.
23 A man hath joy by the answer of his mouth:
and a word spoken in due season, how good is it!
24 The way of life is above to the wise,
that he may depart from hell beneath.
25 The Lord will destroy the house of the proud:
but he will establish the border of the widow.
26 The thoughts of the wicked are an abomination to the Lord:
but the words of the pure are pleasant words.
27 He that is greedy of gain troubleth his own house;
but he that hateth gifts shall live.
28 The heart of the righteous studieth to answer:
but the mouth of the wicked poureth out evil things.
29 The Lord is far from the wicked:
but he heareth the prayer of the righteous.
30 The light of the eyes rejoiceth the heart:
and a good report maketh the bones fat.
31 The ear that heareth the reproof of life abideth among the wise.
32 He that refuseth instruction despiseth his own soul:
but he that heareth reproof getteth understanding.
33 The fear of the Lord is the instruction of wisdom;
and before honor is humility.

PROVERBS CONCERNING LIFE AND CONDUCT

16 The preparations of the heart in man,
and the answer of the tongue, is from the Lord.
2 All the ways of a man are clean in his own eyes;
but the Lord weigheth the spirits.
3 Commit thy works unto the Lord,

and thy thoughts shall be established.

4 The Lord hath made all things for himself:
yea, even the wicked for the day of evil.

5 Every one that is proud in heart is an abomination to the Lord:
though hand join in hand, he shall not be unpunished.

6 By mercy and truth iniquity is purged:
and by the fear of the Lord men depart from evil.

7 When a man's ways please the Lord,
he maketh even his enemies to be at peace with him.

8 Better is a little with righteousness,
than great revenues without right.

9 A man's heart deviseth his way:
but the Lord directeth his steps.

10 A divine sentence is in the lips of the king:
his mouth transgresseth not in judgment.

11 A just weight and balance are the Lord's:
all the weights of the bag are his work.

12 It is an abomination to kings to commit wickedness:
for the throne is established by righteousness.

13 Righteous lips are the delight of kings;
and they love him that speaketh right.

14 The wrath of a king is as messengers of death:
but a wise man will pacify it.

15 In the light of the king's countenance is life;
and his favor is as a cloud of the latter rain.

16 How much better is it to get wisdom than gold!
and to get understanding rather to be chosen than silver!

17 The highway of the upright is to depart from evil:
he that keepeth his way preserveth his soul.

18 Pride goeth before destruction,
and a haughty spirit before a fall.

19 Better it is to be of an humble spirit with the lowly,
than to divide the spoil with the proud.

20 He that handleth a matter wisely shall find good:
and whoso trusteth in the Lord, happy is he.

21 The wise in heart shall be called prudent:
and the sweetness of the lips increaseth learning.

22 Understanding is a wellspring of life unto him that hath it:
but the instruction of fools is folly.

23 The heart of the wise teacheth his mouth,
and addeth learning to his lips.

24 Pleasant words are as a honeycomb,
sweet to the soul, and health to the bones.

25 There is a way that seemeth right unto a man;
but the end thereof are the ways of death.

26 He that laboreth, laboreth for himself;
   for his mouth craveth it of him.

27 An ungodly man diggeth up evil:
   and in his lips there is as a burning fire.

28 A froward man soweth strife:
   and a whisperer separateth chief friends.

29 A violent man enticeth his neighbor,
   and leadeth him into the way that is not good.

30 He shutteth his eyes to devise froward things:
   moving his lips he bringeth evil to pass.

31 The hoary head is a crown of glory,
   if it be found in the way of righteousness.

32 He that is slow to anger is better than the mighty;
   and he that ruleth his spirit than he that taketh a city.

33 The lot is cast into the lap;
   but the whole disposing thereof is of the Lord.

22 A good name is rather to be chosen than great riches,
   and loving favor rather than silver and gold.

2 The rich and poor meet together:
   the Lord is the maker of them all.

3 A prudent man foreseeth the evil, and hideth himself:
   but the simple pass on, and are punished.

4 By humility and the fear of the Lord are riches, and honor, and life.

5 Thorns and snares are in the way of the froward:
   he that doth keep his soul shall be far from them.

6 Train up a child in the way he should go:
   and when he is old, he will not depart from it.

7 The rich ruleth over the poor,
   and the borrower is servant to the lender.

8 He that soweth iniquity shall reap vanity:
   and the rod of his anger shall fail.

9 He that hath a bountiful eye shall be blessed;
   for he giveth of his bread to the poor.

10 Cast out the scorner, and contention shall go out;
   yea, strife and reproach shall cease.

11 He that loveth pureness of heart,
   for the grace of his lips the king shall be his friend.

12 The eyes of the Lord preserve knowledge;
   and he overthroweth the words of the transgressor.

13 The slothful man saith, There is a lion without,
   I shall be slain in the streets.

14 The mouth of strange women is a deep pit:
   he that is abhorred of the Lord shall fall therein.

15 Foolishness is bound in the heart of a child;
   but the rod of correction shall drive it far from him.

16 He that oppresseth the poor to increase his riches,
and he that giveth to the rich, shall surely come to want.

PRECEPTS AND WARNINGS

17 Bow down thine ear, and hear the words of the wise,
and apply thine heart unto my knowledge.
18 For it is a pleasant thing if thou keep them within thee;
they shall withal be fitted in thy lips.
19 That thy trust may be in the Lord,
I have made known to thee this day, even to thee.
20 Have not I written to thee excellent things
in counsels and knowledge,
21 that I might make thee know the certainty of the words of truth;
that thou mightest answer the words of truth to them that send unto
thee?
22 Rob not the poor, because he is poor:
neither oppress the afflicted in the gate:
23 for the Lord will plead their cause,
and spoil the soul of those that spoiled them.
24 Make no friendship with an angry man;
and with a furious man thou shalt not go;
25 lest thou learn his ways,
and get a snare to thy soul.
26 Be not thou one of them that strike hands,
or of them that are sureties for debts.
27 If thou hast nothing to pay, why should he take away thy bed from
under thee?
28 Remove not the ancient landmark, which thy fathers have set.
29 Seest thou a man diligent in his business?
He shall stand before kings;
he shall not stand before mean men.

THE OBSERVATIONS OF AGUR

30 The words of Agur the son of Jakeh,
even the prophecy.
The man spake unto Ith'i-el, even unto Ith'i-el and Ucal,
2 Surely I am more brutish than any man,
and have not the understanding of a man.
3 I neither learned wisdom,
nor have the knowledge of the holy.
4 Who hath ascended up into heaven, or descended?
Who hath gathered the wind in his fists?

Who hath bound the waters in a garment?
Who hath established all the ends of the earth?
What is his name, and what is his son's name, if thou canst tell?
5 Every word of God is pure:
he is a shield unto them that put their trust in him.
6 Add thou not unto his words,
lest he reprove thee, and thou be found a liar.
7 Two things I have required of thee;
deny me them not before I die:
8 remove far from me vanity and lies;
give me neither poverty nor riches;
feed me with food convenient for me:
9 lest I be full, and deny thee,
and say, Who is the Lord?
or lest I be poor, and steal,
and take the name of my God in vain.
10 Accuse not a servant unto his master,
lest he curse thee, and thou be found guilty.
11 There is a generation that curseth their father,
and doth not bless their mother.
12 There is a generation that are pure in their own eyes,
and yet is not washed from their filthiness.
13 There is a generation, O how lofty are their eyes!
And their eyelids are lifted up.
14 There is a generation, whose teeth are as swords,
and their jaw teeth as knives,
to devour the poor from off the earth,
and the needy from among men.
15 The horseleech hath two daughters, crying, Give, give.
There are three things that are never satisfied,
yea, four things say not, It is enough:
16 the grave; and the barren womb;
the earth that is not filled with water;
and the fire that saith not, It is enough.
17 The eye that mocketh at his father,
and despiseth to obey his mother,
the ravens of the valley shall pick it out,
and the young eagles shall eat it.
18 There be three things which are too wonderful for me,
yea, four which I know not:
19 the way of an eagle in the air;
the way of a serpent upon a rock;
the way of a ship in the midst of the sea;
and the way of a man with a maid.

20 Such is the way of an adulterous woman;
    she eateth, and wipeth her mouth,
    and saith, I have done no wickedness.
21 For three things the earth is disquieted,
    and for four which it cannot bear:
22 for a servant when he reigneth;
    and a fool when he is filled with meat;
23 for an odious woman when she is married;
    and a handmaid that is heir to her mistress.
24 There be four things which are little upon the earth,
    but they are exceeding wise:
25 the ants are a people not strong,
    yet they prepare their meat in the summer;
26 the conies are but a feeble folk,
    yet make they their houses in the rocks;
27 the locusts have no king,
    yet go they forth all of them by bands;
28 the spider taketh hold with her hands,
    and is in kings' palaces.
29 There be three things which go well,
    yea, four are comely in going:
30 a lion, which is strongest among beasts,
    and turneth not away for any;
31 a greyhound; a he goat also;
    and a king, against whom there is no rising up.
32 If thou hast done foolishly in lifting up thyself,
    or if thou hast thought evil,
    lay thine hand upon thy mouth.
33 Surely the churning of milk bringeth forth butter,
    and the wringing of the nose bringeth forth blood:
    so the forcing of wrath bringeth forth strife.

THE WISDOM OF SOLOMON

1 Love righteousness, ye that be judges of the earth,
think of the Lord with a good (heart),
and in simplicity of heart seek him.

2 For he will be found of them that tempt him not;
and sheweth himself unto such as do not distrust him.

3 For froward thoughts separate from God,
and his power, when it is tried, reproveth the unwise.

4 For into a malicious soul wisdom shall not enter,
nor dwell in the body that is subject unto sin.

5 For the holy spirit of discipline will flee deceit,
and remove from thoughts that are without understanding,
and will not abide when unrighteousness cometh in.

6 For wisdom is a loving spirit,
and will not acquit a blasphemer of his words,
for God is witness of his reins,
and a true beholder of his heart,
and a hearer of his tongue.

7 For the Spirit of the Lord filleth the world,
and that which containeth all things hath knowledge of the voice.

8 Therefore he that speaketh unrighteous things cannot be hid;
neither shall vengeance, when it punisheth, pass by him.

9 For inquisition shall be made into the counsels of the ungodly,
and the sound of his words shall come unto the Lord for the mani-
festation of his wicked deeds.

10 For the ear of jealousy heareth all things,
and the noise of murmurings is not hid.

11 Therefore beware of murmuring, which is unprofitable,
and refrain your tongue from backbiting;
for there is no word so secret, that shall go for nought;
and the mouth that belieth slayeth the soul.

12 Seek not death in the error of your life,
and pull not upon yourselves destruction with the works of your
hands.

13 For God made not death;
neither hath he pleasure in the destruction of the living.

14 For he created all things, that they might have their being,
and the generations of the world were healthful;

and there is no poison of destruction in them,
nor the kingdom of death upon the earth;
15 for righteousness is immortal.
16 but ungodly men with their works and words called it to them;
for when they thought to have it their friend, they consumed to
nought,
and made a covenant with it,
because they are worthy to take part with it.

2 For the ungodly said, reasoning with themselves, but not aright,
Our life is short and tedious, and in the death of a man there is no
remedy;
neither was there any man known to have returned from the grave.
2 For we are born at all adventure, and we shall be hereafter as though
we had never been;
for the breath in our nostrils is as smoke,
and a little spark in the moving of our heart:
3 which being extinguished, our body shall be turned into ashes,
and our spirit shall vanish as the soft air;
4 and our name shall be forgotten in time,
and no man shall have our works in remembrance,
and our life shall pass away as the trace of a cloud,
and shall be dispersed as a mist that is driven away with the beams
of the sun,
and overcome with the heat thereof.
5 For our time is a very shadow that passeth away,
and after our end there is no returning;
for it is fast sealed, so that no man cometh again.
6 Come on therefore, let us enjoy the good things that are present,
and let us speedily use the creatures like as in youth.
7 Let us fill ourselves with costly wine and ointments,
and let no flower of the spring pass by us;
8 let us crown ourselves with rosebuds, before they be withered;
9 let none of us go without his part of our voluptuousness;
let us leave tokens of our joyfulness in every place,
for this is our portion, and our lot is this.
10 Let us oppress the poor righteous man,
let us not spare the widow,
nor reverence the ancient gray hairs of the aged.
11 Let our strength be the law of justice;
for that which is feeble is found to be nothing worth.
12 Therefore let us lie in wait for the righteous,
because he is not for our turn, and he is clean contrary to our doings;
he upbraideth us with our offending the law,
and objecteth to our infamy the transgressions of our education.

13 He professeth to have the knowledge of God,
   and he calleth himself the child of the Lord.
14 He was made to reprove our thoughts.
15 He is grievous unto us even to behold,
   for his life is not like other men's, his ways are of another fashion.
16 We are esteemed of him as counterfeits;
   he abstaineth from our ways as from filthiness,
   he pronounceth the end of the just to be blessed,
   and maketh his boast that God is his father.
17 Let us see if his words be true,
   and let us prove what shall happen in the end of him.
18 For if the just man be the son of God, he will help him,
   and deliver him from the hand of his enemies.
19 Let us examine him with despitefulness and torture,
   that we may know his meekness, and prove his patience.
20 Let us condemn him with a shameful death,
   for by his own saying he shall be respected.
21 Such things they did imagine, and were deceived,
   for their own wickedness hath blinded them.
21 As for the mysteries of God, they knew them not;
   neither hoped they for the wages of righteousness,
   nor discerned a reward for blameless souls.
23 For God created man to be immortal,
   and made him to be an image of his own eternity.
24 Nevertheless through envy of the devil came death into the world;
   and they that do hold of his side do find it.

3 But the souls of the righteous are in the hand of god,
   and there shall no torment touch them.
2 In the sight of the unwise they seemed to die,
   and their departure is taken for misery,
3 and their going from us to be utter destruction;
   but they are in peace.
4 For though they be punished in the sight of men,
   yet is their hope full of immortality.
5 And having been a little chastised, they shall be greatly rewarded;
   for God proved them, and found them worthy for himself.
6 As gold in the furnace hath he tried them,
   and received them as a burnt offering.
7 And in the time of their visitation they shall shine,
   and run to and fro like sparks among the stubble.
8 They shall judge the nations, and have dominion over the people,
   and their Lord shall reign for ever.
9 They that put their trust in him shall understand the truth,
   and such as be faithful in love shall abide with him,

for grace and mercy is to his saints,
and he hath care for his elect.

10 But the ungodly shall be punished according to their own imagina-
tions,
which have neglected the righteous, and forsaken the Lord.

11 For whoso despiseth wisdom and nurture, he is miserable,
and their hope is vain, their labours unfruitful, and their works
unprofitable;

12 their wives are foolish, and their children wicked;

13 their offspring is cursed.
Wherefore blessed is the barren that is undefiled,
which hath not known the sinful bed;
she shall have fruit in the visitation of souls.

14 And blessed is the eunuch which with his hands hath wrought no
iniquity,
nor imagined wicked things against God;
for unto him shall be given the special gift of faith,
and an inheritance in the temple of the Lord more acceptable to his
mind.

15 For glorious is the fruit of good labours,
and the root of wisdom shall never fall away.

16 As for the children of adulterers, they shall not come to their
perfection,
and the seed of an unrighteous bed shall be rooted out.

17 For though they live long, yet shall they be nothing regarded;
and their last age shall be without honour.

18 Or, if they die quickly, they have no hope,
neither comfort in the day of trial.

19 For horrible is the end of the unrighteous generation.

4 Better it is to have no children, and to have virtue,
for the memorial thereof is immortal;
because it is known with God, and with men.

2 When it is present, men take example at it,
and when it is gone, they desire it;
it weareth a crown, and triumpheth for ever,
having gotten the victory, striving for undefiled rewards.

3 But the multiplying brood of the ungodly shall not thrive,
nor take deep rooting from bastard slips,
nor lay any fast foundation.

4 For though they flourish in branches for a time,
yet standing not fast, they shall be shaken with the wind,
and through the force of winds they shall be rooted out.

5 The imperfect branches shall be broken off,
their fruit unprofitable, not ripe to eat,

yea, meet for nothing.

6 For children begotten of unlawful beds are witnesses of wickedness
against their parents in their trial.

7 But though the righteous be prevented with death, yet shall he be
in rest.

8 For honourable age is not that which standeth in length of time,
nor that is measured by number of years.

9 But wisdom is the gray hair unto men,
and an unspotted life is old age.

10 He pleased God, and was beloved of him,
so that living among sinners he was translated.

11 Yea, speedily was he taken away, lest that wickedness should alter
his understanding,
or deceit beguile his soul.

12 For the bewitching of naughtiness doth obscure things that are
honest;
and the wandering of concupiscence doth undermine the simple
mind.

13 He, being made perfect in a short time, fulfilled a long time,

14 for his soul pleased the Lord;
therefore hasted he to take him away from among the wicked.

15 This the people saw, and understood it not,
neither laid they up this in their minds,
that his grace and mercy is with his saints,
and that he hath respect unto his chosen.

16 Thus the righteous that is dead shall condemn the ungodly which
are living;
and youth that is soon perfected the many years and old age of the
unrighteous.

17 For they shall see the end of the wise,
and shall not understand what God in his counsel hath decreed of
him,
and to what end the Lord hath set him in safety.

18 They shall see him, and despise him,
but God shall laugh them to scorn;
and they shall hereafter be a vile carcase,
and a reproach among the dead for evermore.

19 For he shall rend them, and cast them down headlong, that they
shall be speechless;
and he shall shake them from the foundation,
and they shall be utterly laid waste, and be in sorrow;
and their memorial shall perish.

20 And when they cast up the accounts of their sins, they shall come
with fear;
and their own iniquities shall convince them to their face.

5 Then shall the righteous man stand in great boldness
before the face of such as have afflicted him,
and made no account of his labours.

2 When they see it, they shall be troubled with terrible fear,
and shall be amazed at the strangeness of his salvation, so far beyond all that they looked for.

3 And they repenting and groaning for anguish of spirit shall say within themselves,

4 This was he, whom we had sometimes in derision,
and a proverb of reproach;
we fools accounted his life madness,
and his end to be without honour.

5 How is he numbered among the children of God,
and his lot is among the saints!

6 Therefore have we erred from the way of truth,
and the light of righteousness hath not shined unto us,
and the sun of righteousness rose not upon us.

7 We wearied ourselves in the way of wickedness and destruction;
yea, we have gone through deserts, where there lay no way;
but as for the way of the Lord, we have not known it.

8 What hath pride profited us?
Or what good hath riches with our vaunting brought us?

9 All those things are passed away like a shadow,
and as a post that hasted by;

10 and as a ship that passeth over the waves of the water,
which when it is gone by, the trace thereof cannot be found,
neither the pathway of the keel in the waves;

11 or as when a bird hath flown through the air,
there is no token of her way to be found,
but the light air being beaten with the stroke of her wings,
and parted with the violent noise and motion of them, is passed
through,
and therein afterwards no sign where she went is to be found;

12 or like as when an arrow is shot at a mark,
it parteth the air, which immediately cometh together again,
so that a man cannot know where it went through.

13 Even so we in like manner, as soon as we were born,
began to draw to our end, and had no sign of virtue to shew,
but were consumed in our own wickedness.

14 For the hope of the ungodly is like dust that is blown away with the
wind,
like a thin froth that is driven away with the storm;
like as the smoke which is dispersed here and there with a tempest,
and passeth away as the remembrance of a guest that tarrieth but
a day.

15 But the righteous live for evermore;
   their reward also is with the Lord,
   and the care of them is with the most High.
16 Therefore shall they receive a glorious kingdom,
   and a beautiful crown from the Lord's hand;
   for with his right hand shall he cover them,
   and with his arm shall he protect them.
17 He shall take to him his jealousy for complete armour,
   and make the creature his weapon for the revenge of his enemies.
18 He shall put on righteousness as a breastplate,
   and true judgment instead of an helmet.
19 He shall take holiness for an invincible shield.
20 His severe wrath shall he sharpen for a sword,
   and the world shall fight with him against the unwise.
21 Then shall the right aiming thunderbolts go abroad;
   and from the clouds, as from a well drawn bow, shall they fly to the
      mark.
22 And hailstones full of wrath shall be cast as out of a stone bow,
   and the water of the sea shall rage against them,
   and the floods shall cruelly drown them.
23 Yea, a mighty wind shall stand up against them,
   and like a storm shall blow them away;
   thus iniquity shall lay waste the whole earth,
   and ill dealing shall overthrow the thrones of the mighty.

6 Hear therefore, O ye kings, and understand;
   learn, ye that be judges of the ends of the earth.
2 Give ear, ye that rule the people,
   and glory in the multitude of nations.
3 For power is given you of the Lord,
   and sovereignty from the Highest,
   who shall try your works,
   and search out your counsels.
4 Because, being ministers of his kingdom, ye have not judged aright,
   nor kept the law,
   nor walked after the counsel of God,
5 horribly and speedily shall he come upon you;
   for a sharp judgment shall be to them that be in high places.
6 For mercy will soon pardon the meanest;
   but mighty men shall be mightily tormented.
7 For he which is Lord over all shall fear no man's person,
   neither shall he stand in awe of any man's greatness;
   for he hath made the small and great,
   and careth for all alike.
8 But a sore trial shall come upon the mighty.

9 Unto you therefore, O kings, do I speak,
   that ye may learn wisdom, and not fall away.
10 For they that keep holiness holily shall be judged holy;
   and they that have learned such things shall find what to answer.
11 Wherefore set your affection upon my words;
   desire them, and ye shall be instructed.
12 Wisdom is glorious, and never fadeth away;
   yea, she is easily seen of them that love her,
   and found of such as seek her.
13 She preventeth them that desire her, in making herself first known
   unto them.
14 Whoso seeketh her early shall have no great travail,
   for he shall find her sitting at his doors.
15 To think therefore upon her is perfection of wisdom;
   and whoso watcheth for her shall quickly be without care.
16 For she goeth about seeking such as are worthy of her,
   sheweth herself favourably unto them in the ways, and meeteth them
   in every thought.
17 For the very true beginning of her is the desire of discipline;
   and the care of discipline is love;
18 and love is the keeping of her laws;
   and the giving heed unto her laws is the assurance of incorruption;
19 and incorruption maketh us near unto God:
20 therefore the desire of wisdom bringeth to a kingdom.
21 If your delight be then in thrones and sceptres, O ye kings of the
   people,
   honour wisdom, that ye may reign for evermore.
22 As for wisdom, what she is, and how she came up, I will tell you,
   and will not hide mysteries from you,
   but will seek her out from the beginning of her nativity,
   and bring the knowledge of her into light,
   and will not pass over the truth.
23 Neither will I go with consuming envy;
   for such a man shall have no fellowship with wisdom.
24 But the multitude of the wise is the welfare of the world,
   and a wise king is the upholding of the people.
25 Receive therefore instruction through my words, and it shall do you
   good.

7 I myself also am a mortal man, like to all,
   and the offspring of him that was first made of the earth,
2 and in my mother's womb was fashioned to be flesh in the time of
   ten months,
   being compacted in blood, of the seed of man, and the pleasure that
   came with sleep.

3 And when I was born, I drew in the common air,
  and fell upon the earth, which is of like nature,
  and the first voice which I uttered was crying, as all others do.
4 I was nursed in swaddling clothes, and that with cares.
5 For there is no king that had any other beginning of birth.
6 For all men have one entrance into life, and the like going out.
7 Wherefore I prayed, and understanding was given me;
  I called upon God, and the spirit of wisdom came to me.
8 I preferred her before sceptres and thrones,
  and esteemed riches nothing in comparison of her.
9 Neither compared I unto her any precious stone,
  because all gold in respect of her is as a little sand,
  and silver shall be counted as clay before her.
10 I loved her above health and beauty,
  and chose to have her instead of light;
  for the light that cometh from her never goeth out.
11 All good things together came to me with her,
  and innumerable riches in her hands.
12 And I rejoiced in them all, because wisdom goeth before them;
  and I knew not that she was the mother of them.
13 I learned diligently, and do communicate her liberally;
  I do not hide her riches.
14 For she is a treasure unto men that never faileth,
  which they that use become the friends of God,
  being commended for the gifts that come from learning.
15 God hath granted me to speak as I would,
  and to conceive as is meet for the things that are given me;
  because it is he that leadeth unto wisdom,
  and directeth the wise.
16 For in his hand are both we and our words;
  all wisdom also, and knowledge of workmanship.
17 For he hath given me certain knowledge of the things that are,
  namely, to know how the world was made, and the operation of the
    elements;
18 the beginning, ending, and midst of the times;
  the alterations of the turning of the sun, and the change of seasons;
19 the circuits of years, and the positions of stars;
20 the natures of living creatures, and the furies of wild beasts;
  the violence of winds, and the reasonings of men;
  the diversities of plants, and the virtues of roots;
21 and all such things as are either secret or manifest, them I know.
22 For wisdom, which is the worker of all things, taught me;
  for in her is an understanding spirit, holy, one only, manifold, subtil,
  lively, clear, undefiled, plain, not subject to hurt, loving the thing
  that is good, quick, which cannot be letted, ready to do good,

23 kind to man, stedfast, sure, free from care, having all power, over-
seeing all things, and going through all understanding, pure, and
most subtil, spirits.

24 For wisdom is more moving than any motion;
she passeth and goeth through all things by reason of her pureness.

25 For she is the breath of the power of God,
and a pure influence flowing from the glory of the Almighty;
therefore can no defiled thing fall into her.

26 For she is the brightness of the everlasting light,
the unspotted mirror of the power of God,
and the image of his goodness.

27 And being but one, she can do all things;
and remaining in herself, she maketh all things new;
and in all ages entering into holy souls, she maketh them friends of
God, and prophets.

28 For God loveth none but him that dwelleth with wisdom.

29 For she is more beautiful than the sun, and above all the order of
stars;
being compared with the light, she is found before it.

30 For after this cometh night;
but vice shall not prevail against wisdom.

8 Wisdom reacheth from one end to another mightily,
and sweetly doth she order all things.

2 I loved her, and sought her out from my youth,
I desired to make her my spouse,
and I was a lover of her beauty.

3 In that she is conversant with God, she magnifieth her nobility;
yea, the Lord of all things himself loved her.

4 For she is privy to the mysteries of the knowledge of God,
and a lover of his works.

5 If riches be a possession to be desired in this life,
what is richer than wisdom, that worketh all things?

6 And if prudence work,
who of all that are is a more cunning workman than she?

7 And if a man love righteousness, her labours are virtues;
for she teacheth temperance and prudence, justice and fortitude,
which are such things, as men can have nothing more profitable in
their life.

8 If a man desire much experience,
she knoweth things of old, and conjectureth aright what is to come;
she knoweth the subtilties of speeches, and can expound dark
sentences;
she foreseeth signs and wonders, and the events of seasons and
times.

9 Therefore I purposed to take her to me to live with me,
knowing that she would be a counsellor of good things,
and a comfort in cares and grief.
10 For her sake I shall have estimation among the multitude,
and honour with the elders, though I be young.
11 I shall be found of a quick conceit in judgment,
and shall be admired in the sight of great men.
12 When I hold my tongue, they shall bide my leisure,
and when I speak, they shall give good ear unto me;
if I talk much, they shall lay their hands upon their mouth.
13 Moreover by the means of her I shall obtain immortality,
and leave behind me an everlasting memorial to them that come
after me.
14 I shall set the people in order,
and the nations shall be subject unto me.
15 Horrible tyrants shall be afraid, and when they do but hear of me;
I shall be found good among the multitude, and valiant in war.
16 After I am come into mine house, I will repose myself with her;
for her conversation hath no bitterness,
and to live with her hath no sorrow, but mirth and joy.
17 Now when I considered these things in myself,
and pondered them in my heart,
how that to be allied unto wisdom is immortality,
18 and great pleasure it is to have her friendship,
and in the works of her hands are infinite riches,
and in the exercise of conference with her, prudence,
and in talking with her, a good report,
I went about seeking how to take her to me.
19 For I was a witty child, and had a good spirit.
20 Yea rather, being good, I came into a body undefiled.
21 Nevertheless, when I perceived that I could not otherwise obtain
her, except God gave her me;
and that was a point of wisdom also to know whose gift she was;
I prayed unto the Lord, and besought him, and with my whole heart
I said,

9 O God of my fathers, and Lord of mercy, who hast made all things
with thy word,
2 and ordained man through thy wisdom,
that he should have dominion over the creatures which thou hast
made,
3 and order the world according to equity and righteousness,
and execute judgment with an upright heart:
4 give me wisdom, that sitteth by thy throne,
and reject me not from among thy children;

5 for I thy servant and son of thine handmaid am a feeble person, and
of a short time,
and too young for the understanding of judgment and laws.

6 For though a man be never so perfect among the children of men,
yet if thy wisdom be not with him, he shall be nothing regarded.

7 Thou hast chosen me to be a king of thy people,
and a judge of thy sons and daughters.

8 Thou hast commanded me to build a temple upon thy holy mount,
and an altar in the city wherein thou dwellest,
a resemblance of the holy tabernacle, which thou hast prepared
from the beginning.

9 And wisdom was with thee, which knoweth thy works,
and was present when thou madest the world,
and knew what was acceptable in thy sight,
and right in thy commandments.

10 O send her out of thy holy heavens,
and from the throne of thy glory,
that being present she may labour with me,
that I may know what is pleasing unto thee.

11 For she knoweth and understandeth all things,
and she shall lead me soberly in my doings,
and preserve me in her power.

12 So shall my works be acceptable,
and then shall I judge thy people righteously,
and be worthy to sit in my father's seat.

13 For what man is he that can know the counsel of God?
Or who can think what the will of the Lord is?

14 For the thoughts of mortal men are miserable,
and our devices are but uncertain.

15 For the corruptible body presseth down the soul,
and the earthy tabernacle weigheth down the mind that museth
upon many things.

16 And hardly do we guess aright at things that are upon earth,
and with labour do we find the things that are before us;
but the things that are in heaven who hath searched out?

17 And thy counsel who hath known, except thou give wisdom,
and send thy Holy Spirit from above?

18 For so the ways of them which lived on the earth were reformed,
and men were taught the things that are pleasing unto thee,
and were saved through wisdom.

THE FIRST EPISTLE OF PAUL THE APOSTLE
TO THE CORINTHIANS
(1:17-2:16)

17 For Christ sent me not to baptize, but to preach the gospel: not with wisdom of words, lest the cross of Christ should be made of none effect.

CHRIST THE POWER AND WISDOM OF GOD

18 For the preaching of the cross is to them that perish, foolishness; but unto us which are saved, it is the power of God. ¹⁹ For it is written,

I will destroy the wisdom of the wise,
and will bring to nothing the understanding of the prudent.

²⁰ Where is the wise? where is the scribe? where is the disputer of this world? hath not God made foolish the wisdom of this world? ²¹ For after that in the wisdom of God the world by wisdom knew not God, it pleased God by the foolishness of preaching to save them that believe. ²² For the Jews require a sign, and the Greeks seek after wisdom: ²³ but we preach Christ crucified, unto the Jews a stumblingblock, and unto the Greeks foolishness; ²⁴ but unto them which are called, both Jews and Greeks, Christ the power of God, and the wisdom of God. ²⁵ Because the foolishness of God is wiser than men; and the weakness of God is stronger than men.

26 For ye see your calling, brethren, how that not many wise men after the flesh, not many mighty, not many noble, are called: ²⁷ but God hath chosen the foolish things of the world to confound the wise; and God hath chosen the weak things of the world to confound the things which are mighty; ²⁸ and base things of the world, and things which are despised, hath God chosen, yea, and things which are not, to bring to nought things that are: ²⁹ that no flesh should glory in his presence. ³⁰ But of him are ye in Christ Jesus, who of God is made unto us wisdom, and righteousness, and sanctification, and redemption: ³¹ that, according as it is written, He that glorieth, let him glory in the Lord.

PROCLAIMING CHRIST CRUCIFIED

2 And I, brethren, when I came to you, came not with excellency of speech or of wisdom, declaring unto you the testimony of God.

² For I determined not to know any thing among you, save Jesus Christ, and him crucified. ³ And I was with you in weakness, and in fear, and in much trembling. ⁴ And my speech and my preaching was not with enticing words of man's wisdom, but in demonstration of the Spirit and of power: ⁵ that your faith should not stand in the wisdom of men, but in the power of God.

THE REVELATION BY GOD'S SPIRIT

6 Howbeit we speak wisdom among them that are perfect: yet not the wisdom of this world, nor of the princes of this world, that come to nought: ⁷ but we speak the wisdom of God in a mystery, even the hidden wisdom, which God ordained before the world unto our glory; ⁸ which none of the princes of this world knew: for had they known it, they would not have crucified the Lord of glory. ⁹ But as it is written,

> Eye hath not seen, nor ear heard,
> neither have entered into the heart of man,
> the things which God hath prepared for them that love him.

¹⁰ But God hath revealed them unto us by his Spirit: for the Spirit searcheth all things, yea, the deep things of God. ¹¹ For what man knoweth the things of a man, save the spirit of man which is in him? even so the things of God knoweth no man, but the Spirit of God. ¹² Now we have received, not the spirit of the world, but the Spirit which is of God; that we might know the things that are freely given to us of God. ¹³ Which things also we speak, not in the words which man's wisdom teacheth, but which the Holy Ghost teacheth; comparing spiritual things with spiritual.

14 But the natural man receiveth not the things of the Spirit of God: for they are foolishness unto him: neither can he know them, because they are spiritually discerned. ¹⁵ But he that is spiritual judgeth all things, yet he himself is judged of no man. ¹⁶ For who hath known the mind of the Lord, that he may instruct him? But we have the mind of Christ.

MEDITATIONS*
Section IV

Marcus Aurelius (121–180 A.D.)

That which rules within, when it is according to nature, is so affected with respect to the events which happen, that it always easily adapts itself to that which is possible and is presented to it. For it requires no definite material, but it moves towards its purpose, under certain conditions however; and it makes a material for itself out of that which opposes it, as fire lays hold of what falls into it, by which a small light would have been extinguished: but when the fire is strong, it soon appropriates to itself the matter which is heaped on it, and consumes it, and rises higher by means of this very material.

2 Let no act be done without a purpose, nor otherwise than according to the perfect principles of art.

3 Men seek retreats for themselves, houses in the country, seashores and mountains; and thou too art wont to desire such things very much. But this is altogether a mark of the most common sort of men, for it is in thy power whenever thou shalt choose to retire into thyself. For nowhere, either with more quiet or more freedom from trouble, does a man retire than into his own soul, particularly when he has within him such thoughts that by looking into them he is immediately in perfect tranquillity; and I affirm that tranquillity is nothing else than the good ordering of the mind. Constantly then give to thyself this retreat, and renew thyself; and let thy principles be brief and fundamental, which, as soon as thou shalt recur to them, will be sufficient to cleanse the soul completely, and to send thee back free from all discontent with the things to which thou returnest. For with what art thou discontented? With the badness of men? Recall to thy mind this conclusion, that rational animals exist for one another, and that to endure is a part of justice, and that men do wrong involuntarily; and consider how many already, after mutual enmity, suspicion, hatred and fighting, have been stretched dead, reduced to ashes; and be quiet at last.—But perhaps thou art dissatisfied with that which is assigned to thee out of the universe.—Recall to thy recollection this alternative; either there is

* Translated by George Long.

providence or atoms [fortuitous concurrence of things]; or remember the arguments by which it has been proved that the world is a kind of a political community [and be quiet at last].—But perhaps corporeal things will still fasten upon thee.—Consider then further that the mind mingles not with the breath, whether moving gently or violently, when it has once drawn itself apart and discovered its own power, and think also of all that thou hast heard and assented to about pain and pleasure [and be quiet at last].—But perhaps the desire of the thing called fame will torment thee.—See how soon everything is forgotten, and look at the chaos of infinite time on each side of [the present], and the emptiness of applause, and the changeableness and want of judgment in those who pretend to give praise, and the narrowness of the space within which it is circumscribed [and be quiet at last]. For the whole earth is a point, and how small a nook in it is this thy dwelling, and how few are there in it, and what kind of people are they who will praise thee.

This then remains: Remember to retire into this little territory of thy own, and, above all, do not distract or strain thyself, but be free, and look at things as a man, as a human being, as a citizen, as a mortal. But among the things readiest to thy hand to which thou shalt turn, let there be these, which are two. One is that things do not touch the soul, for they are external and remain immovable; but our perturbations come only from the opinion which is within. The other is that all these things, which thou seest, change immediately and will no longer be; and constantly bear in mind how many of these changes thou hast already witnessed. The universe is transformation: life is opinion.

4 If our intellectual part is common, the reason also, in respect of which we are rational beings, is common: if this is so, common also is the reason which commands us what to do, and what not to do; if this is so, there is a common law also; if this is so, we are fellow-citizens; if this is so, we are members of some political community; if this is so, the world is in a manner a state. For of what other common political community will any one say that the whole human race are members? And from thence, from this common political community comes also our very intellectual faculty and reasoning faculty and our capacity for law; or whence do they come? For as my earthly part is a portion given to me from certain earth, and that which is watery from another element, and that which is hot and fiery from some peculiar source (for nothing comes out of that which is nothing, as nothing also returns to non-existence), so also the intellectual part comes from some source.

5 Death is such as generation is, a mystery of nature; a composition out of the same elements, and a decomposition into the same; and altogether not a thing of which any man should be ashamed, for it is not contrary to [the nature of] a reasonable animal, and not contrary to the reason of our constitution.

6 It is natural that these things should be done by such persons, it is a matter of necessity; and if a man will not have it so, he will not allow the fig-tree to have juice. But by all means bear this in mind, that within a very short time both thou and he will be dead; and soon not even your names will be left behind.

7 Take away thy opinion, and then there is taken away the complaint, "I have been harmed." Take away the complaint, "I have been harmed," and the harm is taken away.

8 That which does not make a man worse than he was, also does not make his life worse, nor does it harm him either from without or from within.

9 The nature of that which is [universally] useful has been compelled to do this.

10 Consider that everything which happens, happens justly, and if thou observest carefully, thou wilt find it to be so. I do not say only with respect to the continuity of the series of things, but with respect to what is just, and as if it were done by one who assigns to each thing its value. Observe then as thou hast begun; and whatever thou doest, do it in conjunction with this, the being good, and in the sense in which a man is properly understood to be good. Keep to this in every action.

11 Do not have such an opinion of things as he has who does thee wrong, or such as he wishes thee to have, but look at them as they are in truth.

12 A man should always have these two rules in readiness; the one, to do only whatever the reason of the ruling and legislating faculty may suggest for the use of men; the other, to change thy opinion, if there is any one at hand who sets thee right and moves thee from any opinion. But this change of opinion must proceed only from a certain persuasion, as of what is just or of common advantage, and the like, not because it appears pleasant or brings reputation.

13 Hast thou reason? I have.—Why then dost not thou use it? For if this does its own work, what else dost thou wish?

14 Thou hast existed as a part. Thou shalt disappear in that which produced thee; but rather thou shalt be received back into its seminal principle by transmutation.

15 Many grains of frankincense on the same altar; one falls before, another falls after; but it makes no difference.

16 Within ten days thou wilt seem a god to those to whom thou art now a beast and an ape, if thou wilt return to thy principles and the worship of reason.

17 Do not act as if thou wert going to live ten thousand years. Death hangs over thee. While thou livest, while it is in thy power, be good.

18 How much trouble he avoids who does not look to see what his neighbour says or does or thinks, but only to what he does himself, that it may be just and pure; or as Agathon says, look not round at the de-

praved morals of others, but run straight along the line without deviating from it.

19 He who has a vehement desire for posthumous fame does not consider that every one of those who remember him will himself also die very soon; then again also they who have succeeded them, until the whole remembrance shall have been extinguished as it is transmitted through men who foolishly admire and perish. But suppose that those who will remember are even immortal, and that the remembrance will be immortal, what then is this to thee? And I say not what is it to the dead, but what is it to the living. What is praise, except indeed so far as it has a certain utility? For thou now rejectest unseasonably the gift of nature, clinging to something else. . . .

20 Everything which is in any way beautiful is beautiful in itself, and terminates in itself, not having praise as part of itself. Neither worse then nor better is a thing made by being praised. I affirm this also of the things which are called beautiful by the vulgar; for example, material things and works of art. That which is really beautiful has no need of anything; not more than law, not more than truth, not more than benevolence or modesty. Which of these things is beautiful because it is praised, or spoiled by being blamed? Is such a thing as an emerald made worse than it was, if it is not praised? or gold, ivory, purple, a lyre, a little knife, a flower, a shrub?

21 If souls continue to exist, how does the air contain them from eternity?—But how does the earth contain the bodies of those who have been buried from time so remote? For as here the mutation of these bodies after a certain continuance, whatever it may be, and their dissolution make room for other dead bodies; so the souls which are removed into the air after subsisting for some time are transmuted and diffused, and assume a fiery nature by being received into the seminal intelligence of the universe, and in this way make room for the fresh souls which come to dwell there. And this is the answer which a man might give on the hypothesis of souls continuing to exist. But we must not only think of the number of bodies which are thus buried, but also of the number of animals which are daily eaten by us and the other animals. For what a number is consumed, and thus in a manner buried in the bodies of those who feed on them? And nevertheless this earth receives them by reason of the changes [of these bodies] into blood, and the transformations into the aërial, or the fiery element.

What is the investigation into the truth in this matter? The division into that which is material and that which is the cause of form [the formal].

22 Do not be whirled about, but in every movement have respect to justice, and on the occasion of every impression maintain the faculty of comprehension [or understanding].

23 Everything harmonizes with me, which is harmonious to thee, O

Universe. Nothing for me is too early nor too late, which is in due time for thee. Everything is fruit to me which thy seasons bring, O Nature: from thee are all things, in thee are all things, to thee all things return. The poet says, Dear City of Cecrops; and wilt not thou say, Dear city of Zeus?

24 Occupy thyself with few things, says the philosopher, if thou wouldst be tranquil.—But consider if it would not be better to say, Do what is necessary, and whatever the reason of the animal which is naturally social requires, and as it requires. For this brings not only the tranquillity which comes from doing well, but also that which comes from doing few things. For the greatest part of what we say and do being unnecessary, if a man takes this away, he will have more leisure and less uneasiness. Accordingly on every occasion a man should ask himself, Is this one of the unnecessary things? Now a man should take away not only unnecessary acts but also unnecessary thoughts, for thus superfluous acts will not follow after.

25 Try how the life of a good man suits thee, the life of him who is satisfied with his portion out of the whole, and satisfied with his own just acts and benevolent disposition.

26 Hast thou seen those things? Look also at these. Do not disturb thyself. Make thyself all simplicity. Does any one do wrong? It is to himself that he does the wrong. Has anything happened to thee? Well, out of the universe from the beginning everything which happens has been apportioned and spun out to thee. In a word, thy life is short. Thou must turn to profit the present by the aid of reason and justice. Be sober in thy relaxation.

27 Either it is a well arranged universe or a chaos huddled together, but still a universe. But can a certain order subsist in thee, and disorder in the All? And this, too, when all things are so separated and diffused and sympathetic?

28 A black character, a womanish character, a stubborn character, bestial, childish, animal, stupid, counterfeit, scurrilous, fraudulent, tyrannical.

29 If he is a stranger to the universe who does not know what is in it, no less is he a stranger who does not know what is going on in it. He is a runaway, who flies from social reason; he is blind, who shuts the eyes of the understanding; he is poor, who has need of another, and has not from himself all things which are useful for life. He is an abscess on the universe who withdraws and separates himself from the reason of our common nature through being displeased with the things which happen, for the same nature produces this, and has produced thee too; he is a piece rent asunder from the state, who tears his own soul from that of reasonable animals, which is one.

30 The one is a philosopher without a tunic, and the other without a

book: here is another half-naked: Bread I have not, he says, and I abide by reason. And I do not get the means of living out of my learning, and I abide [by my reason].

31 Love the art, poor as it may be, which thou hast learned, and be content with it; and pass through the rest of life like one who has intrusted to the gods with his whole soul all that he has, making thyself neither the tyrant nor the slave of any man.

32 Consider, for example, the times of Vespasian. Thou wilt see all these things, people marrying, bringing up children, sick, dying, warring, feasting, trafficking, cultivating the ground, flattering, obstinately arrogant, suspecting, plotting, wishing for some to die, grumbling about the present, loving, heaping up treasure, desiring consulship, kingly power. Well, then, that life of these people no longer exists at all. Again, remove to the times of Trajan. Again, all is the same. Their life, too, is gone. In like manner view also the other epochs of time and of whole nations, and see how many after great efforts soon fell and were resolved into the elements. But chiefly thou shouldst think of those whom thou hast thyself known distracting themselves about idle things, neglecting to do what was in accordance with their proper constitution, and to hold firmly to this and to be content with it. And herein it is necessary to remember that the attention given to everything has its proper value and proportion. For thus thou wilt not be dissatisfied, if thou appliest thyself to smaller matters no further than is fit.

33 The words which were formerly familiar are now antiquated; so also the names of those who were famed of old, are now in a manner antiquated: Camillus, Caeso, Volesus, Leonnatus, and a little after also Scipio and Cato, then Augustus, then also Hadrianus and Antoninus. For all things soon pass away and become a mere tale, and complete oblivion soon buries them. And I say this of those who have shone in a wondrous way. For the rest, as soon as they have breathed out their breath, they are gone, and no man speaks of them. And, to conclude the matter, what is even an eternal remembrance? A mere nothing. What, then, is that about which we ought to employ our serious pains? This one thing, thoughts just, and acts social, and words which never lie, and a disposition which gladly accepts all that happens, as necessary, as usual, as flowing from a principle and source of the same kind.

34 Willingly give thyself up to Clotho [one of the fates], allowing her to spin thy thread into whatever things she pleases.

35 Everything is only for a day, both that which remembers and that which is remembered.

36 Observe constantly that all things take place by change, and accustom thyself to consider that the nature of the Universe loves nothing so much as to change the things which are and to make new

things like them. For everything that exists is in a manner the seed of that which will be. But thou art thinking only of seeds which are cast into the earth or into a womb: but this is a very vulgar notion.

37 Thou wilt soon die, and thou art not yet simple, nor free from perturbations, nor without suspicion of being hurt by external things, nor kindly disposed towards all; nor dost thou yet place wisdom only in acting justly.

38 Examine men's ruling principles, even those of the wise, what kind of things they avoid, and what kind they pursue.

39 What is evil to thee does not subsist in the ruling principle of another; nor yet in any turning and mutation of thy corporeal covering. Where is it then? It is in that part of thee in which subsists the power of forming opinions about evils. Let this power then not form [such] opinions, and all is well. And if that which is nearest to it, the poor body, is cut, burnt, filled with matter and rottenness, nevertheless let the part which forms opinions about these things be quiet, that is, let it judge that nothing is either bad or good which can happen equally to the bad man and the good. For that which happens equally to him who lives contrary to nature and to him who lives according to nature, is neither according to nature nor contrary to nature.

40 Constantly regard the universe as one living being, having one substance and one soul; and observe how all things have reference to one perception, the perception of this one living being; and how all things act with one movement; and how all things are the co-operating causes of all things which exist; observe too the continuous spinning of the thread and the contexture of the web.

41 Thou art a little soul bearing about a corpse, as Epictetus used to say.

42 It is no evil for things to undergo change, and no good for things to subsist in consequence of change.

43 Time is like a river made up of the events which happen, and a violent stream; for as soon as a thing has been seen, it is carried away, and another comes in its place, and this will be carried away too.

44 Everything which happens is as familiar and well known as the rose in spring and the fruit in summer; for such is disease, and death, and calumny, and treachery, and whatever else delights fools or vexes them.

45 In the series of things those which follow are always aptly fitted to those which have gone before; for this series is not like a mere enumeration of disjointed things, which has only a necessary sequence, but it is a rational connection: and as all existing things are arranged together harmoniously, so the things which come into existence exhibit no mere succession, but a certain wonderful relationship.

46 Always remember the sayings of Heraclitus, that the death of earth is to become water, and the death of water is to become air, and

the death of air is to become fire, and reversely. And think too of him who forgets whither the way leads, and that men quarrel with that with which they are most constantly in communion, the reason which governs the universe; and the things which they daily meet with seem to them strange: and consider that we ought not to act and speak as if we were asleep, for even in sleep we seem to act and speak; and that we ought not, like children who learn from their parents, simply to act and speak as we have been taught.

47 If any god told thee that thou shalt die to-morrow, or certainly on the day after to-morrow, thou wouldst not care much whether it was on the third day or on the morrow, unless thou wast in the highest degree mean-spirited—for how small is the difference?—so think it no great thing to die after as many years as thou canst name rather than to-morrow.

48 Think continually how many physicians are dead after often contracting their eyebrows over the sick; and how many astrologers after predicting with great pretensions the deaths of others; and how many philosophers after endless discourses on death or immortality; how many heroes after killing thousands; and how many tyrants who have used their power over men's lives with terrible insolence as if they were immortal; and how many cities are entirely dead, so to speak, Helice and Pompeii and Herculaneum, and others innumerable. Add to the reckoning all whom thou hast known, one after another. One man after burying another has been laid out dead, and another buries him; and all this in a short time. To conclude, always observe how ephemeral and worthless human things are, and what was yesterday a little mucus, to-morrow will be a mummy or ashes. Pass then through this little space of time conformably to nature, and end thy journey in content, just as an olive falls off when it is ripe, blessing nature who produced it, and thanking the tree on which it grew.

49 Be like the promontory against which the waves continually break, but it stands firm and tames the fury of the water around it.

Unhappy am I, because this has happened to me—Not so, but Happy am I, though this has happened to me, because I continue free from pain, neither crushed by the present nor fearing the future. For such a thing as this might have happened to every man; but every man would not have continued free from pain on such an occasion. Why, then, is that rather a misfortune than this a good fortune? And dost thou in all cases call that a man's misfortune, which is not a deviation from man's nature? And does a thing seem to thee to be a deviation from man's nature, when it is not contrary to the will of man's nature? Well, thou knowest the will of nature. Will then this which has happened prevent thee from being just, magnanimous, temperate, prudent, secure against inconsiderate opinions and falsehood; will it prevent thee from having modesty, freedom, and everything else, by the presence of which man's nature obtains all that is its own? Remember, too, on every occasion which leads thee to vexation to apply this principle: not that this is a misfortune, but that to bear it nobly is good fortune.

50 It is a vulgar but still a useful help towards contempt of death, to pass in review those who have tenaciously stuck to life. What more then have they gained than those who have died early? Certainly they lie in their tombs somewhere at last, Cadicianus, Fabius, Julianus, Lepidus, or any one else like them, who have carried out many to be buried, and then were carried out themselves. Altogether the interval is small [between birth and death]; and consider with how much trouble, and in company with what sort of people, and in what a feeble body this interval is laboriously passed. Do not then consider life a thing of any value. For look to the immensity of time behind thee, and to the time which is before thee, another boundless space. In this infinity then what is the difference between him who lives three days and him who lives three generations?

51 Always run to the short way; and the short way is the natural: accordingly say and do everything in conformity with the soundest reason. For such a purpose frees a man from trouble, and warfare, and all artifice and ostentatious display.

THE CITY OF GOD*
Book XX   Chapter 3

St. Augustine

What Solomon, in the book of Ecclesiastes, says
regarding the things which happen alike to good and wicked men.

Solomon, the wisest king of Israel, who reigned in Jerusalem, thus commences the book called Ecclesiastes, which the Jews number among their canonical Scriptures: "Vanity of vanities, said Ecclesiastes, vanity of vanities; all is vanity. What profit hath a man of all his labour which he hath taken under the sun?" [1] And after going on to enumerate, with this as his text, the calamities and delusions of this life, and the shifting nature of the present time, in which there is nothing substantial, nothing lasting, he bewails, among the other vanities that are under the sun, this also, that though wisdom excelleth folly as light excelleth darkness, and though the eyes of the wise man are in his head, while the fool walketh in darkness,[2] yet one event happeneth to them all, that is to say, in this life under the sun, unquestionably alluding to those evils which we see befall good and bad men alike. He says, further, that the good suffer the ills of life as if they were evil-doers, and the bad enjoy the good of life as if they were good. "There is a vanity which is done upon the earth; that there be just men unto whom it happeneth according to the work of the wicked: again, there be wicked men, to whom it happeneth according to the work of the righteous. I said, that this also is vanity." [3] This wisest man devoted this whole book to a full exposure of this vanity, evidently with no other object than that we might long for that life in which there is no vanity under the sun, but verity under Him who made the sun. In this vanity, then, was it not by the just and righteous judgment of God that man, made like to vanity, was destined to pass away? But in these days of vanity it makes an important difference whether he resists or yields to the truth, and whether he is destitute of

* Translated by Marcus Dods.
[1] Eccles. i. 2, 3.
[2] Eccles. ii. 13, 14.
[3] Eccles. viii. 14.

true piety or a partaker of it,—important not so far as regards the acquirement of the blessings or the evasion of the calamities of this transitory and vain life, but in connection with the future judgment which shall make over to good men good things, and to bad men bad things, in permanent, inalienable possession. In fine, this wise man concludes this book of his by saying, "Fear God, and keep His commandments: for this is every man. For God shall bring every work into judgment, with every despised person, whether it be good, or whether it be evil." [4] What truer, terser, more salutary enouncement could be made? "Fear God," he says, "and keep His commandments: for this is every man." For whosoever has real existence, is this, is a keeper of God's commandments; and he who is not this, is nothing. For so long as he remains in the likeness of vanity, he is not renewed in the image of the truth. "For God shall bring into judgment every work,"—that is, whatever man does in this life,— "whether it be good or whether it be evil, with every despised person," —that is, with every man who here seems despicable, and is therefore not considered; for God sees even him, and does not despise him nor pass him over in His judgment.

[4] Eccles. xii. 13, 14.

SERMON XIX*

A Sermon of Valediction at my going into Germany, at Lincolns-Inne, April 18. 1619.

by John Donne

Remember now thy creator
in the dayes of thy youth—Ecclesiast 12:1.

Wee may consider two great virtues, one for the society of this life, Thankfulness, and the other for attaining the next life, Repentance; as the two pretious Mettles, Silver and Gold: Of Silver (of the virtue of thankfulness) there are whole Mines, books written by Philosophers, and a man may grow rich in that mettle, in that virtue, by digging in that Mine, in the Precepts of moral men; of this Gold (this virtue of Repentance) there is no Mine in the Earth; in the books of Philosophers, no doctrine of Repentance; this Gold is for the most part in the washes; this Repentance in matters of tribulation; but God directs thee to it in this Text, before thou come to those waters of Tribulation, remember now thy Creator before those evill dayes come, and then thou wilt repent the not remembring him till now. Here then the holy-Ghost takes the neerest way to bring a man to God, by awaking his memory; for, for the understanding, that requires long and cleer instruction; and the will requires an instructed understanding before, and is in it self the blindest and boldest faculty; but if the memory doe but fasten upon any of those things which God hath done for us, it is the neerest way to him. Remember therefore, and remember now, though the Memory be placed in the hindermost part of the brain, defer not thou thy remembring to the hindermost part of thy life, but doe that now *in die*, in the day, whil'st thou hast light, now *in diebus*, in the days, whilst God presents thee many lights, many means; and *in diebus juventutis*, in the days of thy youth, of strength, whilst thou art able to doe that which thou purposest to thy self; And as the word imports, *Bechurotheica, in diebus*

* From XXVI *Sermons* (London, 1660).

Electionum tuarum, in the dayes of thy choice, whilst thou art able to make thy choyce, whilst the Grace of God shines so brightly upon thee, as that thou maist choose the way, and so powerfully upon thee, as that thou maist walke in that way. Now, *in this day*, and *in these dayes* Remember first the Creator, That all these things which thou laborest for, and delightest in, were created, made of nothing; and therfore thy memory looks not far enough back, if it stick only upon the Creature, and reach not to the Creator, Remember the Creator, and remember thy Creator; and in that, first that he made thee, and then what he made thee; He made thee of nothing, but of that nothing he hath made thee such a thing as cannot return to nothing, but must remain for ever; whether happy or miserable, that depends upon thy *Remembring thy Creator now in the dayes of thy youth.*

First *remember*; which word is often used in the Scripture for considering and taking care: for, God remembred *Noah* and every beast with him in the Ark; as the word which is contrary to that, forgetting, is also for the affection contrary to it, it is neglecting, *Can a woman forget her child, and not have compassion on the son of her womb?* But here we take not remembring so largly, but restrain it to the exercise of that one faculty, the memory; for it is *Stomachus animae.* The memory sayes St. *Bernard*, is the stomach of the soul, it receives and digests, and turns into good blood, all the benefits formerly exhibited to us in particular, and exhibited to the whole Church of God: present that which belongs to the understanding, to that faculty, and the understanding is not presently setled in it; present any of the prophecies made in the captivity, and a Jews understanding takes them for deliverances from *Babylon*, and a Christians understanding takes them for deliverances from sin and death, by the Messias Christ Jesus; present any of the prophecies of the Revelation concerning Antichrist, and a Papist will understand it of a single, and momentane, and transitory man, that must last but three yeer and a half; and a Protestant may understand it of a succession of men, that have lasted so 1000. yeers already: present but the name of Bishop or of elder, out of the Acts of the Apostle[s], or their Epistles, and other men will take it for a name of equality, and parity, and we for a name and office of distinction in the Hierarchy of Gods Church. Thus it is in the understanding that's often perplexed; consider the other faculty, the will of man, by those bitternesses which have passed between the Jesuits and the Dominicans, (amongst other things belonging to the will) whether the same proportion of grace, offered to men alike disposed, must necessarily work alike upon both their wills? And amongst persons neerer to us, whether that proportion of grace, which doth convert a man, might not have been resisted by perversness of his will? By all these difficulties we may see, how untractable, and untameable a faculty the wil of man is. But come not with matter of law, but matter of fact, *Let God make his wonderful works to be had in* remembrance: present the history of Gods protection of his children, from the beginning, in the ark, in both captivities, in infinite dangers; present this to the memory, and howsoever the understanding be beclouded, or the will perverted, yet both Jew and Christian, Papist and Protestant, Puritan and Protestant, are affected with a thankfull acknowledgment of his former mercies and benefits, this issue of that faculty of their memory is alike in them all: And therefore God in giving the law, works upon no other faculty but this, *I am the Lord thy God which brought thee out of the land of Egypt;* He only presents to their memory what he had done for them. And so in delivering the Gospel in one principal seal thereof, the sacrament of his body, he recommended it only to their memory, *Do this in remembrance of me.* This is the faculty that God desires to work upon; And therefore if thine understanding cannot reconcile differences in all Churches, if thy will cannot submit it self to the ordinances of thine own Church, go to thine own memory; for as St. Bernard calls that the stomach of the soul, we may be bold to call it the Gallery of the soul, hang'd with so many, and so lively pictures of the goodness and mercies of thy God to thee, as that every one of them shall be a catachism to thee, to instruct thee in all thy duties to him for those mercies: And as a well made, and well plac'd picture, looks alwayes upon him that looks upon it; so shall thy God look upon thee, whose memory is thus contemplating him, and shine upon thine understanding, and rectifie thy will too. If thy memory cannot comprehend his mercy at large shewed to his whole Church, (as it is almost an incomprehensible thing, that in so few yeers he made us of the Reformation, equall even in number to our adversaries of the Roman Church,) If thy memory have not held that picture of our general deliverance from the Navy; (if that mercy be written in the water and in the sands, where it was perform'd, and not in thy heart) if thou remember not our deliverance from that artificiall Hell, the Vault, (in which, though his instruments failed in their plot, they did not blow us up; yet the Devil goes forward with his plot, if ever he can blow out; if he can get that deliverance to be forgotten.) If these be too large pictures for thy gallery, for thy memory, yet every man hath a pocket picture about him, a manuall, a bosome book, and if he will turn over but one leaf, and remember what God hath done for him even since yesterday, he shall find even by that little branch a navigable river, to sail into that great and endless Sea of Gods mercies towards him, from the beginning of his being.

Do but remember, but remember now: Of his own wil begat he us with the word of truth, that we should be as the first fruits of his creatures: That as we consecrate all his creatures to him, in a sober, and religious use of them, so as the first fruits of all, we should principally consecrate our selves to his service betimes. Now there were three payments of first fruits appointed by God to the Jews: The first was, *Primitiae*

Spicarum, of their Ears of Corn, and this was early about *Easter*; The second was *Primitiae panum*, of Loaves of Bread, after their corn was converted to that use; and this, though it were not so soon, yet it was early too, about *Whitsontide;* The third was *Primitiae frugum*, of all their Fruits and Revenues; but this was very late in *Autumn*, at the fall of the leaf, in the end of the yeer. The two first of these, which were offered early, were offered partly to God, and partly to Man, to the Priest; but in the last, which came late, God had no part: He had his part in the corn, and in the loaves, but none in the latter fruits. Offer thy self to God; first, as *Primitias spicarum*, (whether thou glean in the world, or bind up whole sheaves, whether thy increase be by little and little, or apace;) And offer thy self, as *primitias panum*, (when thou hast kneaded up riches, and honor, and favour in a setled and established fortune) offer at thy *Easter*, whensoever thou hast any resurrection, any sense of raising thy soul from the shadow of death; offer at thy Pentecost, when the holy Ghost visits thee, and descends upon thee in a fiery tongue, and melts thy bowels by the power of his word; for if thou defer thy offering til thy fal, til thy winter, til thy death, howsoever they may be thy first fruits, because they be the first that ever thou gavest, yet they are such, as are not acceptable to God; God hath no portion in them, if they be not offered til then; offer thy self now; for that's an easie request; yea offer to thy self now, that's more easie; *Viximus mundo; vivamus reliquum nobis ipsis;* Thus long we have served the world; let us serve our selves the rest of our time, that is, the best part of our selves, our souls. *Expectas ut febris te vocet ad poenitentiam?* Hadst thou rather a sickness should bring thee to God, than a sermon? hadst thou rather be beholden to a Physitian for thy salvation, than to a Preacher? thy business is to remember; stay not for thy last sickness, which may be a Lethargy in which thou mayest forget thine own name, and his that gave thee the name of a Christian, Christ Jesus himself: thy business is to remember, and thy time is now; stay not till that Angel come which shall say and swear, that time shall be no more.

Remember then, and remember now; *In Die*, in the day; The Lord will hear us *In die qua invocaverimus*, in the day that we shall call upon him; and *in quacunque die*, in what day soever we call, and *in quacunque die velociter exaudiet*, as soon as we call in any day. But all this is *Opus diei*, a work for the day; for in the night, in our last night, those thoughts that fall upon us, they are rather dreams, then true remembrings; we do rather dream that we repent, then repent indeed, upon our death-bed. To him that travails by night a bush seems a tree, and a tree seems a man, and a man a spirit; nothing hath the true shape to him; to him that repents by night, on his death-bed, neither his own sins, nor the mercies of God have their true proportion. Fool, saies Christ, this night they will fetch away thy soul; but he neither tels him, who they be that shall fetch it, nor whether they shall carry it; he hath no light but lightnings; a sodain flash of horror first, and then he goes into fire without light. *Numquid Deus nobis ignem paravit? non, sed Diabolo, et Angelis:* did God ordain hell fire for us? no, but for the Devil, and his Angels. And yet we that are vessels so broken, as that there is not a sheard left, to fetch water at the pit, that is, no means in our selves, to derive one drop of Christs blood upon us, nor to wring out one tear of true repentance from us, have plung'd our selves into this everlasting, and this dark fire, which was not prepared for us: A wretched covetousness, to be intruders upon the Devil; a wretched ambition, to be usurpers upon damnation. God did not make the fire for us; but much less did he make us for that fire; that is, make us to damn us. But now the Judgment is given, *Ite maledicti,* go ye accursed; but yet this is the way of Gods justice, and his proceeding, that his Judgments are not alwaies executed, though they be given. The Judgments and Sentences of Medes and Persians are irrevocable, but the Judgments and Sentences of God, if they be given, if they be published, they are not executed. The Ninevites had perished, if the sentence of their destruction had not been given; and the sentence preserv'd them; so even in this cloud of *Ite maledicti,* go ye accursed, we may see the day break, and discern beams of saving light, even in this Judgment of eternal darkness; if the contemplation of his Judgment brings us to remember him in that day, in the light and apprehension of his anger and correction.

For this circumstance is enlarged; it is not *in die,* but *in diebus,* not in one, but in many dayes; for God affords us many dayes, many lights to see and remember him by. This remembrance of God is our regeneration, by which we are new creatures; and therefore we may consider as many dayes in it, as in the first creation. The first day was the making of light; and our first day is the knowledg of him, who saies of himself, *ego sum lux mundi,* I am the light of the world, and of whom St. John testifies, *Erat lux vera,* he was the true light, that lighteth every man into the world. This is then our first day the true profession of Christ Jesus. God made light first, that the other creatures might be seen; *Frustra essent si non viderentur,* It had been to no purpose to have made creatures, if there had been no light to manifest them. Our first day is the light and love of the Gospel; for the noblest creatures of Princes, (that is, the noblest actions of Princes, war, and peace, and treaties) *frustra sunt,* they are good for nothing, they are nothing, if they be not shew'd and tried by this light, by the love and preservation of the Gospel of Christ Jesus: God made light first, that his other works might appear, and he made light first, that himself (for our example) might do all his other works in the light: that we also, as we had that light shed upon us in our baptism, so we might make all our future actions justifiable by that light, and not *Erubescere Evangelium,* not be ashamed of being too jealous in this profession of his truth. Then God saw that the light was good:

the seeing implies a consideration; that so a religion be not accepted blindly, nor implicitly; and the seeing it to be good implies an election of that religion, which is simply good in it self, and not good by reason of advantage, or conveniency, or other collateral and by-respects. And when God had seen the light, and seen that it was good, then he severed light from darkness; and he severed them, *non tanquam duo positiva*, not as two essential, and positive, and equal things; not so, as that a brighter and a darker religion, (a good and a bad) should both have a beeing together, but *tanquam positivum et primitivum*, light and darkness are primitive, and positive, and figure this rather, that a true religion should be established, and continue, and darkness utterly removed; and then, and not till then, (till this was done, light severed from darkness) there was a day; And since God hath given us this day, the brightness of his Gospel, that this light is first presented, that is, all great actions begun with this consideration of the Gospel; since all other things are made by this light, that is, all have relation to the continuance of the Gospel, since God hath given us such a head, as is sharp-sighted in seeing the several lights, wise in discerning the true light, powerful in resisting forraign darkness; since God hath given us this day, *qui non humiliabit animam suam in die hac*, as *Moses* speaks of the dayes of Gods institution, he that will not remember God now in this day, is impious to him, and unthankful to that great instrument of his, by whom this day spring from on high hath visited us.

To make shorter dayes of the rest, (for we must pass through all the six dayes in a few minuts) God in the second day made the firmament to divide between the waters above, and the waters below; and this firmament in us, is *terminus cognoscibilium*, the limits of those things which God hath given man means and faculties to conceive, and understand: he hath limited our eyes with a firmament beset with stars, our eyes can see no farther: he hath limited our understanding in matters of religion with a starry firmament too; that is, with the knowledg of those things, *quae ubique, quae semper*, which those stars which he hath kindled in his Church, the Fathers and Doctors, have ever from the beginning proposed as things necessary to be explicitely believ'd, for the salvation of our souls; for the eternal decrees of God, and his unreveal'd mysteries, and the inextricable perplexities of the School, they are waters above the firmament: here *Paul* plants, and here *Apollo* waters; here God raises up men to convey to us the dew of his grace, by waters under the firmament; by visible sacraments, and by the word so preach'd, and so interpreted, as it hath been constantly, and unanimously from the beginning of the Church. And therefore this second day is perfited in the third, in the *congregentur aquae*, let the waters be gathered together; God hath gathered all the waters, all the waters of life in one place; that is, all the doctrine necessary for the life to come, into his Church: And then *producet terra*, here in this world are produced to us all herbs and fruits, all that is necessary for the soul to feed upon. And in this third daies work God repeats here that testimony, *vidit quod bonum*, he saw that it was good; good, that here should be a gathering of waters in one place, that is, no doctrine receiv'd that had not been taught in the Church; and *vidit quod bonum*, he saw it was good, that all herbs and trees should be produced that bore seed; all doctrines that were to be proseminated and propagated, and to be continued to the end, should be taught in the Church: but for doctrines which were but to vent the passion of vehement men, or to serve the turns of great men for a time, which were not seminal doctrines, doctrines that bore seed, and were to last from the beginning to the end; for these interlineary doctrines, and marginal, which were no part of the first text, here's no testimony that God sees that they are good. And, *In diebus istis*, if in these two daies, the day when God makes thee a firmament, shewes thee what thou art, to limit thine understanding and thy faith upon, and the day where God makes thee a sea, a collection of the waters, (showes thee where these necessary things must be taught in the Church) if in those daies thou wilt not remember thy Creator, it is an irrecoverable Lethargy.

In the fourth daies work, let the making of the Sun to rule the day be the testimony of Gods love to thee, in the sunshine of temporal prosperity, and the making of the Moon to shine by night, be the refreshing of his comfortable promises in the darkness of adversity; and then remember that he can make thy sun to set at noon, he can blow out thy taper of prosperity when it burns brightest, and he can turn the Moon into blood, he can make all the promises of the Gospel, which should comfort thee in adversity, turn into despair and obduration. Let the fift daies work, which was the creation *Omnium reptibilium*, and *omnium volatilium*, of all creeping things, and of all flying things, produc'd out of water, signifie and denote to thee, either thy humble devotion, in which thou saist of thy self to God, *vermis ego et non homo*, I am a worm and no man; or let it be the raising of thy soul in that, *pennas columbae dedisti*, that God hath given thee the wings of a dove to fly to the wilderness, in a retiring from, or a resisting of tentations of this world; remember still that God can suffer even thy humility to stray, and degenerate into an uncomly dejection and stupidity, and senselessness of the true dignity and true liberty of a Christian: and he can suffer this retiring thy self from the world, to degenerate into a contempt and despising of others, and an overvaluing of thine own perfections. Let the last day in which both man and beasts were made out of the earth, but yet a living soul breath'd into man, remember thee that this earth which treads upon thee, must return to that earth which thou treadst upon; thy body, that loads thee, and oppresses thee to the grave, and thy spirit to him that gave it. And when the Sabbath day hath also remembered thee, that God hath given thee a temporal Sabbath, plac'd

thee in a land of peace, and an ecclesiastical Sabbath, plac'd in a
Church of peace, perfect all in a spirituall Sabbath, a conscience of
peace, by remembring now thy Creator, at least in one of these daies of
the week of thy regeneration, either as thou hast light created in thee,
in the first day, that is, thy knowledg of Christ; or as thou hast a firmament created in thee the second day, that is, thy knowledg what to seek
concerning Christ, things appertaining to faith and salvation; or as thou
hast a sea created in thee the third day, that is, a Church where all the
knowledg is reserv'd and presented to thee; or as thou hast a sun and
moon in the fourth day, thankfulness in prosperity, comfort in adversity,
or as thou hast *reptilem humilitatem*, or *volatilem fiduciam*, a humiliation in thy self, or an exaltation in Christ in thy fift day, or as thou hast
a contemplation of thy mortality and immortality in the sixth day, or a
desire of a spiritual Sabbath in the seaventh, In those daies remember
thou thy Creator.

Now all these daies are contracted into less room in this text, *In
diebus Bechurotheica*, is either, *in the daies of thy youth*, or *electionum
tuarum*, in the daies of thy hearts desire, when thou enjoyest all that
thou couldest wish. First, therefore if thou wouldest be heard in *Davids*
prayer; *Delicta juventutis*; O Lord remember not the sins of my youth;
remember to come to this prayer, *In diebus juventutis*, in the dayes of
thy youth. *Job* remembers with much sorrow, how he was in the dayes
of his youth, when Gods providence was upon his Tabernacle: and it is
a late, but a sad consideration, to remember with what tenderness of
conscience, what scruples, what remorces we entred into sins in our
youth, how much we were afraid of all degrees and circumstances of
sin for a little while, and how indifferent things they are grown to us,
and how obdurate we are grown in them now. This was *Jobs* sorrow,
and this was *Tobias* comfort, when I was but young, all my Tribes fell
away; but I alone went after to *Jerusalem*. Though he lacked the counsail, and the example of his Elders, yet he served God; for it is good for
a man, that he bear his yoke in his youth: For even when God had delivered over his people purposely to be afflicted, yet himself complains
in their behalf, *That the persecutor laid the very heaviest yoke upon the
ancient*: It is a lamentable thing to fall under a necessity of suffering in
our age. *Labore fracta instrumenta, ad Deum ducis, quorum nullus usus?*
wouldest thou consecrate a Chalice to God that is broken? no man
would present a lame horse, a disordered clock, a torn book to the King.
Carojumentum, thy body is thy beast; and wilt thou present that to God,
when it is lam'd and tir'd with excesse of wantonness? when thy clock,
(the whole course of thy time) is disordered with passions, and perturbations; when thy book (the history of thy life,) is torn, 1000.
sins of thine own torn out of thy memory, wilt thou then present thy
self thus defac'd and mangled to almighty God? *Temperantia non est
temperantia in senectute, sed impotentia incontinentiae*, chastity is not

chastity in an old man, but a disability to be unchast; and therefore thou dost not give God that which thou pretendest to give, for thou hast no chastity to give him. *Senex bis puer*, but it is not *bis juvenis*; an old man comes to the infirmities of childhood again; but he comes not to the strength of youth again.

Do this then *In diebus juventutis*, in thy best strength, and when thy natural faculties are best able to concur with grace; but do it *In diebus electionum*, in the dayes when thou hast thy hearts desire; for if thou have worn out this word, in one sense, that it be too late now, *to remember him in the dayes of youth*, (that's spent forgetfully) yet as long as thou art able to make a new choise, to chuse a new sin, that when thy heats of youth are not overcome, but burnt out, then thy middle age chooses ambition, and thy old age chooses covetousness; as long as thou art able to make thy choice thou art able to make a better than this; God testifies that power, that he hath given thee; *I call heaven and earth to record this day, that I have set before you life and death: choose life*: If this choice like you not, *If it seem evil unto you to serve the Lord*, saith *Josuah* then, *choose ye this day whom ye will serve.* Here's the election day; bring that which ye would have, into comparison with that which ye should have; that is, all that this world keeps from you, with that which God offers to you; and what will ye choose to prefer before him? for honor, and favor, and health, and riches, perchance you cannot have them though you choose them; but can you have more of them than they have had, to whom those very things have been occasions of ruin? The Market is open till the bell ring; till thy last bell ring the Church is open, grace is to be had there: but trust not upon that rule, that men buy cheapest at the end of the market, that heaven may be had for a breath at last, when they that hear it cannot tel whether it be a sigh or a gasp, a religious breathing and anhelation after the next life, or natural breathing out, and exhalation of this; but find a spiritual good husbandry in that other rule, that the prime of the market is to be had at first: for howsoever, in thine age, there may be by Gods strong working, *Dies juventutis*, A day of youth, in making thee then a new creature; (for as God is *antiquissimus dierum*, so in his school no man is super-annated,) yet when age hath made a man impotent to sin, this is not *Dies electionum*, it is not a day of choice; but remember God now, when thou hast a choice, that is, a power to advance thy self, or to oppress others by evil means; now *in die electionum*, in those thy happy and sun-shine dayes, *remember him.*

This is then the faculty that is excited, the memory; and this is the time, now, now whilest ye have power of election: The object is, the Creator, *Remember the Creator*: First, because the memory can go no farther then the creation; and therefore we have no means to conceive, or apprehend any thing of God before that. When men therefore speak of decrees of reprobation, decrees of condemnation, before decrees of creation; this is beyond the counsail of the holy Ghost here, *Memento creatoris*, Remember the Creator, for this is to remember God a condemner before he was a creator: This is to put a preface to *Moses* his *Genesis*, not to be content with his *in principio*, to know that *in the beginning God created heaven and earth*, but we must remember what he did *ante principium*, before any such beginning was. *Moses* his *in principio*, that beginning, the creation we can remember; but St. *Johns in principio*, that beginning, eternity, we cannot; we can remember Gods *fiat* in *Moses*, but not Gods *erat* in St. *John*: what God hath done for us, is the object of our memory, not what he did before we were: and thou hast a good and perfect memory, if it remember all that the holy Ghost proposes in the Bible; and it determines in the *memento Creatoris*: There begins the Bible, and there begins the Creed, *I believe in God the Father, maker of Heaven and Earth*; for when it is said, *The holy Ghost was not given, because Jesus was not glorified*, it is not truly *Non erat datus*, but *non erat*; for, *non erat nobis antequam operaretur*; It is not said there, the holy Ghost was not given, but it is the holy Ghost was not: for he is not, that is, he hath no being to us ward, till he works in us, which was first in the creation: *Remember the Creator* then, because thou canst remember nothing backward beyond him, and remember him so too, that thou maist stick upon nothing on this side of him, That so neither *height, nor depth, nor any other creature may separate thee from God*; not only not separate thee finally, but not separate so, as to stop upon the creature, but to make the best of them, thy way to the Creator; We see ships in the river; but all their use is gone, if they go not to sea; we see men fraighted with honor, and riches, but all their use is gone, if their respect be not upon the honor and glory of the Creator; and therefore sayes the Apostle, *Let them that suffer, commit their souls to God, as to a faithful Creator*; that is, He made them, and therefore will have care of them. This is the true contracting, and the true extending of the memory, to *Remember the Creator*, and stay there, because there is no prospect farther, and to *Remember the Creator*, and get thither, because there is no safe footing upon the creature, til we come so far.

Remember then the Creator, and *remember thy Creator*, for, *Quis magis fidelis Deo?* who is so faithful a Counsailor as God? *Quis prudentior Sapiente?* who can be wiser than wisdome? *Quis utilior bono?* or better than goodness? *Quis conjunctior Creatore?* or neerer then our Maker? and therefore remember him. What purposes soever thy parents or thy Prince have to make thee great, how had all those purposes been frustrated, and evacuated if God had not made thee before? this very being is thy greatest degree; as in Arithmatick how great a number soever a man expresse in many figures, yet when we come to number all, the very first figure is the greatest and most of all; so what degrees or titles soever a man have in this world, the greatest and the foundation of all, is, that he had a being by creation: For the distance from nothing to a little, is ten thousand times more, than from it to the highest degree in this life: and therefore *remember thy Creator*, as by being so, he hath done more for thee than all the world besides; and remember him also, with this consideration, that whatsoever thou art now, yet once thou wast nothing.

He created thee, *ex nihilo*, he gave thee a being, there's matter of exaltation, and yet all this from nothing; thou wast worse then a worm, there's matter of humiliation; but he did not create thee *ad nihilum*, to return to nothing again, and there's matter for thy consideration, and study, how to make thine immortality profitable unto thee; for it is a deadly immortality, if thy immortality must serve thee for nothing but to hold thee in immortal torment. To end all, that being which we have from God shall not return to nothing, nor the being which we have from men neither. As St. *Bernard* sayes of the Image of God in mans soul, *uri potest in gehenna, non exuri*, That soul that descends to hell, carries the Image [of] God in the faculties of that soul thither, but there that Image can never be burnt out, so those Images and those impressions, which we have received from men, from nature, from the world, the image of a Lord, the image of a Counsailor, the image of a Bishop, shall all burn in Hell, and never burn out; not only these men, but these offices are not to return to nothing; but as their being from God, so their being from man, shal have an everlasting being, to the aggravating of their condemnation. And therefore *remember thy Creator*, who, as he is so, by making thee of nothing, so he will ever be so, by holding thee to his glory, though to thy confusion, from returning to nothing; for the Court of Heaven is not like other Courts, that after a surfet of pleasure or greatness, a man may retire; after a surfet of sin there's no such retiring, as a dissolving of the soul into nothing; but God is from the beginning the Creator, he gave all things their being, and he is still thy Creator, thou shalt evermore have that being, to be capable of his Judgments.

Now to make up a circle, by returning to our first word, remember: As we remember God, so for his sake, let us remember one another. In my long absence, and far distance from hence, remember me, as I shall do you in the ears of that God, to whom the farthest East, and the farthest West are but as the right and left ear in one of us; we hear with both at once, and he hears in both at once; remember me, not my abilities; for when I consider my Apostleship that I was sent to you, I am in St. *Pauls quorum, quorum ego sum minimus*, the least of them that have been sent; and when I consider my infirmities, I am in his *quorum*, in another commission, another way, *Quorum ego maximus*;

the greatest of them; but remember my labors, and endeavors, at least my desire, to make sure your salvation. And I shall remember your religious cheerfulness in hearing the word, and your christianly respect towards all them that bring that word unto you, and towards myself in particular far [a]bove my merit. And so as your eyes that stay here, and mine that must be far of, for all that distance shall meet every morning, in looking upon that same Sun, and meet every night, in looking upon that same Moon; so our hearts may meet morning and evening in that God, which sees and hears every where; that you may come thither to him with your prayers, that I, (if I may be of use for his glory, and your edification in this place) may be restored to you again; and may come to him with my prayer that what *Paul* soever plant amongst you, or what *Apollos* soever water, God himself will give the increase: That if I never meet you again till we have all passed the gate of death, yet in the gates of heaven, I may meet you all, and there say to my Saviour and your Saviour, that which he said to his Father and our Father, *Of those whom thou hast given me, have I not lost one.* Remember me thus, you that stay in this Kingdome of peace, where no sword is drawn, but the sword of Justice, as I shal remember you in those Kingdomes, where ambition on one side, and a necessary defence from unjust persecution on the other side hath drawn many swords; and Christ Jesus remember us all in his Kingdome, to which, though we must sail through a sea, it is the sea of his blood, where no soul suffers shipwrack; though we must be blown with strange winds, with sighs and groans for our sins, yet it is the Spirit of God that blows all this wind, and shall blow away all contrary winds of diffidence or distrust in Gods mercy; where we shall be all Souldiers of one Army, the Lord of Hostes, and Children of one Quire, the God of Harmony and consent: where all Clients shall retain but one Counsellor, our Advocate Christ Jesus, nor present him any other fee but his own blood, and yet every Client have a Judgment on his side, not only in a not guilty, in the remission of his sins, but in a *Venite benedicti*, in being called to the participation of an immortal Crown of glory: where there shall be no difference in affection, nor in mind, but we shall agree as fully and perfectly in our *Allelujah*, and *gloria in excelsis*, as God the Father, Son, and Holy Ghost agreed in the *faciamus hominem* at first; where we shall end, and yet begin but then; where we shall have continuall rest, and yet never grow lazie; where we shall be stronger to resist, and yet have no enemy; where we shall live and never die, where we shall meet and never part.

THOUGHTS*

Blaise Pascal, 1670

432

Scepticism is true; for, after all, men before Jesus Christ did not know where they were, nor whether they were great or small. And those who have said the one or the other, knew nothing about it, and guessed without reason and by chance. They also erred always in excluding the one or the other.

Quod ergo ignorantes quaeritis, religio annuntiat vobis.[1]

433

After having understood the whole nature of man.—That a religion may be true, it must have knowledge of our nature. It ought to know its greatness and littleness, and the reason of both. What religion but the Christian has known this?

434

The chief arguments of the sceptics—I pass over the lesser ones—are that we have no certainty of the truth of these principles apart from faith and revelation, except in so far as we naturally perceive them in ourselves. Now this natural intuition is not a convincing proof of their truth; since, having no certainty, apart from faith, whether man was created by a good God, or by a wicked demon, or by chance, it is doubtful whether these principles given to us are true, or false, or uncertain, according to our origin. Again, no person is certain, apart from faith, whether he is awake or sleeps, seeing that during sleep we believe as firmly as we do that we are awake; we believe that we see space, figure, and motion; we are aware of the passage of time, we measure it; and in fact we act as if we were awake. So that half of our life being passed in

---

* From Section VII, "Morality and Doctrine." Translated by W. F. Trotter from the text of Brunschvicg. Passages erased by Pascal are enclosed in square brackets.

[1] "What therefore ye ignorantly seek, religion proclaims to you."—Cf. Acts, xvii. 23.

sleep, we have on our own admission no idea of truth, whatever we may imagine. As all our intuitions are then illusions, who knows whether the other half of our life, in which we think we are awake, is not another sleep a little different from the former, from which we awake when we suppose ourselves asleep?

[And who doubts that, if we dreamt in company, and the dreams chanced to agree, which is common enough, and if we were always alone when awake, we should believe that matters were reversed? In short, as we often dream that we dream, heaping dream upon dream, may it not be that this half of our life, wherein we think ourselves awake, is itself only a dream on which the others are grafted, from which we wake at death, during which we have as few principles of truth and good as during natural sleep, these different thoughts which disturb us being perhaps only illusions like the flight of time and the vain fancies of our dreams?]

These are the chief arguments on one side and the other.

I omit minor ones, such as the sceptical talk against the impressions of custom, education, manners, country, and the like. Though these influence the majority of common folk, who dogmatise only on shallow foundations, they are upset by the least breath of the sceptics. We have only to see their books if we are not sufficiently convinced of this, and we shall very quickly become so, perhaps too much.

I notice the only strong point of the dogmatists, namely, that, speaking in good faith and sincerely, we cannot doubt natural principles. Against this the sceptics set up in one word the uncertainty of our origin, which includes that of our nature. The dogmatists have been trying to answer this objection ever since the world began.

So there is open war among men, in which each must take a part, and side either with dogmatism or scepticism. For he who thinks to remain neutral is above all a sceptic. This neutrality is the essence of the sect; he who is not against them is essentially for them. [In this appears their advantage.] They are not for themselves; they are neutral, indifferent, in suspense as to all things, even themselves being no exception.

What then shall man do in this state? Shall he doubt everything? Shall he doubt whether he is awake, whether he is being pinched, or whether he is being burned? Shall he doubt whether he doubts? Shall he doubt whether he exists? We cannot go so far as that; and I lay it down as a fact there never has been a real complete sceptic. Nature sustains our feeble reason, and prevents it raving to this extent.

Shall he then say, on the contrary, that he certainly possesses truth —he who, when pressed ever so little, can show no title to it, and is forced to let go his hold?

What a chimera then is man! What a novelty! What a monster, what a chaos, what a contradiction, what a prodigy! Judge of all things, imbecile worm of the earth; depositary of truth, a sink of uncertainty and error; the pride and refuse of the universe!

Who will unravel this tangle? Nature confutes the sceptics, and reason confutes the dogmatists. What then will you become, O men! who try to find out by your natural reason what is your true condition? You cannot avoid one of these sects, nor adhere to one of them.

Know then, proud man, what a paradox you are to yourself. Humble yourself, weak reason; be silent, foolish nature; learn that man infinitely transcends man, and learn from your Master your true condition, of which you are ignorant. Hear God.

For in fact, if man had never been corrupt, he would enjoy in his innocence both truth and happiness with assurance; and if man had always been corrupt, he would have no idea of truth or bliss. But, wretched as we are, and more so than if there were no greatness in our condition, we have an idea of happiness, and cannot reach it. We perceive an image of truth, and possess only a lie. Incapable of absolute ignorance and of certain knowledge, we have thus been manifestly in a degree of perfection from which we have unhappily fallen.

It is, however, an astonishing thing that the mystery furthest removed from our knowledge, namely, that of the transmission of sin, should be a fact without which we can have no knowledge of ourselves. For it is beyond doubt that there is nothing which more shocks our reason than to say that the sin of the first man has rendered guilty those, who, being so removed from this source, seem incapable of participation in it. This transmission does not only seem to us impossible, it seems also very unjust. For what is more contrary to the rules of our miserable justice than to damn eternally an infant incapable of will, for a sin wherein he seems to have so little a share, that it was committed six thousand years before he was in existence? Certainly nothing offends us more rudely than this doctrine; and yet, without this mystery, the most incomprehensible of all, we are incomprehensible to ourselves. The knot of our condition takes its twists and turns in this abyss, so that man is more inconceivable without this mystery than this mystery is inconceivable to man.

[Whence it seems that God, willing to render the difficulty of our existence unintelligible to ourselves, has concealed the knot so high, or, better speaking, so low, that we are quite incapable of reaching it; so that it is not by the proud exertions of our reason, but by the simple submission of reason, that we can truly know ourselves.

These foundations, solidly established on the inviolable authority of religion, make us know that there are two truths of faith equally certain: the one, that man, in the state of creation, or in that of grace, is raised above all nature, made like unto God and sharing in His divinity; the other, that in the state of corruption and sin, he is fallen from this state and made like unto the beasts.

These two propositions are equally sound and certain. Scripture manifestly declares this to us, when it says in some places: "My delights were to be with the children of men" [Proverbs vii. 31]. "I will pour out my spirit upon all flesh" [Joel ii. 28]. "You are gods and all of you the sons of the most high" [Psalms lxxxi. 6]. "All flesh is grass" [Isaiah lx. 6]. "Man is compared to senseless beasts, and is become like to them" [Psalms xlvii. 13]. "I said in my heart concerning the sons of man that God would prove them and show them to be like beasts" [Ecclesiastes iii. 18].

Whence it clearly seems that man by grace is made like unto God, and a partaker in His divinity, and that without grace he is like unto the brute beasts.]

THE VANITY OF HUMAN WISHES
In Imitation of the Tenth Satire of Juvenal

Samuel Johnson, 1749

Let Observation, with extensive view,
Survey mankind, from China to Peru;
Remark each anxious toil, each eager strife,
And watch the busy scenes of crowded life;
Then say how hope and fear, desire and hate
O'erspread with snares the clouded maze of fate,
Where wav'ring man, betray'd by vent'rous pride
To tread the dreary paths without a guide,
As treach'rous phantoms in the mist delude,
Shuns fancied ills, or chases airy good;   10
How rarely Reason guides the stubborn choice,
Rules the bold hand, or prompts the suppliant voice;
How nations sink, by darling schemes oppress'd,
When Vengeance listens to the fool's request.
Fate wings with ev'ry wish th' afflictive dart,
Each gift of nature, and each grace of art;
With fatal heat impetuous courage glows,
With fatal sweetness elocution flows,
Impeachment stops the speaker's powerful breath,
And restless fire precipitates on death.   20
　　But scarce observ'd, the knowing and the bold
Fall in the gen'ral massacre of gold;
Wide-wasting pest! that rages unconfin'd,
And crowds with crimes the records of mankind;
For gold his sword the hireling ruffian draws,
For gold the hireling judge distorts the laws;
Wealth heap'd on wealth, nor truth nor safety buys,
The dangers gather as the treasures rise.
　　Let Hist'ry tell where rival kings command,
And dubious title shakes the madded land,   30
When statutes glean the refuse of the sword,
How much more safe the vassal than the lord,

Low skulks the hind beneath the rage of power,
And leaves the wealthy traitor in the Tower,
Untouch'd his cottage, and his slumbers sound,
Tho' confiscation's vultures hover round.
    The needy traveller, serene and gay,
Walks the wild heath, and sings his toil away.
Does envy seize thee? crush th' upbraiding joy,
Increase his riches and his peace destroy;   40
New fears in dire vicissitude invade,
The rustling brake alarms, and quiv'ring shade,
Nor light nor darkness bring his pain relief,
One shews the plunder, and one hides the thief.
    Yet still one gen'ral cry the skies assails,
And gain and grandeur load the tainted gales;
Few know the toiling statesman's fear or care,
Th' insidious rival and the gaping heir.
    Once more, Democritus, arise on earth,
With cheerful wisdom and instructive mirth,   50
See motley life in modern trappings dress'd,
And feed with varied fools th' eternal jest:
Thou who couldst laugh where want enchain'd caprice,
Toil crush'd conceit, and man was of a piece;
Where wealth unlov'd without a mourner dy'd;
And scarce a sycophant was fed by pride;
Where ne'er was known the form of mock debate,
Or seen a new-made mayor's unwieldy state;
Where change of fav'rites made no change of laws,
And senates heard before they judg'd a cause;   60
How wouldst thou shake at Britain's modish tribe,
Dart the quick taunt, and edge the piercing gibe?
Attentive truth and nature to descry,
And pierce each scene with philosophic eye,
To thee were solemn toys or empty show
The robes of pleasures and the veils of woe:
All aid the farce, and all thy mirth maintain,
Whose joys are causeless, or whose griefs are vain.
    Such was the scorn that fill'd the sage's mind,
Renew'd at ev'ry glance on human kind;   70
How just that scorn ere yet thy voice declare,
Search ev'ry state, and canvass ev'ry pray'r.
    Unnumber'd suppliants crowd Preferment's gate,
Athirst for wealth, and burning to be great;
Delusive Fortune hears th' incessant call,
They mount, they shine, evaporate, and fall.
On ev'ry stage the foes of peace attend,

Hate dogs their flight, and insult mocks their end.
Love ends with hope, the sinking statesman's door
Pours in the morning worshiper no more;   80
For growing names the weekly scribbler lies,
To growing wealth the dedicator flies;
From ev'ry room descends the painted face,
That hung the bright palladium of the place;
And smok'd in kitchens, or in auctions sold,
To better features yields the frame of gold;
For now no more we trace in ev'ry line
Heroic worth, benevolence divine:
The form distorted justifies the fall,
And detestation rids th' indignant wall.   90

   But will not Britain hear the last appeal,
Sign her foe's doom, or guard her fav'rites' zeal?
Thro' Freedom's sons no more remonstrance rings,
Degrading nobles and controlling kings;
Our supple tribes repress their patriot throats,
And ask no questions but the price of votes;
With weekly libels and septennial ale.
Their wish is full to riot and to rail.

   In full-blown dignity, see Wolsey stand,
Law in his voice, and fortune in his hand: 100
To him the church, the realm, their powers consign,
Through him the rays of regal bounty shine;
Turn'd by his nod the stream of honour flows,
His smile alone security bestows:
Still to new heights his restless wishes tower,
Claim leads to claim, and pow'r advances power;
Till conquest unresisted ceas'd to please,
And rights submitted, left him none to seize.
At length his sov'reign frowns—the train of state
Mark the keen glance, and watch the sign to hate.   110
Where'er turns, he meets a stranger's eye,
His suppliants scorn him, and his followers fly;
At once is lost the pride of awful state,
The golden canopy, the glitt'ring plate,
The regal palace, the luxurious board,
The liv'ried army, and the menial lord.
With age, with cares, with maladies oppress'd,
He seeks the refuge of monastic rest.
Grief aids disease, remember'd folly stings,
And his last sighs reproach the faith of kings.   120

   Speak thou, whose thoughts at humble peace repine,
Shall Wolsey's wealth, with Wolsey's end be thine?

Or liv'st thou now, with safer pride content,
The wisest justice on the banks of Trent?
For why did Wolsey, near the steeps of fate,
On weak foundations raise th' enormous weight?
Why but to sink beneath misfortune's blow,
With louder ruin to the gulfs below?
    What gave great Villiers to th' assassin's knife,
And fix'd disease on Harley's closing life?   130
What murder'd Wentworth, and what exil'd Hyde,
By kings protected and to kings allied?
What but their wish indulg'd in courts to shine,
And pow'r too great to keep or to resign?
    When first the college rolls receive his name,
The young enthusiast quits his ease for fame;
Resistless burns the fever of renown
Caught from the strong contagion of the gown:
O'er Bodley's dome his future labours spread,
And Bacon's mansion trembles o'er his head.   140
Are these thy views? proceed, illustrious youth,
And Virtue guard thee to the throne of Truth!
Yet should thy soul indulge the gen'rous heat,
Till captive Science yields her last retreat;
Should Reason guide thee with her brightest ray,
And pour on misty Doubt resistless day;
Should no false kindness lure to loose delight,
Nor praise relax, nor difficulty fright;
Should tempting Novelty thy cell refrain,
And Sloth effuse her opiate fumes in vain;   150
Should Beauty blunt on fops her fatal dart,
Nor claim the triumph of a letter'd heart;
Should no disease thy torpid veins invade,
Nor Melancholy's phantoms haunt thy shade;
Yet hope not life from grief or danger free,
Nor think the doom of man revers'd for thee:
Deign on the passing world to turn thine eyes,
And pause a while from letters, to be wise;
There mark what ills the scholar's life assail,
Toil, envy, want, the patron, and the gaol.   160
See nations slowly wise, and meanly just,
To buried merit raise the tardy bust.
If dreams yet flatter, once again attend,
Hear Lydiat's life, and Galileo's, end.
    Nor deem, when Learning her last prize bestows,
The glitt'ring eminence exempt from foes;
See when the vulgar 'scapes, despis'd or aw'd,

Rebellion's vengeful talons seize on Laud.
From meaner minds though smaller fines content,
The plunder'd palace, or sequester'd rent;   170
Mark'd out by dang'rous parts he meets the shock,
And fatal Learning leads him to the block:
Around his tomb let Art and Genius weep,
But hear his death, ye blockheads, hear and sleep.
  The festal blazes, the triumphal show,
The ravish'd standard, and the captive foe,
The senate's thanks, the gazette's pompous tale,
With force resistless o'er the brave prevail.
Such bribes the rapid Greek o'er Asia whirl'd,
For such the steady Romans shook the world;   180
For such in distant lands the Britons shine,
And stain with blood the Danube or the Rhine;
This pow'r has praise, that virtue scarce can warm,
Till fame supplies the universal charm.
Yet Reason frowns on War's unequal game,
Where wasted nations raise a single name,
And mortgag'd states their grandsires' wreaths regret
From age to age in everlasting debt;
Wreaths which at last the dear-bought right convey
To rust on medals, or on stones decay.   190
  On what foundation stands the warrior's pride,
How just his hopes, let Swedish Charles decide;
A frame of adamant, a soul of fire,
No dangers fright him, and no labours tire;
O'er love, o'er fear, extends his wide domain,
Unconquer'd lord of pleasure and of pain;
No joys to him pacific sceptres yield,
War sounds the trump, he rushes to the field;
Behold surrounding kings their powers combine,
And one capitulate, and one resign;   200
Peace courts his hand, but spreads her charms in vain;
"Think nothing gain'd," he cries, "till naught remain,
On Moscow's walls till Gothic standards fly,
And all be mine beneath the polar sky."
The march begins in military state,
And nations on his eye suspended wait;
Stern Famine guards the solitary coast,
And Winter barricades the realms of Frost;
He comes, nor want nor cold his course delay;—
Hide, blushing Glory, hide Pultowa's day: 210
The vanquish'd hero leaves his broken bands,
And shows his miseries in distant lands;

Condemn'd a needy supplicant to wait,
While ladies interpose, and slaves debate.
But did not Chance at length her error mend?
Did no subverted empire mark his end?
Did rival monarchs give the fatal wound?
Or hostile millions press him to the ground?
His fall was destin'd to a barren strand,
A petty fortress, and a dubious hand;   220
He left the name at which the world grew pale,
To point a moral, or adorn a tale.

    All times their scenes of pompous woes afford,
From Persia's tyrant to Bavaria's lord.
In gay hostility, and barb'rous pride,
With half mankind embattled at his side,
Great Xerxes comes to seize the certain prey,
And starves exhausted regions in his way;
Attendant Flatt'ry counts his myriads o'er,
Till counted myriads sooth his pride no more;   230
Fresh praise is tried till madness fires his mind,
The waves he lashes, and enchains the wind;
New pow'rs are claim'd, new pow'rs are still bestow'd,
Till rude resistance lops the spreading god;
The daring Greeks deride the martial show,
And heap their valleys with the gaudy foe;
Th' insulted sea with humbler thought he gains,
A single skiff to speed his flight remains;
Th' incumber'd oar scarce leaves the dreaded coast
Through purple billows and a floating host.   240

    The bold Bavarian, in a luckless hour,
Tries the dread summits of Caesarean pow'r,
With unexpected legions bursts away,
And sees defenseless realms receive his sway;
Short sway! fair Austria spreads her mournful charms,
The queen, the beauty, sets the world in arms;
From hill to hill the beacon's rousing blaze
Spreads wide the hope of plunder and of praise;
The fierce Croatian, and the wild Hussar,
With all the sons of ravage crowd the war;   250
The baffled prince, in honour's flatt'ring bloom
Of hasty greatness finds the fatal doom;
His foes' derision, and his subjects' blame,
And steals to death from anguish and from shame.

    Enlarge my life with multitude of days!
In health, in sickness, thus the suppliant prays;
Hides from himself his state, and shuns to know,

That life protracted is protracted woe.
Time hovers o'er, impatient to destroy,
And shuts up all the passages of joy;   260
In vain their gifts the bounteous seasons pour,
The fruit autumnal, and the vernal flower;
With listless eyes the dotard views the store,
He views, and wonders that they please no more;
Now pall the tasteless meats, and joyless wines,
And Luxury with sighs her slave resigns.
Approach, ye minstrels, try the soothing strain,
Diffuse the tuneful lenitives of pain:
No sounds, alas! would touch th' impervious ear,
Though dancing mountains witness'd Orpheus near;   270
Nor lute nor lyre his feeble powers attend,
Nor sweeter music of a virtuous friend,
But everlasting dictates crowd his tongue,
Perversely grave, or positively wrong.
The still returning tale, and ling'ring jest,
Perplex the fawning niece and pamper'd guest,
While growing hopes scarce awe the gath'ring sneer,
And scarce a legacy can bribe to hear;
The watchful guests still hint the last offence;
The daughter's petulance, the son's expense,   280
Improve his heady rage with treach'rous skill,
And mould his passions till they make his will.
    Unnumber'd maladies his joints invade,
Lay siege to life and press the dire blockade;
But unextinguish'd Av'rice still remains,
And dreaded losses aggravate his pains;
He turns, with anxious heart and crippled hands,
His bonds of debt, and mortgages of lands;
Or views his coffers with suspicious eyes,
Unlocks his gold, and counts it till he dies.   290
    But grant, the virtues of a temp'rate prime
Bless with an age exempt from scorn or crime;
An age that melts with unperceiv'd decay,
And glides in modest innocence away;
Whose peaceful day Benevolence endears,
Whose night congratulating Conscience cheers;
The gen'ral fav'rite as the gen'ral friend:
Such age there is, and who shall wish its end?
    Yet ev'n on this her load Misfortune flings,
To press the weary minutes' flagging wings;   300
New sorrow rises as the day returns,
A sister sickens, or a daughter mourns.

Now kindred Merit fills the sable bier,
Now lacerated Friendship claims a tear;
Year chases year, decay pursues decay,
Still drops some joy from with'ring life away;
New forms arise, and diff'rent views engage,
Superfluous lags the vet'ran on the stage,
Till pitying Nature signs the last release,
And bids afflicted worth retire to peace.   310
    But few there are whom hours like these await,
Who set unclouded in the gulfs of Fate.
From Lydia's monarch should the search descend,
By Solon caution'd to regard his end,
In life's last scene what prodigies surprise,
Fears of the brave, and follies of the wise!
From Marlb'rough's eyes the streams of dotage flow,
And Swift expires a driv'ler and a show.
    The teeming mother, anxious for her race,   320
Begs for each birth the fortune of a face:
Yet Vane could tell what ills from beauty spring;
And Sedley curs'd the form that pleas'd a king.
Ye nymphs of rosy lips and radiant eyes,
Whom Pleasure keeps too busy to be wise,
Whom joys with soft varieties invite,
By day the frolic, and the dance by night;
Who frown with vanity, who smile with art,
And ask the latest fashion of the heart;
What care, what rules your heedless charms shall save,
Each nymph your rival, and each youth your slave?   330
Against your frame with fondness hate combines,
The rival batters, and the lover mines.
With distant voice neglected Virtue calls,
Less heard and less, the faint remonstrance falls;
Tir'd with contempt, she quits the slipp'ry reign,
And Pride and Prudence take her seat in vain.
In crowd at once, where none the pass defend,
The harmless freedom, and the private friend.
The guardians yield, by force superior plied:
To Int'rest, Prudence; and to Flatt'ry, Pride.   340
Now Beauty falls betray'd, despis'd, distress'd,
And hissing Infamy proclaims the rest.
    Where then shall Hope and Fear their objects find?
Must dull suspense corrupt the stagnant mind?
Must helpless man, in ignorance sedate,
Roll darkling down the torrent of his fate?
Must no dislike alarm, no wishes rise,

No cries invoke the mercies of the skies?
Inquirer, cease; petitions yet remain,
Which Heaven may hear, nor deem Religion vain.   350
Still raise for good the supplicating voice,
But leave to Heaven the measure and the choice.
Safe in His power, whose eyes discern afar
The secret ambush of a specious prayer.
Implore His aid, in His decisions rest,
Secure, whate'er He gives, He gives the best.
Yet when the sense of sacred presence fires,
And strong devotion to the skies aspires,
Pour forth thy fervours for a healthful mind,
Obedient passions, and a will resign'd;   360
For love, which scarce collective man can fill;
For patience sov'reign o'er transmuted ill;
For faith, that panting for a happier seat,
Counts death kind Nature's signal of retreat:
These goods for man the laws of Heaven ordain,
These goods He grants, who grants the power to gain;
With these celestial Wisdom calms the mind,
And makes the happiness she does not find.

THE AMBITIOUS GUEST*

Nathaniel Hawthorne

One September night a family had gathered round their hearth, and piled it high with the driftwood of mountain streams, the dry cones of the pine, and the splintered ruins of great trees that had come crashing down the precipice. Up the chimney roared the fire, and brightened the room with its broad blaze. The faces of the father and mother had a sober gladness; the children laughed; the eldest daughter was the image of Happiness at seventeen; and the aged grandmother, who sat knitting in the warmest place, was the image of Happiness grown old. They had found the "herb, heart's-ease," in the bleakest spot of all New England. This family were situated in the Notch of the White Hills, where the wind was sharp throughout the year, and pitilessly cold in the winter,—giving their cottage all its fresh inclemency before it descended on the valley of the Saco. They dwelt in a cold spot and a dangerous one; for a mountain towered above their heads, so steep, that the stones would often rumble down its sides and startle them at midnight.

The daughter had just uttered some simple jest that filled them all with mirth, when the wind came through the Notch and seemed to pause before their cottage—rattling the door, with a sound of wailing and lamentation, before it passed into the valley. For a moment it saddened them, though there was nothing unusual in the tones. But the family were glad again when they perceived that the latch was lifted by some traveller, whose footsteps had been unheard amid the dreary blast which heralded his approach, and wailed as he was entering, and went moaning away from the door.

Though they dwelt in such a solitude, these people held daily converse with the world. The romantic pass of the Notch is a great artery, through which the lifeblood of internal commerce is continually throbbing between Maine, on one side, and the Green Mountains and the shores of the St. Lawrence, on the other. The stage-coach always drew up before the door of the cottage. The wayfarer, with no companion but his staff, paused here to exchange a word, that the sense of

* First published in the *New England Magazine*, June, 1835; collected first in *Twice-Told Tales*, 2nd. ed. (1842).

loneliness might not utterly overcome him ere he could pass through the cleft of the mountain, or reach the first house in the valley. And here the teamster, on his way to Portland market, would put up for the night; and, if a bachelor, might sit an hour beyond the usual bedtime, and steal a kiss from the mountain maid at parting. It was one of those primitive taverns where the traveller pays only for food and lodging, but meets with a homely kindness beyond all price. When the footsteps were heard, therefore, between the outer door and the inner one, the whole family rose up, grandmother, children, and all, as if about to welcome some one who belonged to them, and whose fate was linked with theirs.

The door was opened by a young man. His face at first wore the melancholy expression, almost despondency, of one who travels a wild and bleak road, at nightfall and alone, but soon brightened up when he saw the kindly warmth of his reception. He felt his heart spring forward to meet them all, from the old woman, who wiped a chair with her apron, to the little child that held out its arms to him. One glance and smile placed the stranger on a footing of innocent familiarity with the eldest daughter.

"Ah, this fire is the right thing!" cried he; "especially when there is such a pleasant circle round it. I am quite benumbed; for the Notch is just like the pipe of a great pair of bellows; it has blown a terrible blast in my face all the way from Bartlett."

"Then you are going towards Vermont?" said the master of the house, as he helped to take a light knapsack off the young man's shoulders.

"Yes; to Burlington, and far enough beyond," replied he. "I meant to have been at Ethan Crawford's to-night; but a pedestrian lingers along such a road as this. It is no matter; for, when I saw this good fire, and all your cheerful faces, I felt as if you had kindled it on purpose for me, and were waiting my arrival. So I shall sit down among you, and make myself at home."

The frank-hearted stranger had just drawn his chair to the fire when something like a heavy footstep was heard without, rushing down the steep side of the mountain, as with long and rapid strides, and taking such a leap in passing the cottage as to strike the opposite precipice. The family held their breath, because they knew the sound, and their guest held his by instinct.

"The old mountain has thrown a stone at us, for fear we should forget him," said the landlord, recovering himself. "He sometimes nods his head and threatens to come down; but we are old neighbors, and agree together pretty well upon the whole. Besides we have a sure place of refuge hard by if he should be coming in good earnest."

Let us now suppose the stranger to have finished his supper of bear's meat; and, by his natural felicity of manner, to have placed him-

self on a footing of kindness with the whole family, so that they talked
as freely together as if he belonged to their mountain brood. He was of a
proud, yet gentle spirit—haughty and reserved among the rich and
great; but ever ready to stoop his head to the lowly cottage door, and
be like a brother or a son at the poor man's fireside. In the household
of the Notch he found warmth and simplicity of feeling, the pervading
intelligence of New England, and a poetry of native growth, which they
had gathered when they little thought of it from the mountain peaks and
chasms, and at the very threshold of their romantic and dangerous
abode. He had travelled far and alone; his whole life, indeed, had been
a solitary path; for, with the lofty caution of his nature, he had kept
himself apart from those who might otherwise have been his com-
panions. The family, too, though so kind and hospitable, had that consciousness of unity among themselves, and separation from the world
at large, which, in every domestic circle, should still keep a holy place
where no stranger may intrude. But this evening a prophetic sympathy
impelled the refined and educated youth to pour out his heart before
the simple mountaineers, and constrained them to answer him with the
same free confidence. And thus it should have been. Is not the kindred
of a common fate a closer tie than that of birth?

The secret of the young man's character was a high and abstracted
ambition. He could have borne to live an undistinguished life, but not to
be forgotten in the grave. Yearning desire had been transformed to hope;
and hope, long cherished, had become like certainty, that, obscurely as
he journeyed now, a glory was to beam on all his pathway,—though
not, perhaps, while he was treading it. But when posterity should gaze
back into the gloom of what was now the present, they would trace the
brightness of his footsteps, brightening as meaner glories faded, and
confess that a gifted one had passed from his cradle to his tomb with
none to recognize him.

"As yet," cried the stranger—his cheek glowing and his eye flashing
with enthusiasm—"as yet, I have done nothing. Were I to vanish from
the earth to-morrow, none would know so much of me as you: that a
nameless youth came up at nightfall from the valley of the Saco, and
opened his heart to you in the evening, and passed through the Notch
by sunrise, and was seen no more. Not a soul would ask, 'Who was he?
Whither did the wanderer go?' But I cannot die till I have achieved my
destiny. Then, let Death come! I shall have built my monument!"

There was a continual flow of natural emotion, gushing forth amid
abstracted reverie, which enabled the family to understand this young
man's sentiments, though so foreign from their own. With quick sensi-
bility of the ludicrous, he blushed at the ardor into which he had been
betrayed.

"You laugh at me," said he, taking the eldest daughter's hand, and
laughing himself. "You think my ambition as nonsensical as if I were

to freeze myself to death on the top of Mount Washington, only that people might spy at me from the country round about. And, truly, that would be a noble pedestal for a man's statue!"

"It is better to sit here by this fire," answered the girl, blushing, "and be comfortable and contented, though nobody thinks about us."

"I suppose," said her father, after a fit of musing, "there is something natural in what the young man says; and if my mind had been turned that way, I might have felt just the same. It is strange, wife, how his talk has set my head running on things that are pretty certain never to come to pass."

"Perhaps they may," observed the wife. "Is the man thinking what he will do when he is a widower?"

"No, no!" cried he, repelling the idea with reproachful kindness. "When I think of your death, Esther, I think of mine, too. But I was wishing we had a good farm in Bartlett, or Bethlehem, or Littleton, or some other township round the White Mountains; but not where they could tumble on our heads. I should want to stand well with my neighbors and be called Squire, and sent to General Court for a term or two; for a plain, honest man may do as much good there as a lawyer. And when I should be grown quite an old man, and you an old woman, so as not to be long apart, I might die happy enough in my bed, and leave you all crying around me. A slate gravestone would suit me as well as a marble one—with just my name and age, and a verse of a hymn, and something to let people know that I lived an honest man and died a Christian."

"There now!" exclaimed the stranger; "it is our nature to desire a monument, be it slate or marble, or a pillar of granite, or a glorious memory in the universal heart of man."

"We're in a strange way, to-night," said the wife, with tears in her eyes. "They say it's a sign of something, when folks' minds go a wandering so. Hark to the children!"

They listened accordingly. The younger children had been put to bed in another room, but with an open door between, so that they could be heard talking busily among themselves. One and all seemed to have caught the infection from the fireside circle, and were outvying each other in wild wishes, and childish projects of what they would do when they came to be men and women. At length a little boy, instead of addressing his brothers and sisters, called out to his mother.

"I'll tell you what I wish, mother," cried he. "I want you and father and grandma'm, and all of us, and the stranger too, to start right away, and go and take a drink out of the basin of the Flume!"

Nobody could help laughing at the child's notion of leaving a warm bed, and dragging them from a cheerful fire, to visit the basin of the Flume,—a brook, which tumbles over the precipice, deep within the Notch. The boy had hardly spoken when a wagon rattled along the road, and stopped a moment before the door. It appeared to contain two or three men, who were cheering their hearts with the rough chorus of a song, which resounded, in broken notes, between the cliffs, while the singers hesitated whether to continue their journey or put up here for the night.

"Father," said the girl, "they are calling you by name."

But the good man doubted whether they had really called him, and was unwilling to show himself too solicitous of gain by inviting people to patronize his house. He therefore did not hurry to the door; and the lash being soon applied, the travellers plunged into the Notch, still singing and laughing, though their music and mirth came back drearily from the heart of the mountain.

"There, mother!" cried the boy, again. "They'd have given us a ride to the Flume."

Again they laughed at the child's pertinacious fancy for a night ramble. But it happened that a light cloud passed over the daughter's spirit; she looked gravely into the fire, and drew a breath that was almost a sigh. It forced its way, in spite of a little struggle to repress it. Then starting and blushing, she looked quickly round the circle, as if they had caught a glimpse into her bosom. The stranger asked what she had been thinking of.

"Nothing," answered she, with a downcast smile. "Only I felt lonesome just then."

"Oh, I have always had a gift of feeling what is in other people's hearts," said he, half seriously. "Shall I tell the secrets of yours? For I know what to think when a young girl shivers by a warm hearth, and complains of lonesomeness at her mother's side. Shall I put these feelings into words?"

"They would not be a girl's feelings any longer if they could be put into words," replied the mountain nymph, laughing, but avoiding his eye.

All this was said apart. Perhaps a germ of love was springing in their hearts, so pure that it might blossom in Paradise, since it could not be matured on earth; for women worship such gentle dignity as his; and the proud, contemplative, yet kindly soul is oftenest captivated by simplicity like hers. But while they spoke softly, and he was watching the happy sadness, the lightsome shadows, the shy yearnings of a maiden's nature, the wind through the Notch took a deeper and drearier sound. It seemed, as the fanciful stranger said, like the choral strain of the spirits of the blast, who in old Indian times had their dwelling among these mountains, and made their heights and recesses a sacred region. There was a wail along the road, as if a funeral were passing. To chase away the gloom, the family threw pine branches on their fire, till the dry leaves crackled and the flame arose, discovering once again a scene of peace and humble happiness. The light hovered about them fondly, and caressed them all. There were the little faces of the children, peeping from their bed apart, and here the father's frame of strength, the mother's subdued and careful mien, the high-browed youth, the budding girl, and the good old grandam, still knitting in the warmest place. The aged woman looked up from her task, and, with fingers ever busy, was the next to speak.

"Old folks have their notions," said she, "as well as young ones. You've been wishing and planning; and letting your heads run on one thing and another, till you've set my mind a wandering too. Now what should an old woman wish for, when she can go but a step or two before she comes to her grave? Children, it will haunt me night and day till I tell you."

"What is it, mother?" cried the husband and wife at once.

Then the old woman, with an air of mystery which drew the circle closer round the fire, informed them that she had provided her grave-clothes some years before,—a nice linen shroud, a cap with a muslin ruff, and everything of a finer sort than she had worn since her wedding day. But this evening an old superstition had strangely recurred to her. It used to be said, in her younger days, that if anything were amiss with a corpse, if only the ruff were not smooth, or the cap did not set right, the corpse in the coffin and beneath the clods would strive to put up its cold hands and arrange it. The bare thought made her nervous.

"Don't talk so, grandmother!" said the girl, shuddering.

"Now,"—continued the old woman, with singular earnestness, yet smiling strangely at her own folly,—"I want one of you, my children— when your mother is dressed and in the coffin—I want one of you to hold a looking-glass over my face. Who knows but I may take a glimpse at myself, and see whether all's right?"

"Old and young, we dream of graves and monuments," murmured the stranger youth. "I wonder how mariners feel when the ship is sinking, and they, unknown and undistinguished, are to be buried together in the ocean—that wide and nameless sepulchre?"

For a moment, the old woman's ghastly conception so engrossed the minds of her hearers that a sound abroad in the night, rising like the roar of a blast, had grown broad, deep, and terrible, before the fated group were conscious of it. The house and all within it trembled; the foundations of the earth seemed to be shaken, as if this awful sound were the peal of the last trump. Young and old exchanged one wild glance, and remained an instant, pale, affrighted, without utterance, or power to move. Then the same shriek burst simultaneously from all their lips.

"The Slide! The Slide!"

The simplest words must intimate, but not portray, the unutterable horror of the catastrophe. The victims rushed from their cottage, and sought refuge in what they deemed a safer spot—where, in contemplation of such an emergency, a sort of barrier had been reared. Alas! they had quitted their security, and fled right into the pathway of destruction. Down came the whole side of the mountain, in a cataract or ruin. Just before it reached the house, the stream broke into two branches— shivered not a window there, but overwhelmed the whole vicinity, blocked up the road, and annihilated everything in its dreadful course. Long ere the thunder of the great Slide had ceased to roar among the mountains, the mortal agony had been endured, and the victims were at peace. Their bodies were never found.

The next morning, the light smoke was seen stealing from the cottage chimney up the mountain side. Within, the fire was yet smouldering on the hearth, and the chairs in a circle round it, as if the inhabitants had but gone forth to view the devastation of the Slide, and would shortly return, to thank Heaven for their miraculous escape. All had left separate tokens, by which those who had known the family were made to shed a tear for each. Who has not heard their name? The story has been told far and wide, and will forever be a legend of these mountains. Poets have sung their fate.

There were circumstances which led some to suppose that a stranger had been received into the cottage on this awful night, and had shared the catastrophe of all its inmates. Others denied that there were sufficient grounds for such a conjecture. Woe for the high-souled youth, with his dream of Earthly Immortality! His name and person utterly unknown; his history, his way of life, his plans, a mystery never to be solved, his death and his existence equally a doubt! Whose was the agony of that death moment?

THE RUBAIYAT OF OMAR KHAYYAM*

Edward FitzGerald

1

Wake! For the Sun, who scattered into flight
The Stars before him from the Field of Night,
   Drives Night along with them from Heav'n and strikes
The Sultán's Turret with a Shaft of Light.

2

Before the phantom of False morning died,
Methought a Voice within the Tavern cried,
   "When all the Temple is prepared within,
Why nods the drowsy Worshiper outside?"

3

And, as the Cock crew, those who stood before
The Tavern shouted—"Open, then, the Door!
   You know how little while we have to stay,
And, once departed, may return no more."

4

Now the New Year reviving old Desires,
The thoughtful Soul to Solitude retires,
   Where the White Hand of Moses on the Bough
Puts out, and Jesus from the Ground suspires.

5

Iram indeed is gone with all his Rose,
And Jamshyd's Sev'n-ringed Cup where no one knows;
   But still a Ruby kindles in the Vine,
And many a Garden by the Water blows.

* Omar Khayyám (Omar the tent-maker) was a Persian poet of the 11th century. FitzGerald published English verse translations in 1859, 1868, 1872 and 1879, revising and polishing his stanzas.

6

And David's lips are locked; but in divine
High-piping Pehleví, with "Wine! Wine! Wine!
    Red Wine!"—the Nightingale cries to the Rose
That sallow cheek of hers to incarnadine.

7

Come, fill the Cup, and in the fire of Spring
Your Winter-garment of Repentance fling;
    The Bird of Time has but a little way
To flutter—and the Bird is on the Wing.

8

Whether at Naishápúr or Babylon,
Whether the Cup with sweet or bitter run,
    The Wine of Life keeps oozing drop by drop,
The Leaves of Life keep falling one by one.

9

Each Morn a thousand Roses brings, you say;
Yes, but where leaves the Rose of Yesterday?
    And this first Summer month that brings the Rose
Shall take Jamshyd and Kaikobád way.

10

Well, let it take them! What have we to do
With Kaikobád the Great, or Kaikhosrú?
    Let Zál and Rustum bluster as they will,
Or Hátim call to Supper—heed not you.

11

With me along the strip of Herbage strown
That just divides the desert from the sown,
    Where name of Slave and Sultán is forgot—
And Peace to Mahmúd on his golden Throne!

12

A Book of Verses underneath the Bough,
A Jug of Wine, a Loaf of Bread—and Thou
    Besides me singing in the Wilderness—
Oh, Wilderness were Paradise enow!

13

Some for the Glories of This World; and some
Sigh for the Prophet's Paradise to come;   50
   Ah, take the Cash, and let the Credit go,
Nor heed the rumble of a distant Drum!

14

Look to the blowing Rose about us—"Lo,
Laughing," she says, "into the world I blow,
   At once the silken tassel of my Purse   55
Tear, and its Treasure on the Garden throw."

15

And those who husbanded the Golden Grain,
And those who flung it to the winds like Rain,
   Alike to no such aureate Earth are turned
As, buried once, Men want dug up again.   60

16

The Worldly Hope men set their Hearts upon
Turns Ashes—or it prospers; and anon,
   Like Snow upon the Desert's dusty Face,
Lighting a little hour or two—is gone.

17

Think, in this battered Caravanserai   65
Whose Portals are alternate Night and Day,
   How Sultán after Sultán with his Pomp
Abode his destined Hour, and went his way.

18

They say the Lion and the Lizard keep
The Courts where Jamshyd gloried and drank deep;   70
   And Bahrám, that great Hunter—the Wild Ass
Stamps o'er his Head, but cannot break his Sleep.

19

I sometimes think that never blows so red
The Rose as where some buried Caesar bled;
   That every Hyacinth the Garden wears   75
Dropped in her Lap from some once lovely Head.

20

And this reviving Herb whose tender Green
Fledges the River-Lip on which we lean—
    Ah, lean upon it lightly! for who knows
From what once lovely Lip it springs unseen!

21

Ah, my Belovéd, fill the Cup that clears
Today of past Regrets and future Fears:
    Tomorrow!—Why, Tomorrow I may be
Myself with Yesterday's Sev'n thousand Years.

22

For some we loved, the loveliest and the best
That from his Vintage rolling Time hath prest,
    Have drunk their Cup a Round or two before,
And one by one crept silently to rest.

23

And we, that now make merry in the Room
They left, and Summer dresses in new bloom,
    Ourselves must we beneath the Couch of Earth
Descend—ourselves to make a Couch—for whom?

24

Ah, make the most of what we yet may spend,
Before we too into the Dust descend;
    Dust into Dust, and under Dust, to lie,
Sans Wine, sans Song, sans Singer, and—sans End!

25

Alike for those who for Today prepare,
And those that after some Tomorrow stare,
    A Muezzín from the Tower of Darkness cries,
"Fools your Reward is neither Here nor There."

26

Why, all the Saints and Sages who discussed
Of the Two Worlds so wisely—they are thrust
    Like foolish Prophets forth; their Words to Scorn
Are scattered, and their Mouths are stopped with Dust.

27

Myself when young did eagerly frequent
Doctor and Saint, and heard great argument
    About it and about; but evermore
Came out by the same door where in I went.

28

With them the seed of Wisdom did I sow,
And with mine own hand wrought to make it grow;
    And this was all the Harvest that I reaped—
"I came like Water, and like Wind I go."

29

Into this Universe, and *Why* not knowing
Nor *Whence*, like Water willy-nilly flowing;
    And out of it, as Wind along the Waste,
I know not *Whither*, willy-nilly blowing.

30

What, without asking, hither hurried *Whence?*
And, without asking, *Whither* hurried hence!
    Oh, many a Cup of this forbidden Wine
Must drown the memory of that insolence!

31

Up from the Earth's Center through the Seventh Gate
I rose, and on the Throne of Saturn sate,
    And many a Knot unraveled by the Road;
But not the Master-knot of Human Fate.

32

There was the Door to which I found no Key;
There was the Veil through which I might not see;
    Some little talk awhile of Me and Thee
There was—and then no more of Thee and Me.

33

Earth could not answer; nor the Seas that mourn
In flowing Purple, of their Lord forlorn;
    Nor rolling Heaven, with all his Signs revealed
And hidden by the sleeve of Night and Morn.

105

110

115

121

126

130

34

Then of the Thee in Me who works behind
The Veil, I lifted up my hands to find   134
   A lamp amid the Darkness; and I heard,
As from Without—"The Me within Thee blind!"

35

Then to the Lip of this poor earthen Urn
I leaned, the Secret of my Life to learn;
   And Lip to Lip it murmured—"While you live,   140
Drink!—for, once dead, you never shall return."

36

I think the Vessel, that with fugitive
Articulation answered, once did live,
   And drink; and Ah! the passive Lip I kissed,
How many Kisses might it take—and give!

37

For I remember stopping by the way   145
To watch a Potter thumping his wet Clay;
   And with its all-obliterated Tongue
It murmured—"Gently, Brother, gently, pray!"

38

And has not such a Story from of Old
Down Man's successive generations rolled   150
   Of such a clod of saturated Earth?
Cast by the Maker into Human mold?

39

And not a drop that from our Cups we throw
For Earth to drink of, but may steal below
   To quench the fire of Anguish in some Eye
There hidden—far beneath, and long ago.   156

40

As then the Tulip, for her morning sup
Of Heav'nly Vintage, from the soil looks up,
   Do you devoutly do the like, till Heav'n
To Earth invert you—like an empty Cup.   160

41

Perplexed no more with Human or Divine,
Tomorrow's tangle to the winds resign,
    And lose your fingers in the tresses of
The Cypress-slender Minister of Wine.

42

And if the Wine you drink, the Lip you press,
End in what All begins and ends in—Yes;
    Think that you are Today what Yesterday
You were—Tomorrow you shall not be less.

166

43

So when that Angel of the darker Drink
At last shall find you by the river-brink,
    And offering his Cup, invite your Soul
Forth to your Lips to quaff—you shall not shrink.

170

44

Why, if the Soul can fling the Dust aside,
And naked on the Air of Heaven ride,
    Were't not a Shame—were't not a Shame for him
In this clay carcass crippled to abide?

175

45

'Tis but a Tent where takes his one day's rest
A Sultán to the realm of Death addrest;
    The Sultán rises, and the dark Ferrásh
Strikes, and prepares it for another Guest.

180

46

And fear not lest Existence closing your
Account, and mine, should know the like no more;
    The Eternal Sákí from that Bowl has poured
Millions of Bubbles like us, and will pour.

47

When You and I behind the Veil are past,
Oh, but the long, long while the World shall last,
    Which of our Coming and Departure heeds
As the Sea's self should heed a pebble-cast.

185

48

A Moment's Halt—a momentary taste
Of Being from the Well amid the Waste—
And Lo!—the phantom Caravan has reached
The Nothing it set out from—Oh, make haste!

189

49

Would you that spangle of Existence spend
About the secret—quick about it, Friend!
   A Hair perhaps divides the False and True—
And upon what, prithee, does life depend?

195

50

A Hair perhaps divides the False and True—
Yes; and a single Alif were the clue—
   Could you but find it—to the Treasurehouse
And peradventure to The Master too;

200

51

Whose secret Presence, through Creation's veins
Running Quicksilver-like, eludes your pains;
   Taking all shapes from Máh to Máhi; and
They change and perish all—but He remains;

52

A moment guessed—then back behind the Fold
Immersed of Darkness round the Drama rolled
   Which, for the Pastime of Eternity,
He doth Himself contrive, enact, behold.

205

53

But if in vain, down on the stubborn floor
Of Earth, and up to Heav'n's unopening Door,
   You gaze Today, while You are You—how then
Tomorrow, when You shall be You no more?

211

54

Waste not your Hour, nor in the vain pursuit
Of This and That endeavor and dispute;
   Better be jocund with the fruitful Grape
Than sadden after none, or bitter, Fruit.

216

55

You know, my Friends, with what a brave Carouse
I made a Second Marriage in my house;
   Divorced old barren Reason from my Bed,
And took the Daughter of the Vine to Spouse.

56

For "Is" and "Is-not" though with Rule and Line,   ²²¹
And "Up-and-down" by Logic, I define,
   Of all that one should care to fathom, I
Was never deep in anything but—Wine.

57

Ah, but my Computations, People say,   ²²⁵
Reduced the Year to better reckoning?—Nay,
   'Twas only striking from the Calendar
Unborn Tomorrow, and dead Yesterday.

58

And lately, by the Tavern Door agape,
Came shining through the Dusk an Angel Shape   ²³⁰
   Bearing a Vessel on his Shoulder; and
He bid me taste of it; and 'twas—the Grape!

59

The Grape that can with Logic absolute
The Two-and-Seventy jarring Sects confute;
   The sovereign Alchemist that in a trice   ²³⁵
Life's leaden metal into Gold transmute;

60

The mighty Mahmúd, Allah-breathing Lord,
That all the misbelieving and black Horde
   Of fears and Sorrows that infest the Soul
Scatters before him with his whirlwind Sword.

61

Why, be this Juice the growth of God, who dare   ²⁴¹
Blaspheme the twisted tendril as a Snare?
   A Blessing, we should use it, should we not?
And if a Curse—why, then, Who set it there?

62

I must abjure the Balm of Life, I must,
Scared by some After-reckoning ta'en on trust
   Or lured with Hope of some Diviner Drink,
To fill the Cup—when crumbled into Dust!

63

Oh threats of Hell and Hopes of Paradise!
One thing at least is certain—*This* Life flies;
   One thing is certain and the rest is Lies—
The Flower that once has blown forever dies.

64

Strange, is it not? that of the myriads who
Before us passed the door of Darkness through,
   Not one returns to tell us of the Road,
Which to discover we must travel too.

65

The Revelations of Devout and Learned
Who rose before us, and as Prophets burned,
   Are all but Stories, which, awoke from Sleep,
They told their comrades, and to Sleep returned.

66

I sent my Soul through the Invisible,
Some letter of that After-life to spell;
   And by and by my Soul returned to me,
And answered, "I Myself am Heav'n and Hell"—

67

Heav'n but the Vision of fulfilled Desire,
And Hell the Shadow from a Soul on fire
   Cast on the Darkness into which Ourselves,
So late emerged from, shall so soon expire.

68

We are no other than a moving row
Of Magic Shadow-shapes that come and go
   Round with the Sun-illumined Lantern held
In Midnight by the Master of the Show;

69

But helpless Pieces of the Game He plays
Upon this Checker-board of Nights and Days;
  Hither and thither moves, and checks, and slays,
And one by one back in the Closet lays.

70

The Ball no question makes of Ayes and Noes,
But Here or There as strikes the Player goes;
  And He that tossed you down into the Field,
He knows about it all—He knows—HE knows!

71

The Moving Finger writes, and, having writ,
Moves on; nor all your Piety nor Wit
  Shall lure it back to cancel half a Line,
Nor all your Tears wash out a Word of it.

72

And that inverted Bowl they call the Sky,
Whereunder crawling cooped we live and die,
  Lift not your hands to *It* for help—for It
As impotently moves as you or I.

73

With Earth's first Clay They did the Last Man knead,
And there of the Last Harvest sowed the Seed;
  And the first Morning of Creation wrote
What the Last Dawn of Reckoning shall read.

74

Yesterday *This* Day's Madness did prepare;
Tomorrow's Silence, Triumph, or Despair.
  Drink! for you know not whence you came, nor why;
Drink, for you know not why you go, nor where.

75

I tell you this—When, started from the Goal,
Over the flaming shoulders of the Foal
  Of Heav'n Parwín and Mushtarí they flung,
In my predestined Plot of Dust and Soul

76

The Vine had struck a fiber; which about
If clings my Being—let the Dervish flout;
 Of my Base metal may be filed a Key,
That shall unlock the Door he howls without.

77

And this I know: whether the one True Light
Kindle to love, or Wrath-consume me quite,
 One Flash of It within the Tavern caught
Better than in the Temple lost outright.

305

78

What! out of senseless Nothing to provoke
A conscious Something to resent the yoke
 Of unpermitted Pleasure, under pain
Of Everlasting Penalties, if broke!

310

79

What! from his helpless Creature be repaid
Pure Gold for what he lent him dross-allayed—
 Sue for a Debt he never did contract,
And cannot answer—Oh, the sorry trade!

315

80

O Thou, who didst with pitfall and with gin
Beset the Road I was to wander in,
 Thou wilt not with Predestined Evil round
Enmesh, and then impute my Fall to Sin!

320

81

Oh Thou, who Man of Baser Earth didst make,
And ev'n with Paradise devise the Snake,
 For all the Sin wherewith the Face of Man
Is blackened—Man's forgiveness give—and take!

  . . . .

82

As under cover of departing Day
Slunk hunger-stricken Ramazán away,
 Once more within the Potter's house alone
I stood, surrounded by the Shapes of Clay—

325

83

Shapes of all Sorts and Sizes, great and small,
That stood along the floor and by the wall;   330
   And some loquacious Vessels were; and some
Listened perhaps, but never talked at all.

84

Said one among them—"Surely not in vain
My substance of the common Earth was ta'en
   And to this Figure molded, to be broke,   335
Or trampled back to shapeless Earth again."

85

Then said a Second—"Ne'er a peevish Boy
Would break the Bowl from which he drank in joy;
   And He that with his hand the Vessel made
Will surely not in after Wrath destroy."   340

86

After a momentary silence spake
Some Vessel of a more ungainly Make:
   "They sneer at me for leaning all awry;
What! did the Hand, then, of the Potter shake?"

87

Whereat someone of the loquacious Lot—   345
I think a Súfi pipkin—waxing hot—
   "All this of Pot and Potter—Tell me then,
Who is the Potter, pray, and who the Pot?"

88

"Why," said another, "Some there are who tell
Of one who threatens he will toss to Hell   350
   The luckless Pots he marred in making—Pish!
He's a Good Fellow, and 'twill all be well."

89

"Well," murmured one, "Let whoso make or buy,
My Clay with long Oblivion is gone dry;
   But fill me with the old familiar Juice,   355
Methinks I might recover by and by."

90

So while the Vessels one by one were speaking
The little Moon looked in that all were seeking;
   And then they jogged each other, "Brother! Brother!
Now for the Porter's shoulder-knot a-creaking!"   360

.   .   .   .

91

Ah, with the Grape my fading Life provide,
And wash the Body whence the Life has died,
   And lay me, shrouded in the living Leaf,
By some not unfrequented Garden-side—

92

That ev'n my buried Ashes such a snare   365
Of Vintage shall fling up into the Air
   As not a True-believer passing by
But shall be overtaken unaware.

93

Indeed the Idols I have loved so long
Have done my credit in this World much wrong,   370
   Have drowned my Glory in a shallow Cup,
And sold my Reputation for a Song.

94

Indeed, indeed, Repentance oft before
I swore—but was I sober when I swore?
   And then and then came Spring, and Rose-in-hand   375
My thread-bare Penitence apieces tore.

95

And much as Wine has played the Infidel,
And robbed me of my Robe of Honor—Well,
   I wonder often what the Vintners buy
One-half so precious as the stuff they sell.   380

96

Yet Ah, that Spring should vanish with the Rose!
That Youth's sweet-scented manuscript should close!
   The Nightingale that in the branches sang,
Ah whence, and whither flown again, who knows!

97

Would but the Desert of the Fountain yield
One glimpse—if dimly, yet indeed, revealed,
   To which the fainting Traveler might spring,
As springs the trampled herbage of the field!

385

98

Would but some wingéd Angel ere too late
Arrest the yet unfolded Roll of Fate,
   And make the stern Recorder otherwise
Enregister, or quite obliterate!

99

Ah, Love! could you and I with Him conspire
To grasp this sorry Scheme of Things entire,
   Would not we shatter it to bits—and then
Remold it nearer to the Heart's Desire!

396

   .   .   .   .

100

Yon rising Moon that looks for us again—
How oft hereafter will she wax and wane;
   How oft hereafter rising look for us
Through this same Garden—and for one in vain!

400

101

And when like her, O Sákí, you shall pass
Among the Guests Star-scattered on the Grass,
   And in your joyous errand reach the spot
Where I made One—turn down an empty Glass!

EAST COKER*

T. S. Eliot

I

In my beginning is my end. In succession
Houses rise and fall, crumble, are extended,
Are removed, destroyed, restored, or in their place
Is an open field, or a factory, or a by-pass.
Old stone to new building, old timber to new fires,
Old fires to ashes, and ashes to the earth
Which is already flesh, fur and faeces,
Bone of man and beast, cornstalk and leaf.
Houses live and die: there is a time for building
And a time for living and for generation
And a time for the wind to break the loosened pane
And to shake the wainscot where the field-mouse trots
And to shake the tattered arras woven with a silent motto.

In my beginning is my end. Now the light falls
Across the open field, leaving the deep lane
Shuttered with branches, dark in the afternoon,
Where you lean against a bank while a van passes,
And the deep lane insists on the direction
Into the village, in the electric heat
Hypnotised. In a warm haze the sultry light
Is absorbed, not refracted, by grey stone.
The dahlias sleep in the empty silence.
Wait for the early owl.
                              In that open field
If you do not come too close, if you do not come too close,
On a Summer midnight, you can hear the music
Of the weak pipe and the little drum

And see them dancing around the bonfire
The association of man and woman
In daunsinge, signifying matrimonie—
A dignified and commodious sacrament.
Two and two, necessarye coniunction,
Holding eche other by the hand or the arm
Whiche betokeneth concorde. Round and round the fire
Leaping through the flames, or joined in circles,
Rustically solemn or in rustic laughter
Lifting heavy feet in clumsy shoes,
Earth feet, loam feet, lifted in country mirth
Mirth of those long since under earth
Nourishing the corn. Keeping time,
Keeping the rhythm in their dancing
As in their living in the living seasons
The time of the seasons and the constellations
The time of milking and the time of harvest
The time of the coupling of man and woman
And that of beasts. Feet rising and falling.
Eating and drinking. Dung and death.

   Dawn points, and another day
Prepares for heat and silence. Out at sea the dawn wind
Wrinkles and slides. I am here
Or there, or elsewhere. In my beginning.

II

What is the late November doing
With the disturbance of the spring
And creatures of the summer heat,
And snowdrops writhing under feet
And hollyhocks that aim too high
Red into grey and tumble down
Late roses filled with early snow?
Thunder rolled by the rolling stars
Simulates triumphal cars
Deployed in constellated wars
Scorpion fights against the Sun
Until the Sun and Moon go down
Comets weep and Leonids fly
Hunt the heavens and the plains
Whirled in a vortex that shall bring
The world to that destructive fire
Which burns before the ice-cap reigns.

That was a way of putting it—not very satisfactory:
A periphrastic study in a worn-out poetical fashion,
Leaving one still with the intolerable wrestle
With words and meanings. The poetry does not matter.
It was not (to start again) what one had expected.
What was to be the value of the long looked forward to,
Long hoped for calm, the autumnal serenity
And the wisdom of age? Had they deceived us
Or deceived themselves, the quiet-voiced elders,
Bequeathing us merely a receipt for deceit?
The serenity only a deliberate hebetude,
The wisdom only the knowledge of dead secrets
Useless in the darkness into which they peered
Or from which they turned their eyes. There is, it seems to us,
At best, only a limited value
In the knowledge derived from experience.
The knowledge imposes a pattern, and falsifies,
For the pattern is new in every moment
And every moment is a new and shocking
Valuation of all we have been. We are only undeceived
Of that which, deceiving, could no longer harm.
In the middle, not only in the middle of the way
But all the way, in a dark wood, in a bramble,
On the edge of a grimpen, where is no secure foothold,
And menaced by monsters, fancy lights,
Risking enchantment. Do not let me hear
Of the wisdom of old men, but rather of their folly,
Their fear of fear and frenzy, their fear of possession,
Of belonging to another, or to others, or to God.
The only wisdom we can hope to acquire
Is the wisdom of humility: humility is endless.

   The houses are all gone under the sea.

   The dancers are all gone under the hill.

III

O dark dark dark. They all go into the dark,
The vacant interstellar spaces, the vacant into the vacant,
The captains, merchant bankers, eminent men of letters,
The generous patrons of art, the statesmen and the rulers,
Distinguished civil servants, chairmen of many committees,
Industrial lords and petty contractors, all go into the dark,

And dark the Sun and Moon, and the Almanach de Gotha
And the Stock Exchange Gazette, the Directory of Directors,
And cold the sense and lost the motive of action.
And we all go with them, into the silent funeral,
Nobody's funeral, for there is no one to bury.
I said to my soul, be still, and let the dark come upon you
Which shall be the darkness of God.   As, in a theatre,
The lights are extinguished, for the scene to be changed
With a hollow rumble of wings, with a movement of darkness
    on darkness,
And we know that the hills and the trees, the distant panorama
And the bold imposing façade are all being rolled away—
Or as, when an underground train, in the tube, stops too long
    between stations
And the conversation rises and slowly fades into silence
And you see behind every face the mental emptiness deepen
Leaving only the growing terror of nothing to think about;
Or when, under ether, the mind is conscious but conscious of
    nothing—
I said to my soul, be still, and wait without hope
For hope would be hope for the wrong thing; wait without love
For love would be love of the wrong thing; there is yet faith
But the faith and the love and the hope are all in the waiting.
Wait without thought, for you are not ready for thought:
So the darkness shall be the light, and the stillness the dancing.

  Whisper of running streams, and winter lightning.
The wild thyme unseen and the wild strawberry,
The laughter in the garden, echoed ecstasy
Not lost, but requiring, pointing to the agony
Of death and birth.
                        You say I am repeating
Something I have said before. I shall say it again.
Shall I say it again? In order to arrive there,
To arrive where you are, to get from where you are not,
  You must go by a way wherein there is no ecstasy.
In order to arrive at what you do not know
  You must go by a way which is the way of ignorance.
In order to possess what you do not possess
  You must go by the way of dispossession.
In order to arrive at what you are not
  You must go through the way in which you are not.
And what you do not know is the only thing you know
And what you own is what you do not own
And where you are is where you are not.

IV

The wounded surgeon plies the steel
That questions the distempered part;
Beneath the bleeding hands we feel
The sharp compassion of the healer's art
Resolving the enigma of the fever chart.

    Our only health is the disease
If we obey the dying nurse
Whose constant care is not to please
But to remind of our, and Adam's curse,
And that, to be restored, our sickness must grow worse.

    The whole earth is our hospital
Endowed by the ruined millionaire,
Wherein, if we do well, we shall
Die of the absolute paternal care
That will not leave us, but prevents us everywhere.

    The chill ascends from feet to knees,
The fever sings in mental wires.
If to be warmed, then I must freeze
And quake in frigid purgatorial fires
Of which the flame is roses, and the smoke is briars.

    The dripping blood our only drink,
The bloody flesh our only food:
In spite of which we like to think
That we are sound, substantial flesh and blood—
Again, in spite of that, we call this Friday good.

V

So here I am, in the middle way, having had twenty years—
Twenty years largely wasted, the years of *l'entre deux guerres*—
Trying to learn to use words, and every attempt
Is a wholly new start, and a different kind of failure
Because one has only learnt to get the better of words
For the thing one no longer has to say, or the way in which
One is no longer disposed to say it. And so each venture
Is a new beginning, a raid on the inarticulate
With shabby equipment always deteriorating
In the general mess of imprecision of feeling,
Undisciplined squads of emotion. And what there is to conquer

By strength and submission, has already been discovered
Once or twice, or several times, by men whom one cannot hope
To emulate—but there is no competition—
There is only the fight to recover what has been lost
And found and lost again and again: and now, under conditions
That seem unpropitious. But perhaps neither gain nor loss.
For us, there is only the trying. The rest is not our business.

    Home is where one starts from. As we grow older
The world becomes stranger, the pattern more complicated
Of dead and living. Not the intense moment
Isolated, with no before and after,
But a lifetime burning in every moment
And not the lifetime of one man only
But of old stones that cannot be deciphered.
There is a time for the evening under starlight,
A time for the evening under lamplight
(The evening with the photograph album).
Love is most nearly itself
When here and now cease to matter.
Old men ought to be explorers
Here and there does not matter
We must be still and still moving
Into another intensity
For a further union, a deeper communion
Through the dark cold and the empty desolation,
The wave cry, the wind cry, the vast waters
Of the petrel and the porpoise.   In my end is my beginning.

THE RIGHT TIME*

Paul Tillich

> Everything has its appointed hour,
>> there is a time for all things under heaven:
> a time for birth, a time for death,
> a time to plant and a time to uproot,
> a time to kill, a time to heal,
> a time to break down and a time to build,
> a time to cry, a time to laugh,
> a time to mourn, a time to dance,
> a time to scatter and a time to gather,
> a time to embrace, a time to refrain,
> a time to seek, a time to lose,
> a time to keep, a time to throw away,
> a time to tear, a time to sew,
> a time for silence and a time for speech,
> a time for love, a time for hate,
> a time for war, a time for peace.

Ecclesiastes 3:1–8

You have read words of a man who lived about 200 years before the birth of Jesus; a man nurtured in Jewish piety and educated in Greek wisdom; a child of his period—a period of catastrophes and despair. He expresses this despair in words of a pessimism that surpasses most pessimistic writings in world literature. Everything is in vain, he repeats many times. It is vanity, even if you were King Solomon who not only controlled the means for any humanly possible satisfaction but who also could use them with wisdom. But even such a man must say: All is in vain! We do not know the name of the writer of this book who is usually called the Preacher, although he is much more a teacher of wisdom, a practical philosopher. Perhaps we wonder how his dark considerations of man's destiny could become a Biblical book. It took indeed a long time and the overcoming of much protest before it was accepted. But finally synagogue and church accepted it; and now this book is in the Bible beside Isaiah and Matthew and Paul and John. The "all is in vain" has received Biblical authority. I believe that this authority is deserved, that it is not an authority produced by a mistake, but that it is the authority of truth. His description of the human situation is truer than any poetry glorifying man and his destiny. His honesty opens our eyes for those things which are overlooked or covered up by optimists of all kinds. So if you meet people who attack Christianity for having too many illusions tell them that their attacks would be much stronger if they allied themselves with the book of the Preacher. The very fact that this book is a part of the Bible shows clearly that the Bible is a most realistic book. And it cannot be otherwise. For only on this background the message of Jesus as the Christ has meaning. Only if we accept an honest view of the human situation, of man's old reality, can we understand the message that in Christ a new reality has appeared. He who never has said about his life "Vanity of vanities, all is vanity" cannot honestly say with Paul, "In all these things we are more than conquerors through him who loved us."

There is a time, an appointed hour, for all things under heaven, says the Preacher. And in fourteen contrasts he embraces the whole of human existence, showing that everything has its time. What does this mean?

When the Preacher says that everything has its time, he does not forget his ever-repeated statement, "This too is vanity and striving for the wind." The fact that everything has its appointed time only confirms his tragic view. Things and actions have their time. Then they pass and other things and actions have *their* time. But nothing new comes out of this circle in which all life moves. Everything is timed by an eternal law which is above time. We are not able to penetrate into the meaning of this timing. For *us*, it is mystery and what *we* see is vanity and frustration. God's timing is hidden to us, and our toiling and timing are of no ultimate use. Any human attempt to change the rhythm of birth and death, of war and peace, of love and hate and all the other contrasts in the rhythm of life is in vain.

This is the first but it is not the whole meaning of the statement that everything has its appointed hour. If the Preacher says that there is a time to plant and a time to uproot, a time to kill, a time to heal, a time to break down and a time to build, a time to mourn and a time to dance, a time to speak and a time to be silent, he asks us to be aware of the right time, the time to do one thing and not to do another thing. After he has emphasized that everything is timed by an unsurmountable destiny, he asks us to follow this timing from above and to do our own timing according to it. As a teacher of wisdom who gives many wise rules for our acting, he requests right timing. He knows that all our timing is dependent on the timing from above, from the hidden ruler of time; but this does not exclude our acting at the right and not at the wrong moment. The whole ancient world was driven by the belief that for everything we do there is an adequate hour: If you want to build a house or to marry, if you want to travel or to begin a war—for any important enterprise—you must ask for the right moment. You must ask somebody who knows—the priest or the astrologer, the seer or the prophet. On the ground of their oracles about the good season you may or may not act. This was a belief of centuries and millennia. It was one of the strongest forces in human history, from generation to generation. The greatest men of the past waited for the oracle announcing the appointed hour. Jesus Himself says that His hour has not yet come and He went to Jerusalem when He felt that His hour *had* come.

The modern man usually does not ask for oracles. But the modern man knows of the need for timing as much as his predecessors. When in my early years in this country I had to discuss a certain project with an influential American business man he said to me, "Don't forget that the first step to a successful action is the right timing." Innumerable times, when reading about political or commercial actions, I was reminded of these words. In many conversations about activities and plans the problem of timing came up. It is one of the most manifest patterns of our culture, of our industrial civilization. How does it compare with the words of the Preacher?

When the business man spoke to me about timing he thought of what *he* had done and what *he* would do. He betrayed the pride of a man who knows the right hour for his actions, who was successful in his timing, who felt as the master of his destiny, as the creator of new things, as the conqueror of situations. This certainly is not the mood of the Preacher. Even if the Preacher points to the need of right timing he does not give up his great "All is vanity." You must do it, you must grasp the right moment, but ultimately it does not matter. The end is the same for the wise and the fool, for him who toils and for him who enjoys himself, the end is even the same for man and for animals.

The Preacher is first of all conscious that he *is* timed; and he points to our timing as a secondary matter. The modern business man is first of all conscious that *he* has to time, and only vaguely realizes that he *is* timed. Of course, he also is aware that he has not produced the right time, that he is dependent on it, that he may miss it in his calculations and actions. He knows that there is a limit to his timing, that there are economic forces stronger than he, that he also is subject to a final destiny which ends all his planning. He is aware of it, but he disregards it when he plans and acts. Quite different is the Preacher. He starts his enumeration of things that are timed with birth and death. They are beyond human timing. They are signposts which cannot be trespassed. We cannot time them and all our timing is limited by them. This is the reason why in the beginning of our modern era death and sin and hell were removed from the public consciousness. While in the Middle Ages every room, every street, and, more important, every heart and every mind were filled with symbols of the end, of death, it has been today a matter of bad taste even to mention death. The modern man feels that the awareness of the end disturbs and weakens his power of timing. He has, instead of the threatening symbols of death, the clock in every room, on every street, and, more important, in his mind and in his nerves. There is something mysterious about the clock. It determines our daily timing. Without it we could not plan for the next hour, we could not time any of our activities. But the clock also reminds us of the fact that we are timed. It indicates the rush of our time towards it. The voice of the clock has reminded many people of the fact that they are timed. In an old German night-watchman's street song every hour is announced with a special reminder. Of midnight it says: "Twelve—that is the goal of time, give us, O God, eternity." These two attitudes toward the clock indicate two ways of timing—the one as being timed, the other as timing for the next hour, for today and tomorrow. What does the clock tell you? Does it point to the hour of rising and working and eating and talking and going to sleep? Does it point to the next appointment and the next project? Or does it show that another day, another week have passed, that we have become older, that better timing is needed to use our last years for the fulfillment of our plans, for planting and building and finishing before it is too late? Or does the clock make us anticipate the moment in which its voice does not speak any more for us? Have we, the men of the industrial age, the men who are timing every hour from day to day, the courage and the imagination of the Preacher who looks back at all *his* time and all *his* timing and calls it vanity? And if so, what about our timing? Does it not lose any meaning? Must we not say with the Preacher that it is good for man to enjoy life as it is given to him from hour to hour, but that it is better not to be born at all?

There is another answer to the question of human existence, to the question of timing and being timed. It is summed up in the words of Jesus: "The time is fulfilled and the kingdom of God is at hand." In these words, God's timing breaks into our human timing. Something new appears, answering the question of the Preacher as well as the question of the business man. We ask with all generations of thinking men: What is the meaning of the flux of time and the passing away of everything in it? What is the meaning of our toiling and planning when the end of all of us and our works is the same? Vanity? And this is the answer we get: Within this our time something happens that is not of our time but of our eternity, and this times our time! The same power which limits us in time gives eternal significance to our timing. When Jesus says that the right hour has come, that the kingdom of God is at hand, He pronounces the victory over the law of vanity. This hour is not subject to the circle of life and death and all the other circles of vanity. When God Himself appears in a moment of time, when He

Himself subjects Himself to the flux of time, the flux of time is conquered. And if this happens in one moment of time, then all moments of time receive another significance. When the finger of the clock turns around; not one vain moment is replaced by another vain moment, but each moment says to us: The eternal is at hand in this moment. This moment passes, the eternal remains. Whatever in this moment, in this hour, on this day and in this short or long-life-time happens has infinite significance. Our timing from moment to moment, our planning today for tomorrow, the toil of our life-time is not lost. Its deepest meaning lies not ahead where vanity swallows it, but it lies above where eternity affirms it. This is the seriousness of time and timing. Through our timing God times the coming of His kingdom; through our timing He elevates the time of vanity into the time of fulfillment. The activist who is timing with shrewdness and intuition what he has to do in his time and for his time, and for our whole activistic civilization cannot give us the answer. And the Preacher, who himself once was a most successful activist, knows that this is not an answer; he knows the vanity of our timing. And let us be honest. The spirit of the Preacher is strong today in our minds. His mood fills our philosophy and poetry. The vanity of human existence is described powerfully by those who call themselves philosophers or poets of existence. They are all the children of the Preacher, this great existentialist of his period. But neither they nor the Preacher know an answer. They know more than the men of mere acting. They know the vanity of acting and timing. They know that we are timed. But they do not know the answer either. Certainly we must act; we cannot help it. We have to time our lives from day to day. Let us do it as clearly and as successfully as the Preacher when he still followed the example of King Solomon. But let us follow him also when he saw through all this and realized its vanity.

Then, and then alone, are we prepared for the message of the eternal appearing in time and elevating time to eternity. Then we see in the movement of the clock not only the passing of one moment after the other, but also the eternal at hand, threatening, demanding, promising. Then we are able to say: "In spite!" In spite of the fact that the Preacher and all his pessimistic followers today and everywhere and at all times are right, I say yes to time and to toil and to acting. I know the infinite significance of every moment. But again in saying so we should not relapse into the attitude of the activist, not even of the Christian activist—and there are many of them, men and women, in Christendom. The message of the fulfillment of time is not a green light for a new, an assumedly Christian activism. But it makes us say with Paul: "Though our outer nature is wasting away our inner nature is renewed every day—because we look not to the things which are seen but to the things that are unseen. For the things that are seen are transient, but the things that are unseen are eternal." In these words the message of the Preacher and the message of Jesus are united. All is vanity but through this vanity eternity shines into us, comes near to us, draws us to itself. When eternity calls in time, then activism vanishes. When eternity calls in time, then pessimism vanishes. When eternity times us, then time becomes a vessel of eternity. Then we become vessels of that which is eternal.

CONSIDERATIONS AND QUESTIONS
FOR DISCUSSION

GILGAMESH

1. The epic hero, Gilgamesh, has crossed the world in search for immortality. He questions Shamash: "May one who indeed is dead behold yet the radiance of the sun!" But the gods have kept immortal life for themselves leaving only death for mankind. Compare the advice the ale-wife gives to Gilgamesh to that offered by Koheleth.

2. Koheleth is disturbed by death, for the wise man dieth "as the fool" (2:16). Death is described in phrases similar to Ecclesiastes in section vi of *Gilgamesh*, but is the tone as pessimistic? Death can be seen as the end of hatred, class distinction and even fear as in the following lines by Shakespeare from *Cymbeline* (iv, ii 258ff):

> Fear no more the heat o' th' sun,
>   Nor the furious winter's rages;
> Thou thy worldly task hast done,
>   Home art gone, and ta'en thy wages:
> Golden lads and girls all must,
> As chimney-sweepers, come to dust.

Are the emotions described in section vi closer to those of Koheleth or Shakespeare?

A SONG OF THE HARPER

1. Notice that this poem breaks into two parts. In the first half the harper asks where those are who have died before us. In spite of elaborate tombs and preparations for the afterlife, he realizes that death, in the words of Hamlet, takes man to an "undiscovered country, from whose bourn no traveler returns." Compare his attitude towards death to that of Koheleth and Gilgamesh.

2. The second part of the poem changes completely. Since man can be sure of nothing after death he must seize the pleasures of the day. How is this treatment of the *carpe diem* theme similar to that in Gilgamesh and Ecclesiastes?

PSALM 1

1. Psalm 1 presents a clear picture of the two ways presented in the Deuteronomic code; the way of the righteous is contrasted to that of

the ungodly, and each is rewarded or punished in this life. What is Koheleth's reaction to this position?

2. The Psalmist finds delight in contemplating the law of the Lord, probably as epitomized in the Decalogue. Why does he find laws delightful? Do they give a clear sense of order and meaning to life in establishing ultimate values? Is it more than a coincidence that Koheleth does not emphasize the law. What does this tell about his approach to the problems of life?

PROVERBS

1. The wisdom writings of the Old Testament are frequently divided into two categories: prudential or lower wisdom, reflective or higher wisdom. Proverbs and the Wisdom of Solomon fall into the first category for they contain practical advice directed to the young man on ways he can attain the good and successful life. Much of this advice is given in aphoristic form. Ecclesiastes and Job are in the second class for they pose basic questions not treated in the lower wisdom literature. These books probe into the depths of man's anguish about the meaning of life. In lower wisdom writings, wisdom is extolled as the answer to the problems of life. A summary of this position is seen in Proverbs 1:7: "The fear of the Lord is the beginning of knowledge: but fools despise wisdom and instruction." How does Koheleth react to this conclusion? Can man settle his doubts through wisdom?

2. Both Proverbs and Ecclesiastes emphasize the fear of God. The writer in Proverbs in effect says to fear God that you may gain wisdom and knowledge to live a happier and more prosperous life. Koheleth concludes "Fear God, and keep his commandments: for this is the whole duty of man" (12:13). Which fear of God demands the greater faith? Why? Is it possible that the fear of God is the beginning *and* end of wisdom?

3. Wisdom is personified as a woman in Proverbs 1–3 and 8. The advice she gives is practical and emphasizes obedience to the law. The man who is righteous and seeks wisdom "shall inherit glory: but shame shall be the promotion of fools" (3:35). The two ways described in Psalm 1 are emphasized again and again. Compare the treatment of wisdom in Ecclesiastes (particularly in chapters 7–9) to that of Proverbs. How can Koheleth's skepticism be seen even when he accepts some of the maxims from Proverbs?

4. Ecclesiastes 9:2 states "All things come alike to all: there is one event to the righteous, and to the wicked; to the good and to the clean, and to the unclean." Find verses in Proverbs which are diametrically opposed to this position.

5. Many of the maxims of Proverbs are quoted in Ecclesiastes. The aphorism in Proverbs 15:16, 17 and 16:8 is found in Ecclesiastes 4:6. A common idea is expressed in Proverbs 13:18, 15:31 and in Ecclesiastes

7:5. Proverbs 14:29 is similar to the last half of Ecclesiastes 7:8. But notice the first half of the verse: "Better is the end of a thing than the beginning thereof." And Koheleth's proverbs deal with the end, the day of death, sorrow and adversity. Contrast the pessimistic tone of Ecclesiastes 8 to the tone of various chapters of Proverbs.

6. Koheleth writes in the tradition of the earlier Hebrew sages, but he uses their vocabulary and maxims to express his own ideas. The Book of Proverbs supports an ordered existence based on wisdom. Illustrate how Koheleth selects proverbs which help to substantiate his own conclusions about the meaninglessness of existence.

7. What would Koheleth say in answer to Proverbs 22:1: "A good name is rather to be chosen than great riches, and loving favor rather than silver and gold?" Is the problem of death seriously considered in Proverbs?

8. How is the attitude towards wisdom expressed by Agur in the opening verses of Proverbs 30 different from that in the earlier selections? Compare his humility to that of Koheleth who also compares man's position to that of the beast (3:19).

THE WISDOM OF SOLOMON

1. The Wisdom of Solomon illustrates the further development of concepts treated in Proverbs and Ecclesiastes. Wisdom, personified as a beautiful woman in Proverbs, is described here as a "loving spirit." She is "the breath of the power of God, and a pure influence flowing from the glory of the Almighty" (7:25). Contrast this to the picture of wisdom in Proverbs.

2. How does the immortality of man posited in the Wisdom of Solomon answer the problems raised by Koheleth? Some have felt that Chapter 2 is a polemic against the position described in Ecclesiastes. What portions seem aimed at Koheleth's conclusions? Does the writer exaggerate Koheleth's emphasis on finding pleasure in life? Cite verses which illustrate that Koheleth is also very disturbed about the oppressions of the wicked.

3. Compare the picture of the transitory nature of life in Wisdom of Solomon 5 to that of Ecclesiastes. What are some of the images used? Notice that both writers describe life as a shadow. How does each writer use this common base as evidence to support his individual conclusion?

4. Relate the two ways described in Psalm 1 and Proverbs to the conclusions drawn in the Wisdom of Solomon. Notice that "the hope of the ungodly is like dust that is driven away with the wind" (5:14) suggests the chaff of Psalm 1. The punishments and rewards take place in the afterlife rather than on earth.

5. Although the Wisdom of Solomon introduces the concept of immortality to answer the inequities of life, how is the tone of con-

fidence similar to that of Proverbs? Contrast the assertiveness of these works to the skepticism of Ecclesiastes. Which approach to the basic questions of life do you prefer? Why?

6. The Wisdom of Solomon gives positive answers to the problems faced by man. But the emphasis upon "the corruptible body [which] presseth down the soul" (9:15) is a far more negative approach to life than that of Koheleth. Find evidence from the two works to support or refute this statement.

I CORINTHIANS 1:17-2:16

1. What two kinds of wisdom are described in this passage? Would Koheleth agree with the question: "Hath not God made foolish the wisdom of this world?" Find passages which support your conclusion.

2. I Corinthians 2:7 describes the "hidden wisdom" of God. Does Koheleth also recognize this second type of wisdom? In what verses does he speak of the wisdom of God? Is there any hope in Koheleth's writing that this wisdom will be revealed to man?

3. How does the revealed wisdom of Christ represent a continuation of Koheleth's search? Koheleth becomes resigned to the fact that man cannot understand even the works of God. What would be his reaction to the last sentence of this passage: "But we have the mind of Christ"?

MEDITATIONS

1. Matthew Arnold said, "It is impossible to rise from reading Marcus Aurelius without a sense of constraint and melancholy, without feeling that the burden laid upon man is well-nigh greater than he can bear." Do you agree with this conclusion? Is the work more affirmative than Ecclesiastes?

2. Can the tranquillity of mind described by Aurelius in section 3 be equated with Koheleth's definition of wisdom? Is it possible for a man to retreat from the world in the manner described by Aurelius? Is Koheleth more admirable than Aurelius because he does not lift himself above the problem of good and evil?

3. Aurelius is comforted by the fact "that within a very short time both thou and he will be dead; and soon not even your names will be left behind" (section 6). What is Koheleth's response to death? Account for the differences in the reactions of the two men.

4. Section 32 develops the *ubi sunt* theme: where are those who have gone before us? How is this passage similar to parts of the Egyptian *A Song of the Harper*? Does Koheleth agree with Aurelius that the brevity of life puts all things in their proper perspective?

5. Koheleth feels that reputation after death is vanity: "For there is no remembrance of the wise more than of the fool for ever; seeing that which now is in the days to come shall be forgotten" (2:16). What does the Roman emperor, Marcus Aurelius, conclude about eternal remembrance?

6. Aurelius is encouraged by the harmony found in the repetition of natural cycles in sections 43–45. Koheleth also describes the cycle of nature in chapter 1. What is his reaction? Why doesn't this pattern give him the confidence it does Aurelius?

7. The statement "Do not then consider life a thing of value" (section 50) of the *Meditations* can be contrasted to "For to him that is joined to all living there is hope" (9:4) of Ecclesiastes. Differentiate between the attitudes towards life expressed by the two writers.

THE CITY OF GOD

1. When Rome was sacked by the Goths in 410 A.D., many Christians thought that the destruction of "the Eternal City" meant the end of their faith. To assuage these fears, St. Augustine wrote *The City of God* contrasting the city of this world (equated with Rome and earthly societies in general) to the city of God (made up of Christians on earth and ultimately the heavenly city, New Jerusalem). This division is analagous to the contrast between the wisdom of this world and the mind of Christ pointed out in I Corinthians 1:13–2:17. Why does Augustine select Ecclesiastes to support his theme? Which "city" is described by Koheleth?

2. Why does Koheleth devote his "whole book to a full exposure of . . . vanity"? Augustine implies that the book makes the reader long for a better life. Does Koheleth himself give expression to this longing?

3. Does man find his identity in the vanity of this life through fearing God and keeping His commandments? What does Augustine mean by the following statement: "For so long as he remains in the likeness of vanity, he is not renewed in the image of the truth"?

4. Compare St. Augustine's interpretation of Ecclesiastes to later related writings in the Christian tradition such as Donne's *Sermon XIX*, Johnson's *The Vanity of Human Wishes* and T. S. Eliot's *East Coker*.

DONNE, SERMON XIX

1. Donne goes through the text, "Remember now thy Creator in the dayes of thy youth," in an exegetic manner, that is he interprets it word by word. Does this help you to understand the meaning of the whole? Would we today consider many of his analogies from other parts of the Bible relevant?

2. Find sections of the sermon which present interpretations with which we would no longer agree. Is Donne's method at all similar to that described by E. H. Plumptre in *Jewish Interpreters of Ecclesiastes*, Part III of this casebook?

3. Donne entitles this "A Sermon of Valediction" or a farewell sermon. How does he introduce his coming journey in the sermon? Does he relate this to the passage?

4. Do you find it ironic that a sermon based on a text from Ecclesiastes, a book in which the writer feels that death is the end of everything, should end with a ringing affirmation of eternal life?

5. Contrast this sermon to *The Right Time* by Paul Tillich. What changes in the structure of sermons have taken place in the last three centuries? Notice that the style of Tillich's sermon is more informal than the poetic cadences of Donne's. Does this mean that Tillich's sermon is less thought-provoking than Donne's?

THOUGHTS

1. Pascal says "there never has been a real complete sceptic," for no man can doubt everything. Does Koheleth come close to being a complete skeptic? When he closes every observation with "all is vanity and vexation of spirit," doesn't he really, in the words of Pascal, "doubt whether he doubts"?

2. Alexander Pope in *An Essay on Man* (1773–34) describes man as follows:

> He hangs between; in doubt to act, or rest;
> In doubt to deem himself a god, or beast;
> In doubt his mind or body to prefer;
> Born but to die, and reasoning but to err;
> Alike in ignorance, his reason such,
> Whether he thinks too little, or too much:
> Chaos of thought and passion, all confused;
> Still by himself abused, or disabused;
> Created half to rise, and half to fall;
> Great lord of all things, yet a prey to all,
> Sole judge of truth, in endless error hurled:
> The glory, jest, and riddle of the world!

Compare this passage to Pascal's writing which describes man as a chaos, a contradiction, "the pride and refuse of the universe." How would Koheleth react to these descriptions of man?

3. Can Koheleth be described as a man who perceives "an image of truth" and possesses only "a lie"? Is he "incapable of absolute ignorance and of certain knowledge"? Does this explain why at times Koheleth seems almost to envy the fool?

4. Pascal argues that even skeptics must exercise faith in some areas of their lives. Would Koheleth have agreed with this position?

THE VANITY OF HUMAN WISHES

1. Koheleth purposes "to search out by wisdom . . . all things which are done under heaven" (1:13), but really limits his discussion to the problems of man. Johnson, likewise sets out "with extensive view [to] Survey mankind, from China to Peru." He traces the vanity of desire for wealth, power, wisdom, military glory, beauty and long life in various parts of the poem. Compare his categories to those of Koheleth.

2. Johnson's poem is more specific in its references than Ecclesiastes. Do the concrete examples make the poem come alive or do they detract from the universal appeal which characterizes Ecclesiastes? Would the contemporary references have helped eighteenth-century readers understand the poem better?

3. Although his poem imitates the structure of Juvenal's tenth satire, the examples are drawn from Johnson's own experiences. The lines "There mark what ills the scholar's life assail, / Toil, envy, want, the patron and the gaol" (159–160) picture Johnson's own position as a scholar. Is his viewpoint narrower than that of Koheleth who writes as "king in Jerusalem" and obviously had the material means to follow his search wherever he desired?

5. Johnson attacks the vanity of desire for long life in lines 255–318. Would Koheleth have agreed with Johnson's conclusions about life?

6. "Still raise for good the supplicating voice, / But leave to Heaven the measure and the choice" (351–352) carries a resignation similar to Koheleth's "God is in heaven, and thou upon earth: therefore let thy words be few" (5:2). But what implications are found in Johnson's lines that are not present in Koheleth's? How are these implications developed in the conclusion of the poem?

THE AMBITIOUS GUEST

1. Koheleth follows a number of paths in his search for meaning in life. In what way does the young man search for meaning in his life? How would Koheleth react to the man's "abstracted ambition"?

2. The young man feels that his life must have some definite purpose which he will discover before death. He says, "I cannot die till I have achieved my destiny." How does the young man's desire affect the other characters in the story? Name the goals of the various members of the family, however modest they are. Even the children "seemed to have caught the infection from the fireside circle, and were outvying each other in wild wishes, and childish projects of what they would do when they came to be men and women."

3. The young man states that "it is our nature to desire a monument, be it slate or marble, or a pillar of granite, or a glorious memory

in the universal heart of man." Man searches for some way of per-
petuating himself, for some way to combat the oblivion of death. Does
Koheleth desire such monuments? What does he conclude about them?

4. What does the conclusion illustrate about the desire of man to
achieve a memorable destiny? How does it relate to Koheleth's views
about earthly immortality?

5. The young man is proud and feels that he will achieve a memorable destiny. One might describe him as filled with vanity. How does his
death illustrate the other definition of vanity as breath or nothingness,
the definition used in Ecclesiastes?

THE RUBÁIYÁT OF OMAR KHAYYÁM

1. Like Ecclesiastes, *The Rubáiyát* is not a logically developed philosophical treatise. Each quatrain contains an individual thought and the
progression of the argument is often disconnected. But both works have
a basic pattern which is similar. First, the traditional places where man
finds meaning in life are questioned. When these are found to be vanity,
the writers move to an affirmation of life itself. Although both works
extol the pleasures of a full life, the attitudes of the two authors are
different. Contrast Omar's detailed description of drinking the cup of
life to the bottom to Koheleth's more generalized conclusions. Which
do you prefer?

2. How is Omar's dismissal of reason and wisdom in stanzas 26 ff.
similar to Koheleth's rejection of the wisdom of the Hebrew sages?
Notice the poetic images Omar uses to describe man's ignorance: "the
Master-knot of Human Fate," "the Door to which I found no Key," "the
Veil through which I might not see." Does Koheleth dismiss wisdom as
completely as Omar? Does Koheleth give himself as completely to
pleasure as Omar?

3. Men search for wisdom in nature. But Omar finds that earth, sea
and heaven do not answer the riddle of life (stanza 33). Relate this to
Koheleth's experience with nature.

4. Other important parallels can be found in the two men's searches
for meaning. Omar, like Johnson in *The Vanity of Human Wishes*, dis-
covers that "The Worldly Hope . . . Turns [to] Ashes." How is this
similar to the experience of Koheleth?

5. The description of death, seen as taking place in nature in stanza
23, lacks the bluntness of Koheleth's statement: "How dieth the wise
man? as the fool" (2:16). But does the more beautiful setting of death,
even the possibility of the soul's immortality, make death more acceptable to Omar than to Koheleth?

6. Omar argues from the subjective position in stanzas 66 and 67
when his soul concludes "I myself am Heav'n and Hell." Would
Koheleth accept the implications of this statement?

EAST COKER

1. Part I of *East Coker* contains lines and ideas which are obviously taken from Ecclesiastes 1 and 3. Why does Eliot select Ecclesiastes as a source? How does Koheleth give a picture of life which is a good starting point for Eliot's poem?

2. Although man is mentioned in the Ecclesiastes picture of the cycle of nature (1:8), he is not as closely related to nature as in Eliot's description. If man is closely related to nature, how might this affect the poet's attitude towards death as the complete end of existence?

3. In Part II "the wisdom of age" and the "knowledge derived from experience" are questioned and found wanting. Compare this to the conclusions Koheleth draws in the first two chapters of Ecclesiastes.

4. Eliot describes the difficulty of communicating, "the intolerable wrestle / With words and meanings" in Part II and again in the first stanza of Part V. Does Koheleth's use of the phrase "this also is vanity" at the end of every statement also indicate a questioning of the validity of words?

5. The first two parts of *East Coker* reveal many similarities in content and tone to Ecclesiastes. Koheleth would have agreed with Eliot that "In my beginning is my end." However, the poem begins to move beyond the pessimism of Koheleth in Part III with the reference "to the agony / Of death and birth," for the Hebrew writer sees death as the complete end. What experiences does Eliot describe which enable him to conclude "In my end is my beginning"?

6. Christians have frequently interpreted Ecclesiastes as a picture of life "under the sun," written from an earthly point of view without divine perspective. Koheleth gives a vivid picture of the intelligent man's failure to find meaning or satisfaction in life without the hope of eternal life as proclaimed by Christ. Can *East Coker* be interpreted as a poetic expression of this position?

THE RIGHT TIME

1. In what way does the Preacher give us an honest view of the human situation? Notice that Tillich calls him "this great existentialist of his period" and assumes that the Preacher's message is significant to the twentieth-century reader. How does Tillich make the conclusions of the Preacher relevant to the modern reader? Contrast the relevancy of this sermon to that of Donne's sermon. Does Donne make any attempt to relate the conclusions of Ecclesiastes to his contemporary society?

2. What is the contrast between the attitude of the Preacher and that of the modern business man towards time? Distinguish between being timed and timing? Is this one of the basic distinctions between man and God?

3. Contrast modern man's attitude towards time with that of man in the middle ages. Do we become preoccupied with daily timing because we are afraid of the earlier "symbols of the end, of death"?

4. Eliot talks of the limitations of human language in *East Coker;* Tillich talks of the limitations of man's concept of time in this sermon. Relate both of these limitations to the picture of man given by the writer of Ecclesiastes. Do Eliot and Tillich feel that man can find any escape from these limitations? Does the writer of Ecclesiastes offer hope of an escape?

PART THREE

❋

❋

CRITICAL ESSAYS

INTRODUCTION

The following essays emphasize theological, philosophical and literary interpretations of Ecclesiastes. The first article, *Pessimism and Optimism*, provides a general framework into which Ecclesiastes can be placed. The selections by O. S. Rankin and E. H. Plumptre illustrate the relationships between Ecclesiastes and other Semitic and Greek literature. Mary Ellen Chase, Robert Gordis and Peter Ellis present varying contemporary interpretations of Ecclesiastes in their writings.

Some of the general questions posed by these readings are as follows: In what environment was Ecclesiastes written? Where do we find other early treatments of the same themes? How have interpretations of the book changed throughout history? What are some of the various interpretations of today? Why is Koheleth's approach to the problems of life more acceptable to contemporary readers than to most past readers? Does this indicate anything important about our own society or our present values? In what way does the reader's reaction to the book change if he views it as literature? As philosophy? As theology? Are these different approaches mutually exclusive or can they complement one another?

PESSIMISM AND OPTIMISM*

Alexander Martin

These rival interpretations of existence have one circumstance in common: both are designated by superlatives; and the loose employment of the terms in ordinary phraseology renders it needful to point this out. To justify their use in a philosophical sense it is not enough that a given view of things should dwell by preference on their more forbidding or more engaging aspect respectively. The terms are more strictly opposed than this, and each is to be understood in its literal sense. For pessimistic theory this is the worst of worlds; if it were to be a world, it could not have borne to be worse than it is. Some rudiments of order and well-being Schopenhauer himself will allow to it, since otherwise it could not cohere or continue in existence at all. But, so much being granted, the contention is that its irrationality, misery, and worthlessness could not be more than they are. And optimism also expresses itself in the same unqualified way, maintaining that all is for the best in this best of all possible worlds.

The facts on which the former of these views rests are many and undeniable. Whatever a maturer reflexion may suggest, man and his environment do not, superficially regarded, seem to be well fitted to each other. By the essential conditions of his existence man is subjected to hindrance and disappointment, to suffering, decay, and death, and necessarily his awakening consciousness is painfully arrested by such experiences. An anxious and resentful attitude to life may be said to be the natural reaction of the mind's first contact with reality, and spiritual growth thereafter to signify, at least temporarily, a deepening sense of the unsatisfying nature of the world, its instability, its evanescence, and the inconsideration which it manifests for ends humanly felt to be desirable. Hence not only the elegiac note which pervades so much of the world's most moving literature, but also the strain of world-weariness present in the thinking of every people which has risen above the most elementary level of culture. Every age supplies its instances, more especially among the poets, from Homer, who, for all his healthy-

* Reprinted with the Permission of Charles Scribner's Sons from the *Encyclopedia of Religion and Ethics* edited by James Hastings (1904–1927).

mindedness, can find it in his heart to say that 'there is nothing more wretched than man of all things that breathe and are' (*Il,* xvii, 446 f.), and Sophocles, from whom is wrung the cry that 'not to be born is the most to be desired; but, having seen the light, the next best is to go whence one came as soon as may be' (*Oed. Col.* 1225 f.), to our more passionate modern singers of the pitiless sway of wrong and pain and death. And yet such utterances may be expressive merely of a subjective attitude or mood which is transcended in a larger view. The writer, while not fundamentally rebellious, may derive a pensive satisfaction from the indulgence of morbid feeling, and may even find life worth living while he displays before the world the pageant of his bleeding heart. Or, again, his seeming despair may bring otherwise its more express correction with it. The Hebrew teaching on life, *e.g.,* owing to the intensity of the religious belief present throughout, is in the main of a finely robust and hopeful temper, yet in one signal instance it betrays a different character. Koheleth takes rank as one of the classics of the literature of reflective melancholy; nowhere are the bewilderment, dismay, and exhaustion of human nature, baffled by the contradictions of its lot, realized more poignantly. Nevertheless, there is no sign of spiritual collapse in the book. The conclusion reached does not suggest either the despairing or the immoral mind. On the contrary, the groundtone of the writer's view is furnished by the spiritual tradition which he has inherited. His faith, though semi-paralyzed, holds out, and at least a working solution of the world-riddle is arrived at: if men do not ask too much from life, a sober degree of worthiness may be found in it still. And ultimately his chastened trust in existence expresses itself thus: 'Fear God, and keep his commandments, for this is the whole duty of man; for God will bring every work and every secret thing into judgment, whether it be good or whether it be evil.'

For the most part, then, the instinctive sense of the incongruity between the spirit and its environment, together with the depression of feeling thus occasioned, does not in point of fact give rise to the sceptical view of life, but is, consciously or unconsciously, taken up into a more comprehensive estimate of things. Where, however, this is not the case, the result is pessimism, the doctrine that existence is fundamentally and essentially evil. The theory is found both in Eastern and Western thought. . . .

ECCLESIASTES—FOREIGN INFLUENCES*

O. S. Rankin

Various attempts have been made to show that Ecclesiastes was dependent upon Greek philosophy. Otto Pfleiderer (1886) held that he was indebted to Heraclitus for elements of teaching and language; while the commentaries of Thomas Tyler (1874) and E. H. Plumptre (1881) have regarded the Stoic philosophy as contributing to Koheleth's thought. Tyler was also of the opinion that Koheleth aimed at setting Stoicism and Epicureanism over against each other in order to discredit both.[1] The most impressive of the efforts to prove that Ecclesiastes was influenced by Greeks has been made by Harry Ranston[2] who, judging that Koheleth would more probably be dependent on popular aphoristic writers than on philosophical works, has found in the work of Theognis (*ca.* 520 B.C.) many general parallels of thought and similarities of language which, he maintained, prove their influence on Ecclesiastes. Hertzberg has agreed with Ranston's view so far as to say that "Koheleth knew the work of Theognis, at least indirectly."[3]

The trend of modern criticism is to maintain that in no case has it been proved that Ecclesiastes is dependent on any Greek writing, but that the Jewish book appears to be pervaded by the popular Greek spirit. Barton[4] has pointed out that the motif of *carpe diem,* which has caused some to think of influence upon Ecclesiastes from Epicureanism, occurs in ancient Semitic literature—for instance, in the Babylonian Gilgamesh epic (which provides a very close parallel to 9:7–9). He also shows that the differences between Stoicism and Ecclesiastes are fundamental. And as to the claim of Ranston that Theognis has exercised an indirect but

---

* By O. S. Rankin in *The Interpreter's Bible.* Copyright 1956 by Pierce and Washbaugh. Used by permission of Abingdon Press.

[1] Cf. Adolphe Lods, *The Prophets and the Rise of Judaism* (tr. S. H. Hooke; London: Kegan Paul, Trench, Trubner & Co., 1937), pp. 15, 344–45.

[2] *Ecclesiastes and the Early Greek Wisdom Literature* (London: Epworth Press, 1925), p. 61.

[3] *Der Prediger* (Leipzig: Werner Scholl, 1932), p. 51.

[4] *The Book of Ecclesiastes* (New York: Charles Scribner's Sons, 1908), pp. 34–39.

very sustained influence upon Ecclesiastes, Galling[5] has put forward the view that the parallels of thought which Ranston cited as existing between Theognis and Ecclesiastes are in no single case particularly close, and that the aphorisms selected for comparison have in both books a different setting.

But if the attempts to prove Koheleth dependent on Greek literature have not been conclusive, what are the grounds upon which it may be said that Ecclesiastes shows traces of the Greek spirit? Does this conclusion rest upon the realism of the author's mind? McNeile[6] appears to have held that Koheleth has not come into contact with the Greek mind at all; yet he recognized a close affinity of thought between Koheleth and Xenophanes of Colophon (ca. 570 B.C.), whom Gilbert Murray described as "almost the only outspoken critic of religion preserved to us from Greek antiquity."[7] According to McNeile, Koheleth occupies "the debatable ground between Semitic and Greek thought," and lived at a time when Greek thought and Hebrew thought were of themselves beginning to converge. Thus, "Koheleth's affinities with Greek thought are close and significant"[8] and Ecclesiastes contains many of the "seed-thoughts" from which Stoicism sprang. Therefore, although McNeile[9] dated Ecclesiastes as later than 300 B.C., he approached the opinion held by Galling, namely, that Koheleth lived on the frontier between two periods of history.

A characteristic of that epoch was its individualistic and cosmopolitan spirit. And this spirit, though it characterizes the wisdom literature as a whole, is especially prominent in Ecclesiastes. In every part of the book appeal is made to the individual's reason and judgment, and throughout is the universalistic outlook which is concerned with man and with what man experiences everywhere under the sun—an outlook in conformity with that mingling of peoples caused by the campaigns of Alexander the Great. This mark of the Hellenistic age, which may be accounted the Greek contribution to the spirit of that age, along with Koheleth's realism and logical type of thought[10] may well be all that Ecclesiastes shows of Greek origin or influence. As noted by Blieffert,[11] the thoughts of the Greek philosophers were popularized in the Hel-

---

[5] "Stand und Aufgabe der Kohelet-Forschung," Theologische Rundschav, VI (1934), p. 365.

[6] An Introduction to Ecclesiastes (Cambridge: Cambridge University Press, 1904), pp. 44–53.

[7] A History of Ancient Greek Literature (London: W. Heinemann, 1898), p. 74.

[8] Op. cit., pp. 45, 46.

[9] Ibid., p. 33.

[10] Cf. Johannes Hempel, Die althebräische Literatur (Potsdam: Akademische Verlagsgellschaft, 1930), p. 191.

[11] H. J. Blieffert, Weltanschauung und Gottesglaube in Buch Koheleth (Rostock: R. Beckmann, 1938), p. 89.

lenistic period and became part of general culture, so that knowledge of the ideas were acquired without any acquaintance with books. Lukyn Williams well described Koheleth's contact with Greek thought when he wrote: "Stoicism must have been in the air; its phrases would be current coin. But that is all." [12] Each one therefore is presented with the task of deciding whether Koheleth was aloof from all contact with Greek thought, or whether he was merely breathing a Hellenistic atmosphere. The facts that would seem to emerge from weighing the question are that Koheleth was an original thinker, that he was distinctly affected by the Greek spirit, and that his originality of thought is the quality which makes it uncertain whether his book, which gives no unequivocal evidence of borrowing from the Greek literature, is at all influenced by Greek thought. This may seem to be a meager result, but its meagerness accords with findings that have been made regarding the question of Greek influence in the East during the period in which Koheleth lived. Volz[13] pondered the resemblance of Stoicism and Ecclesiastes in respect of their common deterministic outlook, and he refrained from ascribing any influence of one upon the other, but he connected the determinism in Ecclesiastes with the spirit of the age and the political conditions which produced the all-disposing sovereign states, first the Macedonian and later the Roman. This explanation, however, is far too general. The source of the deterministic belief of Koheleth is probably to be found in the popular stellar religion of the ancient Mesopotamians, according to which the astral divinities—sun, moon, and stars—exercised an influence on the earth and on man, and determined their destiny.[14] A true perspective is not won by thinking only of the possibility of Greek influence upon Koheleth. For in the latter's time a reverse process was taking place, namely, the influence of Oriental thought upon the Greek world.

In Palestine the thought of the Hellenistic period was a mingling not only of Greek but also of Oriental conceptions, under which we must include, besides Chaldean and Iranian, also Egyptian ideas. The influence of Egypt upon Hebrew gnomic teaching is evident from the fact that a considerable section of the book of Proverbs, namely, 22:17–23:11, is a careful adaptation of the Egyptian book, The Wisdom of Amen-em-ope.[15] Besides this one instance of sustained borrowing there are striking parellels of thought between the Hebrew and the Egyptian wisdom writings.

[12] *Ecclesiastes* (Cambridge: Cambridge University Press, 1922; "Cambridge Bible") p. xxxiii.
[13] *Weisheit* (Göttingen: Vandenhoek & Ruprecht, 1911), p. 239.
[14] See Hugo Gressmann, *Die hellenistische Gestirnreligion* (Leipzig: J. C. Hinrichs, 1925), and O. S. Rankin, *Israel's Wisdom Literature* (Edinburgh: T. & T. Clark, 1936), pp. 136–45.
[15] See Rankin, *op. cit.*, pp. 6–7.

Paul Humbert described the kind of Egyptian influence which the Hebrew wisdom writings reveal thus:

> The foreign and especially Egyptian influence is traceable in the use of certain literary forms—the king as fictive author; maxims and a more or less philosophical dialogue with a narrative framework; satires on callings; praise of the wise . . . ; descriptions of the feebleness of old age . . . ; exhortation to enjoyment of life in view of the certainty of death.[16]

Elsewhere[17] he examined the biblical wisdom literature for traces of Egyptian influence, and in particular pointed out many resemblances between Ecclesiastes and the Egyptian gnomic writings. A few of these parallels follow:

1. *The Picture of Old Age:* From *The Instruction of Ptahhotep* (third millennium B.C.).

> Old age hath come and dotage hath descended. The limbs are painful and the state of being old appeareth as something new. Strength hath perished for weariness. The mouth is silent and speaketh not. The eyes are shrunken and the ears deaf. . . . The heart is forgetful and remembereth not yesterday. The bone, it suffereth in old age, and the nose is stopped up and breatheth not. To stand up and to sit down are alike ill. Good is become evil. Every taste hath perished.[18]

Cf. 12:3–7, where the account of old age and its infirmities is highly allegorical. The point of comparison is, however, the theme of old age as affecting the members of the body.

2. *Life's Paradoxes:* From *The Admonitions of an Egyptian Sage.*

> In truth, the poor now possess riches and he who was not even able to make sandals for himself possesses treasures. . . . He who had not any servants is now become master of (many) slaves and he who was a nobleman has now to manage his own affairs.[19]

Cf. 9:11: "I saw that . . . the race is not to the swift, nor the battle to the strong, nor bread to the wise, nor riches to the intelligent." Cf. 10:7: "I have seen slaves on horses, and princes walking on foot like slaves."

3. *Carpe diem:* From the *Song of the Harper.* This song was sung at funerary banquets by the friends of a deceased person gathered in the tomb, partaking there of a meal which was enlivened by wine, music,

---

[16] "Weisheitsdichtung," *Religion in Geschichte und Gegenwart*, Vol. V, col. 1808.

[17] *Recherches sur les sources égyptiennes de la littérature sapientale d'Israël* (Neuchâtel: Secrétariat de l'Université, 1929).

[18] Erman, *Literature of the Ancient Egyptians* (tr. by A. M. Blackman; New York: E. P. Dutton & Co., 1927), p. 55.

[19] A. H. Gardiner, *The Admonitions of an Egyptian Sage* (Leipzig: J. C. Hinrichs, 1909); cf. Humbert, *Recherches*, p. 121.

flowers, singing, and perfumes. This custom enshrined the two phases
—death and the enjoyment of life—which are combined in the reflections of Koheleth (see 2:24; 3:12–13; 5:17; 9:7–9; 11:7–9). The singer
of the song declares:

> None cometh from thence [i.e., from the place of the dead] that he may
> tell us how they fare, that he may tell us what they need, that he may
> set our heart at rest (?), until we also go to the place whither they are
> gone.
>   Be glad. . . . Follow thy desire, so long as thou livest. Put myrrh on
> thine head, clothe thee in fine linen, and anoint thee. . . .
>   Increase yet more the delights that thou hast, and let not thine
> heart grow faint. Follow thy desire, and do good to thyself (?)[20]

Also from the inscription on the tomb of Petosiris (ca. 300 B.C.):

> Drink and be drunken, do not cease to [make] festival. Follow [the
> desires of] your hearts in the time [you are] on the earth. . . . When a
> man goes hence, his goods go from him. He who shall inherit them will
> satisfy his desires as he wishes. For the rich there is no more sun. . . .
> He departs quickly as a dream. There is no one who knows the day
> when [death] will come. It is the work of God to make the heart for-
> getful (?) . . . . God it is who puts . . . into the heart of him whom he
> hates, in order to give his goods to another whom he loves, for he is
> the disposer (?) of [man's] goods.[21]

With these Egyptian texts may be compared the Babylonian parallel
with Koheleth (9:7–9), which the latter may also have known, namely,
the passage from the Gilgamesh epic (ca. 2000 B.C.):

> Since the Gods created men
> Death they ordained for man,
>
> . . . .
>
> Day and night be thou joyful,
> Daily ordain gladness,
> Day and night rage and be merry,
> Let thy garments be bright,
> Thy head purify, wash with water,
> Desire thy children which thy hand possesses,
> A wife enjoy in thy bosom.[22]

4. God is the Giver: From The Instruction of Ptahhotep.

Reverence [the man of repute] in accordance with what hath happened
unto him, for wealth cometh not of itself. . . . It is God that createth
repute . . . The vestibule [of the great] hath its rule . . . . It is God who
assigneth the foremost place.[23]

---

[20] Erman, op. cit., p. 133.
[21] Gustave Lefèbvre, Le tombeau de Pétosiris (Le Caire: Imprimerie de
l'Institut Français d'Archéologie Orientale, 1924), I. 161.
[22] Tablet X, Col. III, ll. 2–13.
[23] Erman, op. cit., pp. 58–59.

Cf. 3:13: "Also . . . it is God's gift to man that every one should eat and drink"; 5:18–19, "Every man also to whom God has given wealth"; see also 6:2. Naturally the various similarities that are brought to light have different degrees of closeness, and some may seem to have little importance as proof of the dependence of Ecclesiastes on Egyptian gnomic works; but it is clear that the Hebrew writer was acquainted with the Egyptian wisdom and that the resemblances mentioned are more tangible and less problematical than those adduced from the Greek sphere. The author of Ecclesiastes did not borrow en bloc. His originality is not impaired by the phrases and pictures which recall the Egyptian background, any more than a speaker's originality is diminished by using expressions that have a biblical context. The knowledge of the source might contribute to the depth and meaning of the speaker's words.

ECCLESIASTES AND THE WISDOM OF SOLOMON*

E. H. Plumptre

The form which . . . [the writer of the Wisdom of Solomon] adopts for his teaching, his personation of the character of Solomon (Wisd. vii. 7–11, viii. 14, ix. 7, 8), shews that he did not shrink from challenging comparison with Ecclesiastes. A closer scrutiny shews, if I mistake not, that a main purpose of his book was to correct either the teaching of that book, or a current misinterpretation of it. Let us remember in what light it must have presented itself to him. It had not, if our conclusion as to its authorship be right, the claim which comes from the reverence due to the authority of a remote antiquity or an unquestioned acceptance. He must have known that it had not been received as canonical without a serious opposition, that the strictest school of Pharisees had been against its reception, that it had seemed to them tainted with the heresy of Epicureanism and Sadduceeism. If it was interpreted then as it has often been interpreted since, it may have seemed to him to sanction a lawless sensuality, to fall in with the thoughts of those who said "let us eat and drink, for tomorrow we die," to throw doubt, if not denial, on the soul's immortality. Was this, he seems to have asked himself, the true ideal of wisdom? Was it not his duty to bring before men another Solomon than that whose experience seemed to end in materialism and pessimism, in the scepticism of an endless doubt? And so he too adopts, without any hesitation, the form of personated authorship. He has indeed less dramatic power than his predecessor. His Solomon is more remote from the Solomon of history than that of Koheleth. The magnificence, the luxury, the voluptuousness, which the earlier writer portrays so vividly, not less than the idolatry which is so prominent in the historical Solomon, are passed over here. The Son of David, as painted by him, is simply an ideal sage, a kind of Numa Pompilius, consecrating his life from beginning to end to the pursuit of wisdom, blameless and undefiled (Wisd. vii. viii.). Looked at from this point of view the opening of his book is in its very form sufficiently significant. He will not call himself an *Ecclesiastes* or *Debater*. It seems to him that the work of a

* From E. H. Plumptre, *Introduction to Ecclesiastes*, The Cambridge Bible (Cambridge: The University Press, 1898), pp. 70–87.

teacher is to teach and not merely to discuss. The wisdom which inspires him is authoritative and queen-like. He is, what Koheleth is not, a "preacher" in the modern sense of the word, and calls on men to listen with attention (Wisd. i. 1). Had his predecessor counselled submission to the tyranny of kings, and accepted the perversion of judgment and justice as inevitable (Eccles. v. 8, x. 4, 20), he, for his part, will call on the judges of the earth and kings, and rebuke them for their oppressions (Wisd. i. 1, vi. 1–10). Had Koheleth spoken of seeking wisdom in wine and revelry, and the "delights" of the sons of men (Eccles. ii. 1–8), he will proclaim that "wisdom will not dwell in the body that is subject unto sin" (Wisd. i. 4) and that "the true beginning of her is the desire of discipline" (Wisd. vii. 17). Had the earlier writer spoken bitter things of men and yet more of women (ch. vii. 28), he will remind his hearers that wisdom is a "loving," a "philanthropic," spirit ($\phi\iota\lambda\acute{\alpha}\nu\theta\rho\omega\pi\sigma\nu\ \pi\nu\epsilon\hat{\upsilon}\mu\alpha$, Wisd. i. 6). To the ever-recurring complaint that all things are "vanity and feeding upon wind" (Eccles. i. 14, 17, ii. 26, et al.) he opposes the teaching that "murmuring is unprofitable" (Wisd. i. 11). The thought that death was better than life, to be desired as an everlasting sleep (Eccles. vi. 4, 5), he meets with the warning "seek not death in the error of your life" (Wisd. i. 12), ventures even on the assertion that "God made not death," that it was an Enemy that had done this, that life and not death was contemplated in the Divine Purpose as the end of man (Wisd. i. 13). It was only the ungodly who counted death their friend (Wisd. i. 16). In the second chapter of the book, there is a still more marked antagonism. He puts into the mouth of the "ungodly" what appears in Ecclesiastes as coming from the writer himself. It is they who say "our life is short and miserable" (Wisd. ii. 6; Eccles. viii. 6), that "we shall be hereafter as though we had never been" (Wisd. ii. 2; Eccles. ix. 5, 6), that death and life are both determined by a random chance, "at all adventure" (Wisd. ii. 2; Eccles. ix. 11), that "our body shall be turned into ashes, and our spirit vanish in the soft air" (Wisd. ii. 3; Eccles. iii. 19, xii. 7), that it was an Enemy that had done this, that life and not death was actions (Wisd. ii. 4; Eccles. i. 11). They take up almost the very words of Koheleth when they say "Let us enjoy the good things that are present . . . Let us fill ourselves with costly wine and ointments" (Wisd. ii. 7; Eccles. ix. 7–9). Had the despondent pessimist mourned over the fact that the "wise man dieth as the fool," that there is one event to the righteous and the wicked" (Eccles. vii. 15, ix. 2), the answer is ready— that it was only "in the sight of the unwise they seemed to die," and that their hope is full of immortality (Wisd. iii. 2). Had he declared that he had not found one righteous woman after all his searching (Eccles. vii. 26), he is met with the half-personal answer that that was but natural, that it was true of all who despised wisdom and nurture that "their wives are foolish and their children wicked" (Wisd. iii. 12). Had he taught, or been thought to teach, a life which was emancipated from all restraints and welcomed on almost equal terms children born in and out of wedlock, . . . entering as it were, a protest against the asceticism which afterwards developed itself into the rule of the more rigid Essenes, the voice of the writer of Wisdom declares that "blessed is the barren who is undefiled" and "the eunuch, which with his hands hath wrought no iniquity" (Wisd. iii. 14), that it is better "to have no children and to have virtue" (Wisd. iv. 1), that "the multiplying brood of the ungodly shall not thrive." Had the sceptical thinker spoken in terms which suggested the thought that he looked on the hope of immortality and the enthusiasm of virtue as no less a form of insanity than the passionate vices of mankind (Eccles. i. 17, ii. 12, vii. 25), the author of the Wisdom of Solomon puts into the mouth of the scoffers the confession "we fools counted his life madness" (Wisd. iv. 4).

And the corrective antagonism of the later writer to the earlier is seen not less clearly in the fact that he gives prominence to what had been before omitted than in these direct protests. It seemed to him a strange defect that a book professing to teach wisdom should contain from first to last no devotional element, and therefore he puts into the mouth of his ideal Solomon a prayer of singular power and beauty for the gift of wisdom (Wisd. ix.). He, an Israelite, proud of the history of his fathers, could not understand a man writing almost as if he had ceased to be an Israelite, one to whom the names of Abraham and Isaac and Jacob were unknown, and therefore he enters on a survey of that history to shew that it had all along been a process manifesting the law at once of a Divine retribution, and of a Divine education (Wisd. x. xi.). He could as little understand how a son of Abraham, writing in Egypt with all the monuments of its old idolatries and later developments of the same tendency to anthropomorphic and theriomorphic worship around him, could have let slip the opportunity of declaring that God is a spirit (Wisd. xii. 1) and must be worshipped in spirit and in truth; that the worship of "fire or wind, or the swift air or the circle of the stars, or the violent water or the lights of heaven" (Wisd. xiii. 1–4) was relatively noble, "less to be blamed" as compared with the gross idolatry which stirred his spirit within him—as that of Athens stirred the spirit of St Paul—as he walked through the streets of Alexandria. The one idea of God presented in Ecclesiastes seemed to him to be that of Power, hardly of Law, predestinating times and seasons (Eccles. iii. 1–10) and the chances and changes of men's lives (Eccles. ix. 11), working out a partial retribution for man's misdeeds within the limits of earthly experience (Eccles. xi. 9, xii. 14), but leaving many wrongs and anomalies unredressed (Eccles. v. 8, viii. 11). He seeks therefore to bring before men that thought of the Fatherhood of God, which was beginning to dawn upon men's minds, some echoes of which (if our conclusion as to the date of the book be right) had perhaps floated to him from the lips that proclaimed that Fatherhood in its fulness. He had heard, it may be, that One had appeared in Galilee and Jerusalem who "professed to have the knowledge of God, and called himself the 'child' or 'servant' ($\pi\alpha\hat{\iota}\delta\alpha$) of the Lord and made his boast that God was his Father" (Wisd. ii. 13–16), that He had been slandered, conspired against, mocked, and put to death, that Sadducean priests had stood by his cross deriding Him, "if the righteous man be the son of God, He will help him and deliver him from the hands of his enemies. Let us examine him with despitefulness and torture and condemn him with a shameful death" (Wisd. ii. 18–20) and that marvellous history had stirred him into a glow of admiration for Him whom as yet he knew not. He could not subside after that into the tone of mind which looks on "life as a pastime and our time here as a market for gain" (Wisd. xv. 12).

It will be seen in the Commentary that follows that I look on the estimate which the author of the Wisdom of Solomon formed of Ecclesiastes as a wrong one, that he was wanting in the insight that sees the real drift which is the resultant of cross currents and conflicting lines of thought. The mystical ascetic who had been trained in the school of Philo, who was, it may be, to develop afterwards, under a higher teaching, into the writer of the Epistle to the Hebrews, lived and moved in a region of thought and feeling altogether different from that of the man who had passed through a multiform experience of wine and wisdom, of love and madness, of passion and "feeding upon wind." But it is not the less instructive to note how such a writer treated the earlier book which also professed to embody the Wisdom of Solomon, of which he could not possibly have been ignorant, and which seemed to him to tend to the popular easy-going Epicureanism that was destructive of all lofty aims and nobleness of character.

JEWISH INTERPRETERS OF ECCLESIASTES

It is, perhaps, natural in dealing with a book which presents so many difficulties both in particular passages and in its general drift, to turn to the interpreters who belonged to the same race and spoke the same language as the writer. How did they understand this or that expression? What did they gather from the book as its chief substantial lesson? And of these we look naturally, in the first instance, with most interest and expectation to the book which gives us the expression, not of an individual opinion, but of the collective wisdom of Israel. We have heard, it may be, high things of the beauty of the Haggadistic mode of interpretation that prevailed in the schools out of which the Mishna, the Gemara, the Targum, and the Midrashim sprang.[1] We open the Midrash, or Commentary, on Koheleth in the hope that we shall see our way through passages that have before been dark, that some light will be thrown on the meaning of words and phrases that have perplexed us. What we actually find are answers to the parable of the blind leading the blind and both falling into the ditch (Matt. xv. 14); rules of interpretation by which anything can be made to mean anything else; legends of inconceivable extravagance passing the utmost limits of credibility; an absolute incapacity for getting at the true meaning of a single paragraph or sentence,—this makes up the store of accumulated wisdom to which we had fondly looked forward. Instead of a "treasure" of "things new and old," the pearls and gems, the silver and the gold, of the wisdom of the past, we find ourselves in an old clothes' shop full of shreds and patches, of rags and tatters. We seem, as we read, to be listening to "old wives' fables" and old men's dreams. A suspicion floats across our mind that the interpretations are *delirantium somnia* in the most literal sense of the word. We involuntarily ask, Can these men have been in their right minds? Are we not listening to a debate of insane Commentators? Is not the Midrash as a *Critici Sacri* compiled and edited within the walls of Colney Hatch? Of other expositions it is true that they "to some faint meaning make pretence." Of this alone, or almost alone, it may be said that it "never deviates into sense."

Would the reader like to judge for himself and try his luck at *Sortes Midrashianae?* I take a few samples at a venture.

(1) Eccles. i. 7, "All the rivers run into the sea, yet the sea is not full." Of this verse we have a wide variety of interpretations: (a) All wisdom is in the heart of man and the heart is not full. (b) The whole law goes into the heart and the heart is not satisfied. (c) All people will join themselves to Israel and yet the number of Israel will still grow. (d) All the dead pass into Hades and Hades is not full. (e) All Israelites go on their yearly pilgrimage to Jerusalem and yet the Temple is never

---

[1] The terms may be briefly explained for the reader to whom they are wholly or comparatively new. The Targums (=Interpretation) are the Chaldee or Aramaic Paraphrases of the Books of the Old Testament. The Mishma (=repetition or study) is a collection of Treatises on various points, chiefly ceremonial or juristic, in the Mosaic Law. The Gemara (=completeness) is a commentary on, or development of, the Mishna, the contents of which have been classified as coming under two categories, (1) the Halachah (=Rule), which includes the enactments of the Mishna in their application to life, and answers accordingly to the casuistic systems of Scholastic Theology, and (2) the Haggadah (=Legend, or *Saga*) which comprises a wide range of legendary, allegorical, and mystical interpretation. The Midrashim (=studies, or expositions) are commentaries, collecting the opinions of distinguished Rabbis on the Books of the Old Testament, and these also contain the Halachah and Haggadah as their chief elements.

crowded. (f) All riches flow into the kingdom of Edom (=Rome), but in the days of the Messiah they shall be brought back.

(2) Eccles. iv. 8, "There is one alone, and there is not a second; yea, he has neither child nor brother." (a) He who is alone is God, the ever-blessed One. (b) Or he is Abraham, who had no son or brother or wife when he was thrown into Nimrod's furnace, when he was told to leave his father's house, and when he was commanded to offer up his only son Isaac; or (c) He who is alone, is the tribe of Levi, who found "no end of all his labour" in erecting the Tabernacle; or (d) that which is alone is the evil lust which leads a man to sin and breaks the ties of kindred; or (e) the words describe Gebini ben Charson who was his mother's only son and was blind and could not see his wealth and had no end of trouble with it.

(3) Eccles. ix. 14–16, "There was a little city and few men within it, and there came a great king and besieged it, and built great bulwarks against it. Now there was found in it a poor wise man, and he by his wisdom delivered the city." Here again the expositions are manifold. (a) The city is the world, and the few men are those that lived at the time of the Flood and the king is Jehovah, and the wise man is Noah. (b) The city is Egypt and the king is Pharaoh, and the poor wise man is Joseph. (c) The city is Egypt and the few men are Joseph's brethren and the king is Joseph, and the wise man is Judah. (d) The city is Egypt and the men are the Israelites, and the king is the Pharaoh of the Exodus, and the wise man is Moses. (e) The city is Sinai, the men are the Israelites and the king is the King of kings, and the bulwarks are the 613 precepts of the Law, and the wise man is Moses. (f) The city is Sinai and the few men are the Israelites, and the king is the lust of the flesh, and the wise man is Moses. (g) The little city is the Synagogue, and the men are the assembly in it, and the king is the King of kings and the wise man is the elder of the Synagogue. (h) The city is the human body, and the men are its limbs, and the king is the lust of the flesh, and the bulwarks are temptations and errors, and the wise man is Conscience.

A few more specimens will be enough to complete the induction. The "dead flies" of Eccles. x. 1 are (a) Korah and his company; or (b) Doeg and Ahithophel. The precept, "give a portion to seven and also to eight" of Eccles. xi. 3, is explained as referring (a) to the Laws of the Sabbath on the seventh day of the week and of Circumcision on the eighth day after birth; or (b) to Moses as in the seventh generation from Abraham and Joshua as representing the eighth; or (c) to the ceremonial precept of Lev. xii. 1–3; or (d) to the seven days of the Feast of Tabernacles and the closing festival of the eighth day. The maxim, "in the morning sow thy seed and in the evening withhold not thine hand" of Eccles. xi. 6, means Marry in thy youth and beget children, and if thy wife dies, marry again in thine age and beget more children. "Rejoice, O young man, in thy youth . . ." "Rejoice in the study of the Law and let thy heart cheer thee with the doctrine of the Mishna and walk in the ways of thy heart, *i.e.* of the higher knowledge of the Talmud." The "evil days" of Eccles. xii. 1 are the days of the Messiah and of the great tribulation that accompanies them. The "mourners that go about the streets" are the worms that feed upon the carcase (Eccles. xii. 5). The "clouds that return after the rain" are the stern prophecies of Jeremiah that came after the destruction of the Temple. The "pitcher broken at the fountain" (Eccles. xii. 6) is the potter's vessel of Jer. xxxvi. 18. The "grasshopper" of Eccles. xii. 6 is the golden image of Nebuchadnezzar.

The student will probably think that he has had enough and more than enough of the insanities of the *Midrash Koheleth.*

If the Midrash fail us, shall we fare better with the Targum, or Paraphrase, of Ecclesiastes? Here at any rate we are not involved in a labyrinth of conflicting interpretations each more monstrous than the other. The mass of opinions has been sifted, and the judicious editor, compiling, as it were, a Commentary for use in families and schools, has selected that which seems to him most in accordance with the meaning of the original, explaining its hard passages so as to make them easy and edifying for the unlearned reader. Let us see what he will find in this instance and how the edification is obtained.

TEXT.	TARGUM.
Eccles. i. 3. What profit hath a man of all his labour which he taketh under the sun?	What advantage is there to a man after his death, from all his labour which he laboured under the sun in this world, except he studied the word of God, in order to receive a good reward in the world to come?
Eccles. i. 11. Neither shall there be any remembrance of things that are to come with those that shall come after.	There will be no remembrance of them among the generations which will be in the days of the King Messiah.
Eccles. i. 17. I the Preacher was king over Israel in Jerusalem.	When king Solomon was sitting upon the throne of his kingdom, his heart became very proud of his riches, and he transgressed the word of God, and he gathered many horses, and chariots, and riders, and he amassed much gold, and silver, and he married from foreign nations; whereupon the anger of the Lord was kindled against him, and he sent to him Ashmodai the king of the demons, who drove him from the throne of his kingdom, and took away the ring from his hand, in order

TEXT.	TARGUM.
	that he should wander about the world to reprove it, and he went about in the provincial towns and cities of the land of Israel, weeping and lamenting, and saying, I am Koheleth whose name was formerly called Solomon, who was king over Israel in Jerusalem.
Eccles. ii. 4. I made me great works: I builded me houses; I planted me vineyards.	I multiplied good works in Jerusalem. I built houses, the Temple, to make atonement for Israel, and a royal palace, and a conclave, and the porch, and a house of judgment of hewn stones where the wise men sit, and the judges to give judgment. I made a throne of ivory for the sitting of royalty. I planted vineyards in Jabne, that I and the Rabbis of the Sanhedrin might drink wine, and also to make libations of wine new and old upon the altar.
Eccles. ii. 10. My wisdom remained with me.	Whatsoever the Rabbis of the Sanhedrin asked of me respecting pure and impure, innocent and guilty, I did not withhold from them any explanation of these things.
Eccles. ii. 18. Because I should leave it unto the man that shall be after me.	Because I must leave it to Rehoboam my son who comes after me, and Jeroboam his servant will come and take away out of his hands ten tribes, and will possess half of his kingdom.
Eccles. iii. 2. A time to be born, and a time to die.	There is a special time for begetting sons and daughters, and a special time for killing disobedient and perverse children, to kill them with stones according to the decree of the judges.
Eccles. iii. 11. He hath made everything beautiful in his time.	King Solomon said by the spirit of prophecy, God made everything beautiful in its time; for it was opportune that there should be the strife which was in the days of Jeroboam son of Nebat: for if it had been in the days of Sheba, son of Bichri, the Temple would not have been

TEXT.	TARGUM.
	built because of the golden calves which the wicked Jeroboam made . . . He concealed from them also the great Name written and expressed on the foundation stone.
Eccles. iii. 19. That which befalleth the sons of men befalleth beasts.	For as to the destiny of the wicked and the destiny of the unclean beast, it is one destiny for both of them.
Eccles. iv. 13. Better is a poor and wise child than an old and foolish king.	Better Abraham, who is the poor youth and in whom is the spirit of prophecy from the Lord, and to whom the Lord was known when three years old, and who would not worship an idol, than the wicked Nimrod who was an old and foolish king. And because Abraham would not worship an idol he threw him into the burning furnace, and a miracle was performed for him of the Lord of the world, and He delivered him from it. . . For Abraham went out from the family of idolators, and reigned over the land of Canaan; for even in the reign of Abraham Nimrod became poor in the world. . . . [Then follows a long prediction like that in the paraphrase of chap. iii. 11 of the revolt of the ten tribes under Jeroboam.]
Eccles. v. 7. In the multitude of dreams and many words there are also divers vanities: but fear thou God.	In the multitude of the dreams of the false prophets, and in the vanities of sorcerers, and in the many words of the wicked, believe not, but serve the wise and just.
Eccles. v. 6. Neither say thou before the angel that it was an error.	In the day of the great judgment thou wilt not be able to say before the avenging angel who exercises dominion over thee, that it is an error.
Eccles. vi. 6. Do not all go to one place?	If he . . . had not studied the law . . . in the day of his death he will go to Gehenna, to the place whither all sinners go.
Eccles. vi. 8. What hath the poor, that knoweth to walk before the living?	What is this poor man to do but to study the law of the Lord, that he may know how he will

TEXT.

TARGUM.

	have to walk in the presence of the righteous in Paradise?

Eccles. vii. 4. The heart of the wise is in the house of mourning.

The heart of the wise mourns over the destruction of the Temple, and grieves over the captivity of the house of Israel.

Eccles. vii. 15. All things have I seen in the days of my vanity.

All this I saw in the days of my vanity, that from the Lord are decreed good and evil to be in the world according to the planets under which men are created.

Eccles. vii. 16. Be not righteous over much.

Be not over-righteous when the wicked is found guilty of death in the court of judgment: so as to have compassion on him, and not to kill him.

Eccles. vii. 24. That which is far off, and exceeding deep, who can find it out?

Who is he that will find out by his wisdom the secret of the day, of death, and the secret of the day when the King Messiah will come?

Eccles. vii. 28. One man among a thousand have I found; but a woman among all those have I not found.

From the days of the first Adam till the righteous Abraham was born, who was found faithful and just among the thousand kings that gathered together to build the tower of Babel? and a woman, as Sarah, among all the wives of those kings I have not found.

Eccles. viii. 14. There be just men to whom it happeneth according to the work of the wicked; again, there be wicked men to whom it happeneth according to the work of the righteous.

There are righteous to whom evil happens as if they had done like the deeds of the wicked; and there are wicked to whom it happens as if they had done like the deeds of the righteous; and I saw by the Holy Spirit that the evil which happens to the righteous in this world is not for their guilt, but to free them from a slight transgression, that their reward may be perfect in the world to come; and the good that comes to sinners in this world is not for their merits, but to render them a reward for the small merit they have acquired, so that they may get their reward in this world, and to destroy their portion in the world to come.

TEXT.

Eccles. ix. 2. All things come alike to all.

Eccles. ix. 8. Let thy garments be always white; and let thy head lack no ointment.

Eccles. ix. 14. There was a little city, and few men within it. . .

Eccles. x. 7. I have seen servants upon horses, and princes walking as servants.

Eccles. xi. 9. Whoso removeth stones shall be hurt therewith; and he that cleaveth wood shall be endangered thereby.

TARGUM.

Everything depends upon the planets; whatever happens to any one is fixed in heaven.

At all times let thy garment be white from all pollution of sin, and acquire a good name, which is likened to anointing oil.

Also this I saw . . . the body of a man which is like a small city . . . and in it are a few mighty men just as the merits in the heart of man are few; and the evil spirit who is like a great and powerful king, enters into the body to seduce it . . . to catch him in the great snares of Gehenna, in order to burn him seven times for his sin. And there is found in the body a good spirit, humble and wise, and he prevails over him and subdues him by his wisdom, and saves the body from the judgment of Gehenna.

King Solomon said by the spirit of prophecy, I saw nations who were before subject to the people of the house of Israel, now prosperous and riding on horses like princes, whilst the people of the house of Israel and their princes walk on the ground like slaves.

King Solomon the prophet said, It is revealed to me that Manasseh, the son of Hezekiah, will sin and worship idols of stone; wherefore he will be delivered into the hands of the king of Assyria, and he will fasten him with halters: because he made void the words of the law which are written on the tables of stone from the beginning, therefore he will suffer from it; and Rabshakeh his brother will worship an image of wood, and forsake the words of the law which are laid in the ark of shittim-wood; therefore he

TEXT.

Eccles. x. 16, 17. Woe to thee, O land, when thy king is a child, and thy princes eat in the morning. Blessed art thou, O land, when thy king is the son of nobles, and thy princes eat in due season.

Eccles. x. 20. Curse not the king, no not in thy thought; and curse not the rich in thy bed-chamber; for a bird of the air shall carry the voice, and that which hath wings shall tell the matter.

Eccles. xii. 5. The mourners go about the streets.

Eccles. xii. 11. The words of the wise are as goads, and as nails fastened by the masters of assemblies, which are given from one shepherd.

TARGUM.

shall be burned in a fire by the angel of the Lord.

Woe to thee, O land of Israel, when wicked Jeroboam shall reign over thee, and remove from thee the morning sacrifices, and thy princes shall eat bread before offering the daily morning sacrifice. Well to thee, O land of Israel, when Hezekiah son of Ahaz, from the family of the house of David, king of Israel, who is mighty in the land, shall reign over thee, and shall perform the obligations of the commandments, and thy nobles, after having brought thee the daily sacrifice, shall eat bread at the fourth hour.

Even in thy mind, in the innermost recesses of thy heart, curse not the king, and in thy bed-chamber revile not a wise man, for the angel Raziel proclaims every day from heaven upon Mount Horeb, and the sound thereof goes into all the world; and Elijah the high-priest hovers in the air like an angel, the king of the winged tribe, and discloses the things that are done in secret to all the inhabitants of the earth.

The angels that seek thy judgment walk about like mourners, walking about the streets, to write the account of thy judgments.

The words of the wise are like goads that prick, and forks which incite those who are destitute of knowledge to learn wisdom as the goad teaches the ox; and so are the words of the rabbis of the Sanhedrin, the masters of the Halachas and Midrashim which were given through Moses the prophet; who alone fed the people of the house of Israel in the wilderness with manna and delicacies.

TEXT.	TARGUM.
Eccles. xii. 12. And further, by these, my son, be admonished; of making many books there is no end, and much study is a weariness of the flesh.	And more than these, my son, take care to make many books of wisdom without an end, to study much the words of the law and to consider the weariness of the flesh.

It will be felt from the extracts thus brought together that the Targum is on the whole pleasanter reading than the Midrash. The traces of discordant interpretation are carefully effaced. All flows on smoothly as if there never had been and never could be any doubt as to what the writer of the original book had meant. Hard sayings are made easy. A spiritual, or at least an ethical, turn is given to words which seemed at first to suggest quite other than spiritual conclusions. The writer of the book, whose identity with Solomon is not questioned for a moment, is made to appear not only as a moral teacher but in the higher character of a prophet. The illustrations drawn from the history of Israel, the introduction of the name of Jehovah, the constant reference to the Shechinah and the Law, give the paraphrase a national and historical character not possessed by the original. The influence of the planets as determining men's characters and the events that fashion them is brought in as a theory of predestination easier to receive than that which ascribes all that happens to the direct and immediate action of the Divine Will. All is done, in one sense, to edification.

This misfortune is, however, that the edification is purchased at the cost of making the writer say just the opposite, in many cases, of what he actually did say. As Koheleth personates Solomon, so the paraphrast personates Koheleth, and the confessions of the Debater, with their strange oscillations and contrasts, become a fairly continuous homily. In all such interpretations, and the Targum of Koheleth is but a sample of a widespread class which includes other than Jewish commentators, there is at once an inherent absence of truthfulness and a want of reverence. The man will not face facts, but seeks to hide them or gloss them over. He assumes that he is wiser than the writer whom he interprets, practically, i.e. he claims for himself a higher inspiration. He prefers the traditions of the school in which he has been brought up to the freshness of the Divine word as it welled forth out of the experience of a human heart.

ECCLESIASTES, OR KOHELETH, THE PREACHER*

Mary Ellen Chase

The man who wrote the book of Ecclesiastes around the year 200 B.C. called himself Koheleth and identified himself as a preacher. From his identification comes the Greek name Ecclesiastes. In his introduction to his essay, which we may call *The Meaning of Life*, he says that he is "the son of David, king of Jerusalem." This statement, which, of course, suggests Solomon as the author, is a mere literary device, not seriously considered even by the editors who prepared his book for insertion among the other books of the Old Testament.

Koheleth wrote his book after many years of what was apparently a fairly happy existence filled with many experiences which had taught him many things. He may be thought of as a radical of his day who had discovered, through keen observation of the processes of nature and of the life of man and through his own reflections upon both, that the Jewish orthodoxy of his time had little meaning and less truth for him and that, on the whole, traditional religion is but wishful thinking. Although his rather magnificent descriptions of his life given in Chapter 2 of his book cannot be taken literally, as he is apparently here continuing his fictitious assumption of Solomon as himself, the tone and atmosphere throughout his twelve chapters would certainly suggest that he was in no sense a poor man. His brilliant command of language and the worldliness evident throughout his sophisticated reflections on life characterize him rather as one who had the means to live comfortably and pleasantly, who was most acceptable socially, and who may well have travelled beyond his native city of Jerusalem. Perhaps, indeed, he knew Alexandria or had even been to school there, for it is evident that Greek thought interested and influenced him. At all events, we should think of him as a cultured and cosmopolitan man, not in any sense as one who from under his own vine and fig tree gave expression to captious thoughts and carping disillusionments.

Disillusioned he surely was, but not to bitterness. Perhaps, like so many others of his race, he was too intensely alive for complete misanthropy. Even although in theory he claims that death, or at least non-existence, is preferable to life, and praises the dead more than the living and even more him "which hath not been," in practice he recommends a full enjoyment of whatever joys life has to offer, bread, wine, clean clothes, marriage, and any work in which one has delight. Nor would he be overzealous for too much wisdom or for too much righteousness, nor for their opposites, wickedness or folly. In a word, since the world is topsy-turvy anyway and since it is plainly impossible to discover, even after much thinking and study, any consistent plan either in nature or in human life, one should serenely and even zestfully enjoy what can be enjoyed before old age and death forever take away the capacities for pleasure.

Koheleth wrote most of his book in prose, although poetry is not lacking in certain portions, notably in his first chapter and in his famous concluding poem. Sometimes, indeed, his prose and his poetry are difficult to distinguish, at least in our translation. Although he was one of the most original thinkers in the Old Testament and has much to say on a great variety of subjects, he rarely arranges his reflections and conclusions in any logical order. The first four chapters of his book have more coherence than the rest, perhaps because within these he has voiced his main conclusions and afterward merely repeats them in one form or another. He states his thesis in the beginning: "Vanity of vanities; all is vanity," and he apparently has great fondness for this witty invention of words, for he repeats them frequently throughout his book.

Although he does not doubt the existence of God as a cosmic force and as that inscrutable spirit which gives life to man, he can discover no just plan for human life and in the monotonous round of nature only futility. Not for him the wonder of Job before the mysteries of the world, the treasures of the snow, the singing of the morning stars. In spite of the beauty of the short poem which follows immediately upon his introduction to his book, one is conscious of something akin to weariness in its lines, or perhaps even of the aimlessness and monotony of which he writes:

> One generation passeth away, and another generation cometh; but the earth abideth forever.
> The sun also ariseth, and the sun goeth down, and hasteth to his place where he arose.
> The wind goeth toward the south, and turneth about unto the north; it whirleth about continually, and the wind returneth again according to his circuits.
> All the rivers run into the sea; yet the sea is not full; unto the place from whence the rivers come, thither they return again.

To Koheleth God's obvious ruling of the world has no relation to His concern for man and his suffering. Apparently, indeed, He has no such concern. The order and the time of all events are determined by God, and yet He and His activity alike are incomprehensible to human intelligence. So far as Koheleth can see, and he has thought and studied all his life, God is not the God of Israel, nor is He a just and merciful ruler of men; He is rather a blind fate, and not only blind but fickle and capricious. One has only to look about him, says Koheleth, to see that the work of man, his righteousness and his goodness, weigh nothing with God. Pleasures and prosperity may be snatched from him, suffering and poverty may come upon him without regard for his worth as a human being. His success or his failure in life is not governed by justice, but merely by chance, for anyone with his eyes and mind open can see that the same fate overtakes both the good man and the wicked one:

> I returned, and saw under the sun, that the race is not to the swift, nor the battle to the strong, neither yet bread to the wise, nor yet riches to men of understanding, nor yet favor to men of skill; but time and chance happeneth to them all.

Nor does Koheleth extoll wisdom for its own sake; in fact, he has tested both wisdom and folly and has discovered that they are equally futile. The search for wisdom cannot give one an understanding of God and of His works, for even "though a wise man think to know it, yet shall he not be able to find it." "For in much wisdom is much grief, and he that increaseth knowledge increaseth sorrow." The way of folly is equally disappointing, for in wine and women, luxury and wealth, there is but vanity and a striving after wind. As a matter of fact, the man who labours with his hands can sleep, for he has no worries, but the rich man must worry in the night hours for fear he will lose his abundance.

Since the future is unknowable, "for who can tell a man what shall be after him under the sun?" and since from all appearances it will be but a repetition of what has been, for "there is no new thing under the sun," it is worse than useless to look for any better order of things. Nor is there the least hope of any redress after death, for "the dead know not anything," "the memory of them is forgotten," "their love, and their hatred, and their envy" are perished. Therefore, as human beings are powerless to change their destiny and as assuredly there is no knowledge nor wisdom in the grave where all must go, the only wise and sensible way to meet the uncertainties and caprices of life is to live as joyfully as possible. The light of the sun is sweet to one's eyes, bread and wine increase merriment in one's heart, and there is joy in living with a woman whom one loves, even though one's days are vanity. After all, to be "a living dog is better than a dead lion."

With more than a touch of ironic humour, Koheleth admits that, though in his search for wisdom he has failed, he has found out one thing: a certain sort of woman, whose heart is like a snare and a net, is more "bitter than death" and only a fool will not run from her! Ironically, too, he warns against overseriousness and against that soulsearching which to him is both unwholesome and a waste of time. Just as it clearly does not pay to be wicked or to indulge in foolishness, it is just as clearly a bad investment to be overconscientious:

> Be not righteous over much, neither make thyself over wise; why shouldest thou destroy thyself?
> Be not over much wicked, neither be thou foolish; why shouldest thou die before thy time?

Koheleth's genius as a poet is shown in the last chapter of his book in his beautiful and justly famous poem on old age. Contrary to the belief of many readers, it is neither a moral nor a religious poem. It is instead a lyric which depicts in startlingly original images and in lines full of cadence and sorrow the pathos of those deprived of their youth by the ceaseless round of time. It begins, not with Chapter 12 with the well-known words, "Remember now thy Creator in the days of thy youth" (which are, in fact, an interpolation by some later editor and not Koheleth's own), but with Verse 9 of Chapter 11, and should read, after the later additions and corrections are taken out, as follows:

> Rejoice, O young man, in thy youth; and let thy heart cheer thee in the days of thy youth, and walk in the ways of thine heart and in the sight of thine eyes.
> Therefore remove sorrow from thy heart, and put away evil from thy flesh
> While the evil days come not, nor the years draw nigh, when thou shalt say, I have no pleasure in them;
> In the day when the keepers of the house shall tremble, and the strong men shall bow themselves, and the grinders cease because they are few, and those that look out of the windows be darkened,
> And the doors shall be shut in the streets, when the sound of the grinding is low, and he shall rise up at the voice of the bird, and all daughters of music shall be brought low;
> Also when they shall be afraid of that which is high, and fears shall be in the way, and the almond tree shall flourish, and the grasshopper shall be a burden, and desire shall fail: because man goeth to his long home, and the mourners go about the streets.
> Or ever the silver cord be loosed, or the golden bowl be broken, or the pitcher be broken at the fountain, or the wheel broken at the cistern.
> Then shall the dust return to the earth as it was; and the spirit shall return unto God who gave it.
> Vanity of vanities, saith the Preacher; all is vanity.

The beauty and significance of this poem are enlarged and deepened once it is understood in all its rich symbolism and allegory. Although there have been many interpretations of its images and metaphors, most scholars are convinced that its vivid descriptions have to do with the physical handicaps and weaknesses of age. The "keepers of the house" are the trembling hands of the old; the "grinders" which cease are the teeth which are gone; the darkened windows are the blinded eyes. The old "rise up at the voice of the bird" because their sleep is so light; they take no pleasure any longer in music; they are afraid of high places and of crowded streets; their hair is as white as the blossoms on the almond tree; and all the desires of youth and its passions have failed and gone from them. Their hands can no longer carry the pitchers to the well, nor can they draw water, nor safely care for the golden bowls and silver cords of their lamps.

This poem is one of the loveliest in biblical literature because of its richness of imagination and wealth of symbolism, which, once understood, endows it with a meaning hitherto obscure. The haunting echoes of its musical notes in a distinctly minor key lend to it a peculiar charm and sadness. In the possession of these we can easily overlook Koheleth's cynicism, since in this poem he reveals the compassion which he felt for all who live from birth to death.

Nor is his cynicism necessarily disillusioning or unpleasant. There is evident throughout his book a light humour which relieves it from darkness; and one can certainly detect, in spite of his scepticism, a keen enjoyment of life. He is neither moping in a corner nor announcing grim facts from housetops.

Many readers and students of his book see in it the influence of Greek thought which by 200 B.C. had surely made itself felt in Palestine. The philosophy of Koheleth may well be tinged with the Epicurean doctrine of making the most of the pleasures of life without overindulgence and possibly with that of the Stoics in his poem on time and the cosmic flow of things. He surely was out of sympathy, as was Job, with the Jewish orthodoxy of his day, with its interpretation of life in terms of rewards and of punishments according to goodness and to evil; but his scepticism, unlike that of Job, stopped short of distress, nor in his hands did it become a steppingstone to impassioned and noble questioning concerning the mysteries of life and of God.

We may well wonder why it was that the book of this Omar Khayyám of the Old Testament should have been allowed inclusion in the Jewish Scriptures. One reason was doubtless that of its popularity in its day. Perhaps, too, the fictitious assumption that it was written by Solomon bore weight with the scholars and editors who made up the Old Testament in its final form. But it assuredly would not have found a place had not certain annotators changed its emphasis in places and added passages and ideas of their own to Koheleth's original work. Worried over his denial of God's retribution on earth, they took upon themselves the responsibility of interpolating their own words in his text. Such an interpolation occurs, for example, in Verse 9 of Chapter 11, which verse introduces Koheleth's great poem on old age: "But know thou, that for all these things God will bring thee into judgment." This thought is directly opposed to his teaching, and lends, as do various other interpolated portions, a note of confusion to his book. Again, in Verse 17 of Chapter 3, the editors, disliking Koheleth's cynical statement in Verse 16 that wickedness is in the place of judgment, added their own words, "God shall judge the righteous and the wicked." Several of these additions give an annoying note of inconsistency to the book; and we can imagine how they would have annoyed and angered Koheleth himself.

The worst instance, however, of this tampering with his work occurs at the close of the symbolic poem with which Koheleth, of course, planned to end his book and in the perfection of which, one can assume, he took great pleasure and satisfaction. Not content with adding the first line of Chapter 12 in order to sound a pious note, the revisers and editors proceeded to tack on to the poem five dull and moralizing precepts. There were apparently two of these meddling annotators. The first in Verses 9 and 10 strives to explain that, after all, the Preacher was wise and wrote words of truth. The second, not yet convinced that Koheleth's book will not do more harm than good and possessed of a sardonic, if grim, humour, admonishes its readers that of making of many books (like this unfortunate one!) there is no end and that, in his opinion, nothing is to be gained except weariness from so much study. He himself has a safe and sane conclusion to the whole matter—and he proceeds to give it!

KOHELETH THE MAN*

Robert Gordis

No other book within the Bible and few outside of it in world literature are as intensely personal as Koheleth. To be sure, he can be properly understood only within the framework of the intellectual life of ancient Israel, which is itself a distinctive part of the larger culture-pattern of the ancient Near East. Nonetheless, his vision of life is definitely his own, the reaction of his personality to the world about him, individual in content and unique in expression.

Modern psychological, economic, and social studies have shed valuable light on the factors entering into the thought-processes of men. Unfortunately, this development has often been carried to extremes and the study of the genesis of an idea has tended to replace the evaluation of its truth and significance. All too often one encounters the tendency to interpret the world-view of thinkers almost exclusively in terms of their personal idiosyncrasies or of their social backgrounds and economic interests.

As though anticipating this development, and seeking to forestall, or at least hinder, this process, the Biblical writers generally give us little information about themselves and their times. The few details we have about Isaiah and the somewhat ampler information we possess about Jeremiah are revealed to us incidentally, in the course of the prophet's career. As a result, the message of the Prophets, rooted though it be in their life and age, confronts the modern man in universal form, as though beyond the limitations of time and space.

In this sense, too, Koheleth was a son of his people. His brief book gives tantalizingly few hints about his personal life, and these have been seized upon and elaborated variously by his readers. Some have regarded the detailed description of luxury in Chapter 2 as autobiographical, and accordingly have pictured him as an extremely wealthy aristocrat, if not as a king. In that passage, however, Koheleth is merely adopting the role of King Solomon as a literary device, in order to use

* From Robert Gordis, *Koheleth—The Man and His World*, Vol. XIX, *Texts and Studies of the Jewish Theological Seminary of America* (New York: Bloch Publishing Co., 1955), pp. 75–86, 112–122. Reprinted by permission.

the career of the great king to emphasize his conclusion as to the in-
adequacy of wealth and wisdom as absolute goals.

The book of Koheleth is not a pseudepigraph, seeking to masquer-
ade as the authentic work of Solomon. If that were the author's inten-
tion, he would have adopted the name "Solomon" outright, instead of
inventing the enigmatic name of "Koheleth," which suggests the identity
only by indirection. It should be remembered, too, that he does not call
himself "son of David"; this phrase occurs only in the opening verse,
which is the title of the book and emanates from an editor. That this
identification played a large part in gaining admission for the book into
the canon is one of the fortunate accidents of literary history, but does
not gainsay the fact that it does not go back to the author.

It has been inferred, on the basis of the difficult passage 5:8, which
seems to glorify agricultural pursuits, that Koheleth was a country
gentleman. Even if the meaning of the verse were certain, it would be
merely a conventional tribute to country life, in which Koheleth is re-
flecting the standpoint of the conservative upper-classes. For the
aristocracy of the ancient world, who lived in luxury in the great urban
centers of Jerusalem, Alexandria or Rome, largely on the income they
derived from their country estates, which were tilled by tenant farmers,
liked to regard themselves as country gentlemen, and looked down upon
the artisans and merchants of the cities.

While these and similar deductions about Koheleth's personal life
seem unwarranted, a few facts may be derived from his book. All signs
point to the fact that Koheleth lived in Jerusalem. The sophistication
which characterizes the book is best sought for in a great cultural center like the capital city. The references to the Temple and the sacrificial
cult (4:17 f.) as being close at hand, and his matter-of-fact familiarity
with the corruption of government (5:7), lend credence to the repeated
mention of Jerusalem (1:12; 2:9; cf. 1:1) as the seat of Koheleth's activity.
Evidence for the Palestinian locale of the book has already been
indicated.

The content and form of his book make it clear that Koheleth was
a teacher in one of the Wisdom academies in Jerusalem, which served
the educational needs of upper-class youth. The internal evidence is
buttressed by the testimony on Koheleth's calling which is to be found
in the Epilogue (12:9–14). These verses were written not by Koheleth,
but by a contemporary, probably a colleague, who knew him personally:

> Not only was Koheleth a sage himself, but he also taught the people
> knowledge, weighing and searching and fashioning many proverbs.
> Koheleth tried to find attractive words and honestly to set down the
> truth.
> The words of the wise are like goads, and like well-fastened nails
> are the collected sayings, coming from one Source.
> Furthermore, my son, be warned: of making many books there is no
> end, and much study wears one's strength away.

From this contemporary source we learn that Koheleth did not limit himself to his professional activity as a Wisdom teacher (*hakham*), but carried on literary activity, collecting (*hikker*, lit. "search out") extant proverbs, and composing (*tikken*) original material as well, being concerned not only with the truth of his teaching (*dibhrē 'emeth*), but with an attractive literary form (*dibhrē hefes*).

As a Wisdom teacher Koheleth was closely identified with the upper-class groups of Jewish society by vocation. It is, of course, possible that he was of lowly origin, and had won his place among the successful groups by his superior abilities, but we should then have expected, in one as sensitive as Koheleth, a greater degree of reaction to social injustice and oppression than we find in this book. It therefore seems most probable that Koheleth belonged to the upper classes by birth and position, for we find no indications that he ever suffered poverty and want. Apparently he enjoyed the benefits of travel and other opportunities that were denied to the poor.

While his range of knowledge may not have equalled that of the author of *Job*, who has been described as the most learned ancient before Plato, he was cultured and well-informed. He was able to draw upon history, contemporary affairs, and the science of his day, in order to express his own world-view. His familiarity with at least some of the fundamental ideas of Greek philosophy, like the four elements and the doctrine of the golden mean, as well as his creative use of these concepts in his own world-view, has already been discussed. In the same original manner he utilizes some basic formulations in the Pentateuch and the Historical Books.

Only a few other facts may be inferred regarding his personal history. Koheleth was a bachelor, or at least a man without children. For he is considerably exercised over the fact that when a man dies he must leave his wealth to "strangers" who never labored to achieve it, and he betrays no sentiment for kith and kin, even when he speaks of the family.

That Koheleth is writing as an old man is clear from the deeply felt Allegory of Old Age in chapter 12. The same vantage-point is reflected in his nostalgic stress upon the joys of youth and upon man's obligation to do all things with might and main before it grows too late forever.

Nothing more is known definitely of the external events of his life. Fortunately, his book permits us to reconstruct the principal phases of his spiritual odyssey, for each of them left his impress upon his philosophy of life. Koheleth entered the world richly endowed in spirit. From earliest youth his intellectual and emotional faculties were exceptionally keen, and they determined the entire course of his development. Fundamental in the boy and the man was a passionate love of life, the universal heritage of the healthy mind and the healthy body. He loved the tang of living. The sight of the sun, the breath of the wind, the good things of the world held him enthralled:

Sweet is the light, and it is good for the eyes to see the sun. (11:7)

The experience of life thrilled him to the core. Women he loved deeply, and even in old age he well remembered the world of sensation to which they beckoned:

Enjoy life with the woman you love. (9:9)

Nor was he a stranger to other sources of material comfort and beauty. The cool spaciousness of gardens and orchards, the nobility of fine houses, the cheer of good food and fine wine, the charm of music and the grace of the dance—Koheleth savored them all. Even after his joy in life had been tempered by later experiences, he still felt that merely to be alive was a boon:

For surely a live dog is better than a dead lion. (9:4)

Had Koheleth possessed no other elements in his spiritual constitution than his love of life, he would have been happy. Possessing the means of gratifying his desires, he might have spent his days in carousing and feasting or in the subtler forms of sensual enjoyment. He could have been a Philistine or an esthete, but in any event a happy man. That happiness eluded him was the result of other facets in his personality.

As a Jew, Koheleth had naturally been reared in the rich religious tradition of Israel, embodied in the books of the Torah and the Prophets, which were in his day already recognized as Sacred Scriptures. These educative influences brought to bear upon him were no mere historical memories. For the teachings of the Torah were being practiced in the Temple cult by the priests, and were being expounded in the academies by the Scribes. As for the Prophets, though their greatest period was over, their teachings were now accepted as integral to Judaism. Moreover, the creative impulse of Prophecy was not altogether spent, expressing itself in the strange, submerged patterns of Apocalyptic literature.

In spite of their varying emphases, both Torah and Prophecy were concerned with justice, the latter with its triumphant enthronement in society, the former, as the social legislation of the Pentateuch indicates, at least with the minimizing of social oppression and want.

The third spiritual current, that of *Hokmah*, richly creative and deeply influential in Koheleth's age, was less passionate on this score, but it also was permeated by the Hebrew quest for righteousness. It is noteworthy that the Prophetic concept of history is most comprehensively stated in the book of *Proverbs* (14:34): "Righteousness exalts a people, but sin is the disgrace of nations." Were this religio-ethical standpoint lacking in Wisdom, it could never have been identified with Torah in the synthesis which was later to produce normative Judaism.

Thus the zest for justice, the hallmark of the spirit of Israel, was early brought to bear upon Koheleth, and he was never again the same carefree, lusty youth. He was too clear-sighted to overlook the widespread scars of suffering on the body politic of society, and too sensitive to remain callous to human misery, merely because he himself was not directly affected. The beauty of nature and the luxury of wealth could not blot out the marks of man's injustice to his fellows:

> Furthermore, I saw under the sun, in the place of judgment, there was wickedness, and in the place of righteousness, wrong. (3:16)

Superimposed upon his innate love of life, there had now come a second great motive power, the love of justice. But there was a cruel difference between the two. While the first could easily be gratified, he was doomed to failure in the second. As he grew older, and became aware of the tragic distance that yawned between the prophetic ideal and the real world, something snapped within him. The magnificent audacity of the Prophets, their unshakable faith in the ultimate triumph of the right, these were not for him. He was too realistic, too sober, perhaps too narrow, for that. Too many years had elapsed since the Prophets had foretold the doom of evil and folly, and still the wicked prospered, while folly sat enthroned in the high places:

> I have seen everything during my vain existence, a righteous man being destroyed for all his righteousness, and a sinner living long for all his wickedness. (7:15)
> Folly is often enthroned on the great heights . . . I have seen slaves on horses, while lords must walk on foot like slaves. (10:6a, 7)

Nor did Koheleth possess the spiritual energy to grow indignant and reprove his God, as did the author of *Job*. At the spectacle of injustice, the Prophets had thundered and pleaded and proclaimed the day of doom, but Koheleth merely smiled. Wrong and corruption, he felt, were eternal, inherent in the scheme of things:

> If you observe the despoiling of the poor and the perversion of justice and right in the state, do not be astonished at the fact, for each guardian of the law is higher than the next, and there are still higher ones above them! (5:7)

Yet Koheleth did not react with a cheap and easy cynicism to human suffering. On other themes he might be light or sarcastic, but here he was in deadly earnest, with a fervor almost prophetic in its intensity:

> Again, I saw all the acts of oppression that are done under the sun. Here are the tears of the oppressed, with none to comfort them; and power in the hands of their oppressors, with none to comfort them. So I praise the dead who have already died, more than the creatures who are still alive. (4:1, 2)

He was yet to encounter other sources of frustration, but none except injustice possessed the power to evoke so bitter a denunciation of life. Henceforth the happiness of a carefree and joyous existence was evermore beclouded for Koheleth by the vision of a world in agony. Koheleth became a cynic, not because he was indifferent to human suffering, but, on the contrary, because he was acutely sensitive to man's cruelty and folly.

But Koheleth had not yet plumbed the full depths of the despair that life was to breed in him. Stronger ever than his love of justice was his love of truth. Possessing a keen mind and a lively curiosity, he eagerly sought after the profounder *Hokmah*, the fundamental insight into the world and its meaning. It was the Wisdom hymned by the Sage, after which Koheleth strove:

> The Lord by Wisdom founded the earth;
> By Understanding He established the heavens. (Pr. 3:19)

Koheleth sought to probe these mysteries, which the more matter-of-fact Ben Sira had advised leaving alone, perhaps because he knew of the perils that lurked in the quest:

> What is too wonderful for you do not seek,
> Nor search after what is hidden from you,
> Seek to understand what is permitted you,
> And have no concern with mysteries. (B. S. 3:20f.)

Job, too, had sought this wisdom in vain:

> Where is Wisdom to be found?
> And where is the place of Understanding? (Job 28:20)

Yet in this very unknowability of the world, Job had found an anodyne for his suffering, a token that there was a rational and just world-order, though on a scale incomprehensible to man. For Job, the grandeur and harmony of the cosmos, created by Divine Wisdom, were signs pointing toward an equally pervasive moral universe, founded on Divine justice. But that faith was not for Koheleth. His fruitless search for justice in human life had grievously wounded his personal happiness. Now came the tragic realization that the all-inclusive Wisdom of the universe was also unattainable:

> I saw that though a man sleep neither by day nor by night, he cannot discover the meaning of God's work which is done under the sun, for the sake of which a man may search hard, but he will not find it; and though a wise man may think he is about to learn it, he will be unable to find it. (8:17)

A deep woe now settled upon the youthful enthusiast, when the futility of his aspirations was borne in upon him. Justice he had sought, but it was nowhere; wisdom he had pursued, but the phantom had vanished. All life was meaningless and futile, and his judgment upon it was devastating:

> Vanity of vanities, says Koheleth, vanity of vanities, all is vanity.
> (1:2, 12:8)
> Hence I hated life, for all the work that is done beneath the sun seemed worthless to me, and everything vanity and a chasing of wind.
> (2:17)

As the spectacle of human cruelty and suffering was revealed to him, he despaired of life:

> More fortunate than both the living and the dead is he who has not yet been born and so has never seen the evil deeds that are being done under the sun. (4:3)

Three great ideas had lighted his way in the world. The love of life was rich with promise of happiness, but the yearning for justice and wisdom had brought him only sorrow and disillusion.

For a space, one can live in a state of complete intellectual nihilism, without values or activities. Few men, however—and Koheleth was not among them—can abide that emptiness indefinitely. The quest for certainty is not abandoned merely because two of its roads have proved blind alleys. Koheleth *had* to discover some definite basis for belief, or at least some rationale of action, if his life was to go on. It could not be wisdom or justice, for these had been weighed and found wanting. He had to retrace his steps to the first great principle of his life, the only law that had not brought him to grief.

So Koheleth returns to his first love, but with a difference. The whole-hearted, instinctive gladness of youth is gone. His love of life is now the result of reflection, the irreducible minimum of his life's philosophy. In the striving for happiness lies the only reasonable goal for human existence. He chants a hymn of joy, but there are overtones

of tragedy, the sad music of the inevitability of old age, the echo of
the cruelty and ignorance of mankind:

> For if a man live many years, let him rejoice in them all, and re-
> member that the days of darkness will be many, and that everything
> thereafter is nothingness. (11:8)
> So I saw that there is nothing better for man than to rejoice in his
> works, for that is his lot, and no one can permit him to see what shall
> be afterwards. (3:22)

Koheleth sets up the attainment of happiness as the goal of human
striving, not merely because he loves life, but because he cannot have
justice and wisdom. Joy is the only purpose that he can find in a
monotonous and meaningless world, in which all human values, such
as wealth, piety, and ability, and vanity, where all men encounter the
same fate and no progress is possible.

To set forth these basic attitudes toward life, the implications of
which will be presented below, Koheleth writes his book in old age,
recapitulating the stages of his spiritual history in the process. As
he contemplates his past career, he has no personal complaint to make;
on the whole, life has been good to him. He has been spared the
degradation of poverty and the terror of insecurity, nor has he ever
had to taste the bitterness of personal tragedy. His charm, insight
and skill have doubtless made him a successful teacher in the Wisdom
academies and brought him tangible as well as intangible rewards.
The competence he has acquired now makes it possible for him to
enjoy the amenities of life—a fine house in Jerusalem, a sense of in-
dependence, and the blessing of unworried leisure. Thus he sits in
the sunset hours of his life, a tiny island of ease and contemplation
within the whirling currents of life in the capital city.

His is a comfortable old age, but there is a quiet loneliness about it.
He has no wife to share either the simple happenings of ordinary
existence or the rare moments of deeper experience. His home has
never reëchoed with the voices of children at play. He has never been
stirred to ecstasy by their laughter or driven to distraction by their
tears. But perhaps, he muses, it is better so, as he recalls the fine brave
rapture of youth and the febrile ambitions of maturity, all now revealed as emptiness and chasing of wind.

From time to time, his former pupils visit him, for Judaism declares it a duty to pay respect to one's former teachers by calling on
them. He looks into the faces of these lads who have since gone forth
to positions of prominence and dignity in the practical world. Some
are important government officials, others are Temple dignitaries,
while others have far-flung economic interests as merchant princes or
landed gentry. As his wise, understanding eyes scan their faces, he
notes that they have paid a high price for success. The shining, care-

free countenances of youth, the sparkling eyes brimful with mischief, are gone. In their stead are worn faces, some drawn, others grown puffy with the years, and tired, unhappy eyes sagging beneath the weight of responsibility. Time was when his pupils were young and he was old, but now the tables are turned. True, Koheleth is a few paces before them in the inexorable procession toward the grave. But in a deeper sense, he is young and they are prematurely old. He knows what they have forgotten, that men's schemes and projects, their petty jealousies and labors, their struggles and heartaches, all are vanity and that joy in life is the one divine commandment.

Before it is too late, he takes pen in hand to transmit the truth, as he sees it, concerning the incomprehensible and indescribably precious blessing called life. For it is his secret wish that men after him, whom his living voice will never reach, may face life with truth as their banner and with a song in their hearts.

> Go, then, eat your bread with joy, and drink your wine with a glad heart, for God has already approved your actions.
> At all times let your clothes be white, and oil on your head not be lacking.
> Enjoy life with the woman you love through all the vain days of your life, which God has given you under the sun, throughout your brief days, for that is your life's reward for your toil under the sun.
> Whatever you are able to do, do with all your might, for there is neither action nor thought nor knowledge nor wisdom in the grave towards which you are moving. (9:7-10)

Doubtless Koheleth would have been the first to confess that in taking such pains to urge the enjoyment of life upon man, at a time when he himself had already passed his prime and reached the days in which there is no pleasure, there lurked more than a little of vanity —in both senses. Fortunately however, the need for self-expression triumphed over the dictates of consistency and so a masterpiece was born.

THE WORLD-VIEW OF KOHELETH

I

The reconstruction of the precise stages in Koheleth's spiritual odyssey that we have proposed is confessedly an act of the imagination, rooted though it be in the facts before us. On the other hand, the conclusions at which he ultimately arrived are clear, for he set them forth in the book he left behind him. Personal experience or reflection, most probably both, had robbed him of the traditional Jewish faith in the triumph of justice in this world, preached by the Prophets, or in the redress of the balance in the hereafter, as affirmed by the forerunners of Pharisaic Judaism, who were his contemporaries. Moreover—and this was a deprivation he felt even more keenly—he had lost the assurance that man could fathom the meaning of life.

The modern reader might expect that Koheleth would be led by his views to deny the existence of God, but that was impossible to an ancient mind, and especially to a Jew. Even the Epicureans, who denied the gods' intervention in human affairs as a fundamental element of their outlook, did not deny their being. In the ancient world, atheism, the denial of God, referred to the view that the gods did not intervene in human affairs. Koheleth, a son of Israel, reared on the words of the Torah, the Prophets and the Sages, could not doubt the reality of God for an instant. For him, the existence of the world was tantamount to the existence of God.

It was on the question of God's relation to men that Koheleth parted company with the conventional teachers of his time. For all the barrage of platitudes of the Wisdom teachers, there was not a shred of proof that God wished to reveal the true *Hokmah,* the secret of life, to men. Similarly, there was tragic evidence to contradict the confident assertion of the moralists:

> Say to the upright that it shall be well with him, for he shall eat the fruit of his doings. Woe to the wicked! It shall be ill with him, for the reward of his hands shall be given him. (*Isa.* 3:10, 11)

The Psalmist had sung:

> I have been young, and now am old, yet I have never seen an upright man forsaken, and his offspring begging bread. (Ps. 37:25)

His words might be a prayer or a pious hope; they were scarcely the result of empirical observation!

With justice in human affairs an illusion, and truth unattainable, Koheleth is left with very little upon which to build. All that is certain is that man has an innate desire for happiness. Since God has created man, He has also created this impulse. It thus becomes clear that God's fundamental purpose for mankind is the furthering of man's pleasure.

We may put it another way: Koheleth's metaphysics postulates the existence of God, coupled with His creative power and limitless sovereignty. But beyond these attributes, Koheleth refuses to affirm anything about his God, except that He has revealed His will to His creatures by implanting in man an ineradicable desire for happiness.

Koheleth's morality accordingly recognizes the pursuit of happiness as the goal. His religion is the combination of his theology and his ethics.

In substance, this is Koheleth's world-view, but setting it forth in systematic abstract categories gives it a lifelessness and a dogmatic cast that are completely alien to Koheleth's personality. For it robs the book of its most attractive qualities, the informality and tentativeness with which the author sets forth his ideas, his amused doubts even with regard to skepticism, his insights into human nature with all its weaknesses and pretenses, and his basic sympathy for men in their lifelong quest for happiness, elusive and fleeting at best. Above all, there is the haunting sadness of one who in earlier years had known and shared larger hopes for man upon earth.

The contradictions that troubled earlier readers are, in part, normal variations in temper and mood and, in part, the consequence of his clearsighted recognition that no one, not even he, has a monopoly on truth. These contrasting passages are not among the least of Koheleth's charms.

Thus the basic theme of the book is its insistence upon the enjoyment of life, of all the good things in the world. There is the love of woman—and the singular is noteworthy—

> Enjoy life with the woman whom you love through all the vain days of your life, which God has given you under the sun,

but the counterpoint of melancholy is never absent:

> Throughout your brief days, for that is your life's reward for your toil under the sun. (9:9)

With a moving sense of the transitoriness of life, he calls for the vigorous and full-blooded enjoyment of all it affords, food and drink, oil and fine clothes, beautiful homes and music:

> Whatever you are able to do, do with all your might, for there is neither action nor thought nor knowledge nor wisdom in the grave toward which you are moving. (9:10)

In practice, Koheleth advocates a moderate course, not very different from the attitude of the Rabbis of the Talmud:

> שלשה דברים מרהיבין דעתו של אדם בית נאה אשה נאה וכלים נאים
> Three things bring a sense of ease and contentment to a man: a beautiful home, an attractive wife, and fine clothes. (Ber. 57b)

What set his standpoint apart from theirs was that his attitude stemmed not from a full-hearted acceptance of the world, as preached by religion, but from a sense of frustration and resignation, induced by his philosophy.

For Koheleth, nothing really counts if truth and righteousness cannot be attained. Yet man lives and God rules, and God's manifest will is man's happiness, not that it matters overmuch, but this at least is certain.

II

In Koheleth, form and substance are so closely interwoven that any restatement becomes a distortion. His view of life is best gathered from his own words, or at least from a summary of the book as he wrote it.

The work opens and closes with his fundamental judgment, "Vanity of vanities, all is vanity" (1:2; 12:8). In the opening section, Koheleth declares that the natural world about us presents a changeless cycle without novelty or progress. The four elements of the universe, the earth, the sun, the wind and the sea, repeat their monotonous courses interminably. Against this background, man's petty strivings are folly (1:2–11).

Koheleth then takes on the role of King Solomon, and tells how he had experimented with wisdom and wealth, goals for which men are wont to struggle and squander their lives. Truth he found unattainable, and wisdom a source of misery. As for physical pleasure, it may offer a temporary satisfaction, but it is not an absolute or enduring good. Nonetheless, it is God who has endowed man with the desire for happiness; to enjoy life is therefore the only commandment of which man can be certain; to fail to obey it is to be a sinner before God (1:12 to 2:26).

Not only are the processes of nature beyond man's power to contravene, but even human actions are preordained. All human activity is useless, above all the search for truth. Only joy remains for man as the gift of God (3:1–15).

Bitterly, Koheleth condemns the world in which the powerful are unjust and the weak victimized. Nor can one be certain of a just retribution in the hereafter, as some would believe. Only joy is a sensible goal in life (3:16 to 4:3).

A favorite doctrine of the preceptors of youth is the value of diligence and hard work. Analysis reveals, however, that the reasons usually advanced for these virtues are worthless. The creative skill in which men glory is largely a disguise for their desire to compete with and outstrip their fellows (4:4). Some men claim to toil for the sake of their families, the advantages of which, Koheleth finds, are much overrated, being largely physical (4:9 ff.). As for the desire for fame, "the last infirmity of noble minds," that is the greatest illusion of all, for all men are quickly forgotten (4:13–16). The conclusion is inescapable—hard work is folly and only ease is sensible (4:4–16).

A few brief comments now follow on the basic institutions of society. Religion is part of the accepted order, and a sensible man should do his duty to the Temple. He should visit the sanctuary at proper intervals, offer his brief prayers, and pay his vows by which the ritual is maintained. Koheleth scorns the religious ecstatic, but even more, the man who evades his obligation (4:17 to 5:6). He then turns to the political scene and finds that corruption is inherent in the very nature of government, with its endless hierarchy of officials. In a difficult verse, he seems to pay tribute to agriculture as the basic pursuit of society (5:7–8).

He now turns to a basic drive in the lives of men. Few vices are more widespread than the lust for wealth, and few bring less genuine satisfaction. Diligence and thrift are hardly more than expressions of greed. Men struggle and toil to amass riches, finding only that the dependents and parasites about them augment their responsibilities, but bring no increased pleasure in life. Greed often drives men into ill-starred ventures that wipe out overnight the patient accumulation of a lifetime. Even if a man does not lose all his fortune, some one else will inherit it all, after he goes down into silence. Whoever his heir, be it his child or kinsman, fundamentally he is a stranger to him (6:2). Hence it is better to seize joy before it is too late forever (5:9 to 6:9).

Man remains incapable of changing the predetermined character of events or even of penetrating the mystery of existence—that is the fundamental tragedy (6:10–12).

There now follows a collection of proverbs dealing with the good life, linked together by the opening word tōbh, "good." These traditional apothegms are made to serve Koheleth's outlook. Man must not expect too much from life in order to avoid disappointment. Since life is unchanging, it is as foolish to weave elaborate hopes for the unborn future as to glorify the dead past. Good and evil are both to be accepted as part of the pattern ordained by God (7:1–14). Man should avoid extremes, whether of saintliness or of wickedness, and strive after "the golden mean." In a world where nothing is predictable to man, hewing close to the center is the safest course (7:15–25).

Koheleth has little confidence in the character of men. Upon women, however, he pours out the vials of his bitterness and wrath —testimony that he had loved them and lost (7:26–29).

With regard to the political status quo, Koheleth urges submission to the king, not merely because of the oath of allegiance that he exacts from his subjects, but because of the royal power. The unpredictability of events and the perils of life in a mysterious universe are reflected and heightened in a royal court, where the ruler's caprice and the intrigues of the courtiers make survival, let alone advancement, a difficult and risky art (8:1–9).

Noting how successful evil-doers are often eulogized as public benefactors in their last rites, Koheleth turns to the problem of reward and punishment. He does not altogether deny the principle of retribution. However, the long delays that occur before God metes out punishment to the sinner and the numerous cases where there is no discernible difference between the lot of the righteous and that of the evil-doer, act as a stimulus for men to do wrong. Hence, the quest for justice is futile—only joy remains (8:10 to 9:3). This latter theme is then expanded in an eloquent call to man to enjoy life with all the zest at his command, before unknown perils crush him and death ends all sensation and activity (9:4–12).

Though Koheleth cannot overcome his natural bias for the wise man as against the fool, he knows how slight is the respect that wisdom commands and how easily all its achievements can be negated by stupidity (9:13 to 10:1).

Another proverb collection, miscellaneous in character, now follows. Koheleth urges the same practical virtues as the conventional Wisdom teachers, but generally on more realistic grounds that are in harmony with his basic viewpoints—man's inability to know the future and his duty to enjoy life while he can (10:2 to 11:6).

In the closing sentences, Koheleth rises to eloquent heights. Joy is God's great commandment for man. The time for joy is youth, the period of vigor and zest. Koheleth, from the vantage point of his own experience, calls upon the youth to "remember his Creator" before the shadows begin to lengthen and presage the end. With the unforgettable "Allegory of Old Age," Koheleth sounds the note of man's inevitable dissolution and death. Vanity of vanities, all is vanity (11:7 to 12:8).

The Epilogue, consisting of the six concluding verses of the book (12:9–14), are an addition by an editor, who knew Koheleth as a Wisdom teacher and a collector and composer of *Hokmah* literature. Fascinated by the book, the editor is fearful lest the reader be led away from the eternal verities and he calls upon him, having heard everything, to fear God and keep His commandments.

III

From this summary it is clear that Koheleth does not present a systematic philosophy in the grand manner of Aristotle, Spinoza, Hegel or Kant, but that is less of a defect than may appear. For nothing is as certain as the fact that the elaborate systems of philosophers upon which they spend their life's energies ultimately pass away, and only scattered insights, minor details in their patterns of thought, become abiding elements in man's approach to reality. Only the flashes of illumination endure to light up men's path in a dark and mysterious world.

Basic to Koheleth, as we have seen, is the skeptical outlook, which, rooted in his temperament, was nurtured also by his position among the well-to-do classes of society. Essentially, a skeptic is one who refuses to be convinced without proof; concerning the shape of things to come, where such evidence cannot be forthcoming, he remains without faith. The skeptic finds it possible to be suspended in a state of perpetual doubt with regard to the future, because as a rule he finds his lot in the present not unbearable. Being generally a beneficiary and not a victim of the status quo, he feels no powerful urge to achieve or even to envisage a better world. That drive tends to arise among the submerged groups in society, who finds existence intolerable without the hope of a change. Koheleth, on the other hand, rejects the older prophetic faith, which expressed itself in such concepts as the End-Time and the Messianic Age. At the same time, he is unable to accept the newer Pharisaic doctrine of life after death or the Apocalyptic faith in the imminent end of the world through a Divine cataclysm. He is, of course, at the farthest remove possible from the mystic, the social reformer or the revolutionary.

Undoubtedly, Koheleth's failure to respond actively to social injustice and political tyranny constitutes a crucial defect, so that our age cannot find in him the motive power toward the building of a better world that is so abundant in the Hebrew prophets. In the face of the towering evils of our own day coupled with the breath-taking vision of a more abundant life for all men, now for the first time within realization, Amos and Isaiah are incomparably more inspiring guides than the disillusioned sage of Jerusalem.

Yet for all Koheleth's remoteness from the fever and the fret of the world and his apparent lack of concern with social problems, his view of life does furnish a basis, at least, for men's age-old struggle against any order in which "man has power over his neighbor to do him harm." For Koheleth, joy is God's categorical imperative for man, not in any anemic or spiritualized sense, but rather as a full-blooded and tangible experience, expressing itself in the play of the body and the activity of the mind, the contemplation of nature and the pleasures of love. Since he insists that the pursuit of happiness with which man has been endowed by his Creator is an escapable sacred duty, it follows that it must be an inalienable right.

To be sure, Koheleth never drew the implications of these premises, in facing the social, economic, and political ills of his day. His conservatism was, as has been noted, an amalgam of intellectual, temperamental and social factors. But had he been confronted by the logic of his position, we may well believe that he would have been too honest to deny the conclusion that a system of society which denies inalienable rights to men is not God-ordained, and that men have the duty as well as the right to change it. He lacked the Prophets' faith that right would triumph, but at least he shared their conviction that it should. His passionate outcry against life because of human oppression (4:1 ff.) should guard us against imagining that he was complacent in the face of oppression. If, as a rule, he deprecated where he should have condemned, he never committed the blasphemy of regarding the status quo as the acme of perfection. He was no apologist for folly enthroned in high places and did not hesitate to call evil by its right name.

Koheleth's principal value, however, lies not in this implication for the social scene, but in his explicit concern with the individual. The temperamental difference between Koheleth and the Prophets must not blind us to the guidance he offers men in meeting those ills that must be transcended because they cannot be transformed. It is true that nowhere does Koheleth preach the virtue of courage in so many words. For him courage is not a conscious ideal, nor even an idea—it is far more, an inborn, pervasive quality. Every line in his book is instinct with the spirit of clear-eyed, brave and joyous acceptance of life, for all its inevitable limitations.

And these limitations are inevitable, however unwilling a youthful and activistic generation may be to confess it. However successful men may become in moulding the pattern of the world nearer heart's desire, they will still encounter pain and frustration in life, in meeting which they will require dignity and courage and the saving grace of good humor. The mounting doubts, fears and tensions of our own day, carried to unconscionable lengths though they may be, have served at least to remind us of this truth.

This need for resignation is independent of any given set of political, social and economic conditions. It inheres in the character of the universe and the nature of man. For he is a creature whose reach is always greater than his grasp, with a boundless imagination weaving hopes and desires far beyond the capacity of his brief, earth-bound existence to fulfill. As Koheleth observes, "All a man's toil is for his wants, but his desires are never satisfied." In teaching men to taste life's joys without self-deception and to face its sorrows without despair, Koheleth performs an everlastingly significant function.

The several factors that played their part in gaining admission for the book of Koheleth to the canon of Scripture have been discussed above. Undoubtedly the tradition of Solomonic authorship and Koheleth's unique style, particularly his unconventional use of a religious vocabulary and his citation of proverbs for his own special purposes, proved decisive factors.

Yet with it all, there was much in the book that was a stumbling-block to the devout. That it was never dislodged may be due in part to the naïveté and lack of historical perspective of many of its readers. But, basically, its preservation is a tribute both to the fascination of the book and to the catholic taste of the creators of the Biblical canon, who saw in every honest seeker after truth a servant of the one source of truth.

Moreover, ancient and medieval readers were not so naïve as their modern successors are wont to believe. That the basic theme of the book was *simhah*, the enjoyment of life, was clearly recognized by Jewish religious authorities who thus explained the custom of reading *Koheleth* in the synagogue on the Feast of Tabernacles, the Season of Rejoicing. But whatever the motives that led to the preservation of the book, we cannot be too grateful.

Koheleth would have been shocked, even amused, to learn that his notebook was canonized as part of Holy Scripture. But the obscure instinct of his people was building more truly than it knew when it stamped his work as sacred. Two millennia after Koheleth's day, a pietistic movement arose in Eastern European Jewry at the farthest possible remove from the temper of the ancient sage of Jerusalem. Yet a classic tale of the Hasidic tradition reveals a remarkable affinity with Koheleth. One day, Rabbi Bunam of Pshysha found his beloved disciple Enoch in tears. The Rabbi asked him, "Why are you weeping?" and Enoch answered, "Am I not a creature of this world, and am I not made with eyes and heart and all limbs, and yet I do not know for what purpose I was created and what good I am in the world." "Fool!" said Rabbi Bunam. "I also go around thus." Thus Koheleth, too, went about, seeking the purpose of life and lamenting his ignorance. His book is the record of his wandering and his sorrow, and of the peace he finally attained.

In the deepest sense, Koheleth is a religious book, because it seeks to grapple with reality. The Psalmist had sung:

> A broken and contrite heart,
> O God, Thou wilt not despise. (Ps. 51:19)

This cry of a sensitive spirit wounded by man's cruelty and ignorance, this distilled essence of an honest and courageous mind, striving to penetrate the secret of the universe, yet unwilling to soar on the wings of faith beyond the limits of the knowable, remains one of man's noblest offerings on the altar of truth.

QOHELETH*

Peter F. Ellis

Almost all we know about Qoheleth is told us by an editor in a brief epilogue. "Besides being wise," he tells us, "Qoheleth taught the people knowledge, and weighed, scrutinized and arranged many proverbs. Qoheleth sought to find pleasing sayings, and write down true sayings with precision" (12:9–10). Unfortunately the description fits any wisdom teacher. However, a further remark of the editor, "The sayings of the wise are like goads" (12:11), is particularly pertinent to Qoheleth and probably reflects the editor's personal reaction to the book.

Qoheleth's sayings are goads and more than goads. They torment the spirit, harass the mind, disturb the heart. They unsettle the complacent, shock the orthodox, and trouble even the wise. It is advisable, therefore, before reading the book, to note the concluding words of this remarkable work: "The last word, when all is heard: Fear God and keep his commandments, for this is man's all; because God will bring to judgment every work, with all its hidden qualities, whether good or bad" (12:13–14).

The reader who does not keep in mind these and other words of Qoheleth (5:1–6; 7:18; 8:12–13; 12:1) may easily misinterpret both the man and his book. We would not be the first to do so. Qoheleth has been labeled among other things: a skeptic, a pessimist, a hedonist, a materialist and, in recent times, the earliest existentialist. He is not any of these for the simple reason that he is a man of faith. He believes in the reality of divine providence (3:11, 14–15; 8:17; 11:5), praises divine wisdom (7:12, 20; 9:13–18), and expects divine judgment (3:17; 11:9; 12:13–14). These things must be remembered if Qoheleth is to be rightly understood.

The name Ecclesiastes is Greek for Qoheleth, a Hebrew word that probably means preacher or leader of the congregation. Possibly he was the head of a group of sages. His remark, "I, Qoheleth, was king over Israel in Jerusalem, and I applied my mind to search and investigate in wisdom all things that are done under the sun" (1:12–13), as well as the

* From *The Men and the Message of the Old Testament* (Collegeville, Minnesota: The Liturgical Press, 1963), pp. 487–490. Reprinted by permission.

title of the book, "The words of David's son, Qoheleth, king in Jerusalem" (1:1), indicate that Qoheleth wished to pose as Solomon, the wise man *par excellence*. It is a poetic fiction as the epilogue clearly indicates (12:9–14). Linguistic indications point to a postexilic origin for the book and most authors would date its composition around 300 B.C.

The theme of the book is the vanity of all things, an expression that means the uselessness, transitoriness, and intrinsic insubstantiality of all things human. A modern author has aptly rendered the expression, "Vanity of vanities," as "the absolute absurdity of it all!" The author pursues this theme relentlessly. All man's labors are vain (1:4–11), wisdom itself only leads to greater perplexity (1:12–18), pleasure brings no enduring satisfaction (2:1–12), the wise man as well as the fool ends up in the grave (2:13–17), the pursuit of wealth is a chase after the wind (2:18–26), the unchanging order of events impresses upon life a lamentable monotony (3:1–13), and the uncertainty of the future places a pall over the present (3:14–22). Thus it goes to the end of the book.

It is a dreary theme for the author. He examines life under the microscope of long experience and finds it unsatisfactory. The realities of life do not correspond to the yearnings of the heart. Man's deepest desires are constantly thwarted by the hard facts of experience, and the timelessness in his heart is frustrated by the time-restricted span of his days. There is a time for everything. And the time for dying sounds a deathknell for his hopes.

It is more than obvious that the author knows nothing about the true nature of the after-life. If he had, he would have said with St. Augustine, "Our hearts are restless, O Lord, until they rest in thee," but he only knows that his heart is restless. He does not know that the timelessness in his heart, the yearning after true satisfaction, the fulfillment of his deepest desires will one day be swallowed up in the timelessness and depthlessness of God.

The basic message of Qoheleth is simple: this world, this life, all its pleasures, all its wonders cannot satisfy the restless heart of man. At bottom, therefore, Qoheleth is concerned with man's happiness as Job is concerned with man's suffering. He can see no lasting, certain, secure happiness in this earthly existence. Even if a man gain the whole world, have all riches, be able to indulge his every desire—even then, Qoheleth would say, he would not be satisfied, he would not be perfectly happy.

The book, therefore, cries out for the revelation of the future life given to the Jews only in the last two centuries before Christ in the books of Daniel (12:2–3), Machabees (6–7), Wisdom (2–5), and in the Gospels. Ignorant of the solution to his insoluble dilemma and his insatiable yearnings, he is forced to satisfy himself with the act of faith contained in the epilogue of his book: "The last word, when all is heard: Fear God and keep his commandments, for this is man's all" (12:3).

It was enough for justification, for Christ stated: "If you keep my commandments, you will abide in my love, as I also have kept my

Father's commandments, and abide in his love." But it was not enough to satisfy Qoheleth's tormented heart. Nor was it the last word. The last word, the word Qoheleth would have rejoiced to hear in his lifetime, was spoken by Christ: "In my Father's house there are many mansions. Were it not so, I should have told you, because I go to prepare a place for you. And if I go and prepare a place for you, I am coming again, and I will take you to myself, that where I am, there you also may be" (John 13:2–3).

It is to the lasting glory of Qoheleth that he sensed and expressed with unforgettable clarity the yearnings of man's heart for the mansions of heaven long before God made them a subject of divine revelation. Indeed, his unflinching appraisal of the hard and inescapable realities of life prepared his readers to answer a resounding "Nothing!" to the question of Christ (Matthew 16:26): "What does it profit a man if he gain the whole world and suffer the loss of his soul?"

The reader must not expect rigid order in Qoheleth. The book does not contain a systematic presentation nor a logical demonstration of the vanity of all things human. It is rather a notebook containing the author's reflections. It may even be the notebook of one of his students. In any event, the book is a collection of more or less related observations after the manner of Pascal's *Pensées*, and it is to be interpreted accordingly.

Anyone who reflects for a moment will realize that proverbs express general truths of experience. They do not always express universal truths. If it is generally true that "absence makes the heart grow fonder," it is equally true to say "out of sight, out of mind." No one ever understood better the relative value of proverbs than Qoheleth. Thus, where we would use adjectives or adverbs to qualify our statements, Qoheleth qualifies one proverb with another. He will say for instance: "Those now dead, I declare more fortunate in death than are the living to be still alive" (4:2); but in another place he qualifies this pessimistic view with the contrary statement: "Indeed, for any among the living there is hope; a live dog is better off than a dead lion" (9:4). Again Qoheleth declares sorrow better than laughter (7:3). Later, however, he commends mirth (8:15).

It would be a mistake to think Qoheleth is contradicting himself. Rather he is dealing with a most delicate subject—the value of life. He knows very well that for some life is a terrible burden. For others the burden is lighter. But for all there is a lack of balance between the good sought for in life and the effort put into the search. The good is never proportionate to the yearnings of man.

Life is essentially vibrant and cannot be pinned down like a butterfly in a laboratory. Qoheleth, therefore, walks around his subject, looks at it from different angles, reflects on it in varying moods. Sometimes his mood inclines him to see the wintry side of life. At other times, it is the springtime that catches his fancy. Sometimes his restlessness is manifested by a subtle inquietude breaking through his reflections and giving them a kind of haunting melancholy. At other times the emptiness of life that afflicts the modern existentialist with a positive nausea gnaws at Qoheleth's vitals and leaves him only the leap of faith to escape the absolute darkness. The key, therefore, to Qoheleth is not a relentlessly logical analysis of his statements but a subtle balancing and weighing of his remarks on the scale provided by the questions: "What does it profit in relation to the restless and timeless spirit of man? Does it result in a permanent, definitive good?"

If the reader will keep this key in mind, he may indeed come to see in Qoheleth "the earliest existentialist." He will not mistake him for a materialist, a hedonist, a pessimist, a stoic, or an epicurean. In the face of the enigma of life, the leap of faith is not a luxury, it is a necessity. "The last word, when all is heard: Fear God and keep his commandments, for this is man's all; because God will bring to judgment every work, with all its hidden qualities, whether good or bad" (12:13–14). Or, as all the wisdom writers tirelessly teach: "The beginning of wisdom is fear of the Lord."

CONSIDERATIONS AND QUESTIONS
FOR DISCUSSION

PESSIMISM AND OPTIMISM

1. Martin states that "for pessimistic theory this is the worst of worlds." Would Koheleth agree with this picture of the world? Notice that later in the essay Martin describes Koheleth as a book of "reflective melancholy." How are the connotations of this phrase different from those evoked by the word pessimism?

2. Can a man become a pessimist by asking too much from life? Is the search for an ultimate meaning or revealed truth more dangerous for a man's mental peace than "doing whatsoever thy hand findeth to do" (9:10)?

3. The pessimist "may derive a pensive satisfaction from the indulgence of morbid feeling." Does Koheleth sit on the sidelines and indulge in melancholy or is he actively concerned with the problems of life?

4. In what places does Koheleth flatly contradict the final definition of pessimism, "the doctrine that existence is fundamentally and essentially evil"? Would it be better to call Koheleth a skeptic than a pessimist?

ECCLESIASTES—FOREIGN INFLUENCES

1. It is important to draw a distinction between parallel themes and influences. Writers from different cultures may express similar ideas which are independently developed because each, as a human being, faces the same problems: the search for meaning in life and an answer for the riddle of death. On the other hand, a thinker may be influenced directly by the writings of his predecessors or indirectly by ideas which are actively discussed by his peers. What ideas in Ecclesiastes are similar to Greek concepts? Egyptian? Babylonian?

2. Should we be surprised to find Greek, Egyptian and Babylonian concepts in one book? If Koheleth had been influenced strongly by Greek philosophy would so many Egyptian and Babylonian ideas be brought in as well? Does the very eclectic nature of the book argue in favor of indirect rather than direct influence? What geographical and historical factors would contribute to the circulation of a common body of knowledge which Koheleth might have used?

3. How does the description by Rankin of the currency of some of the ideas of Koheleth affect your appreciation of the book? Does it help establish the universal appeal of the problems which plague Koheleth and enable the reader to better perceive the truth of the statement "there is no new thing under the sun" (1:9).

ECCLESIASTES AND THE WISDOM OF SOLOMON

1. The affinities of The Wisdom of Solomon with various books of the New Testament, especially the development of the concept of immortality, suggest that the book was written after Ecclesiastes had been received as canonical (at least informally). What is one of the main purposes of the writer of The Wisdom of Solomon according to Plumptre?

2. The author of The Wisdom of Solomon "puts in the mouth of the 'ungodly' what appears in Ecclesiastes as coming from the writer himself." At best, this puts Koheleth in the position of playing the devil's advocate. Can the modern reader accept this interpretation of the book?

3. What are some of the reasons why the opinions of Koheleth were unsatisfactory to the members of the lower wisdom school? Is it because Koheleth refused to draw conclusions or to make any positive statements which he could not support from experience? Must all problems and questions be completely resolved before a work has meaning? Can a clear statement of the questions sometimes be more valuable than patent answers?

4. Does the Book of Ecclesiastes really embody an "easy-going Epicureanism"? Can Koheleth be dismissed as merely a hedonist? In what places does he counsel a moderation far from the popular picture of the Epicurean?

JEWISH INTERPRETERS OF ECCLESIASTES

1. Notice that the Midrash interpretations of Ecclesiastes attempt to find allegorical or literal counterparts to some of the ambiguous passages. What does this effort to force a meaning on a passage which is not clear tell us about man? Koheleth finally decides that man cannot understand the reasons behind life and death. Do readers rebel at being left in such a position?

2. The Targum attempts to give the Book of Ecclesiastes greater meaning in another way. Much information is given about Solomon's position in an attempt to support the historical authority of the writings. There are also attempts to relate Ecclesiastes to other Old Testament books and to draw ethical conclusions. Does this approach also represent

a refusal to accept Koheleth's skeptical conclusions? Is it an effort of man to deny that life may have no meaning which he can understand?

3. Plumptre states that frequently Jewish commentators and interpreters refuse to face facts and assume that they are wiser than the writers they interpret; they claim for themselves "a higher inspiration." How is this illustrated in the Targum paraphrase of Ecclesiastes? If Koheleth on the basis of his experience refuses to make assertive conclusions, is it honest for others to make them for him?

ECCLESIASTES, OR KOHELETH, THE PREACHER

1. In what ways can we consider Koheleth "a radical of his day"? How would he have appeared to his contemporaries? Find parts of Ecclesiastes which express conservative ideas.

2. Why does Koheleth repeat "vanity of vanities; all is vanity" throughout the book? How is this phrase more than a "witty invention of words"?

3. What are some of the interpretations of the images and metaphors found in the picture of old age in Ecclesiastes 11? Does this poem reveal a compassionate side of Koheleth which is not seen in other parts of the book? Relate this passage to the central ideas treated in Ecclesiastes.

4. Are the concluding verses of Ecclesiastes inconsistent with the remainder of the book? What other verses emphasize fear of God and obedience on the part of man?

KOHELETH THE MAN

1. Why is Koheleth's identity important? What can we tell about his life from his writings? Does it affect the meaning of Ecclesiastes if Solomon is not the real author?

2. Proverbs was written by the wisdom academies in Jerusalem. How is Koheleth's relationship to this tradition illustrated in Ecclesiastes? Does he flatly contradict the conclusions of earlier sages or simply question the precepts which are belied by his own experience?

3. Gordis describes Koheleth's "passionate love of life." What parts of the book illustrate this attitude? Can this love of life be reconciled with his pessimistic thoughts?

4. How do Koheleth's love of justice and his profound reaction to the inequities of life illustrate a concern not found in the conclusions of the detached observer who views life from the ivory tower? Quote passages which indicate that even though Koheleth finds evil an inherent part of life, he is greatly disturbed by its presence.

5. Gordis states that after the failure of his search for meaning in life, "Koheleth returns to his first love, but with a difference. The whole-hearted, instinctive gladness of youth is gone." How is this experience analagous to the loss of innocence through the knowledge of good and evil which Adam and Eve experience in the Garden of Eden (Genesis 3)?

THE WORLD-VIEW OF KOHELETH

1. Koheleth has frequently been called a skeptic. In what ways is he skeptical? Does he question the existence of God or does he question man's perception of God? What is the difference between these two questions?

2. What do the contradictions found in Ecclesiastes reveal about truth? Can the lack of consistency in Koheleth's argument be viewed as an added illustration of the lack of any universal truth which man can learn from his own experience?

3. Section II of this chapter is a concise summary of the "form and substance" of Ecclesiastes. Compare this interpretation by Gordis to that of Margoliouth in his article. What important differences do you notice? How has the critical attitude towards the book changed in the last fifty years?

4. In what ways is Koheleth a victim of his age? Does he frequently intellectualize rather than act? How is he caught between the visionary idealism of the older prophetic age and the confident legalism later developed by the Pharisees? Compare ways in which Koheleth's age is similar to our own.

5. What factors were important in the acceptance of Ecclesiastes into the canon of Scripture? Notice that unlike some other commentators, Gordis believes that the creators of the canon were broadminded enough to see "in every honest seeker after truth a servant of the one source of truth."

QOHELETH

1. What verses can you find to justify the following labels for Qoheleth: skeptic, pessimist, hedonist, materialist, existentialist? Would Qoheleth have reacted with "all is vanity"? Can Qoheleth's conclusions really be defined by a single term or even by a single philosophy?

2. Ellis mentions that a contemporary writer has modernized "vanity of vanities" to "the absolute absurdity of it all!" Some existentialists believe that man's efforts to act in a meaningless, "absurd" world often lead to loneliness, anguish and despair. Does Qoheleth react to

his world by concluding that it is absurd, or would he feel that it just seems absurd from man's perspective?

3. In what ways does Ecclesiastes express the restlessness of man in an alien world, a world without fixed values and without hope? Can Qoheleth be contrasted to the Old Testament prophets and the New Testament apostles who move beyond the experiences of this world through faith?

4. Ellis describes Qoheleth as "a man of faith." Do you agree with this statement? In what ways is Qoheleth's faith expressed? How is it a greater act of faith for Qoheleth to conclude "fear God" after discovering the meaninglessness of life than for the lower wisdom writers who expect tangible rewards for their piety?

GENERAL QUESTIONS

1. Is Koheleth a disillusioned idealist? Does he expect too many answers from life? Compare his attitude to that of Gilgamesh, the writer of Proverbs, Marcus Aurelius, the young man in the *Ambitious Guest* and Omar Khayyám.

2. Which of the writings from Part II are pessimistic according to Alexander Martin's definition in *Pessimism and Optimism*? Can you draw any general conclusions about the nature of pessimism from these works?

3. Compare the structure of Ecclesiastes to some of the writings of Part II such as *A Song of the Harper, Meditations,* and *East Coker.* Notice that the first parts question human values and move in the direction of nihilism—the denial of any basis for truth or knowledge. Yet none of the writers stops at this point of emptiness. In what ways do the various works move from this "everlasting no"?

4. Trace the expression of the *carpe diem* theme as an answer to the problems posed in Ecclesiastes and some of the writings in Part II. Which works are hedonistic? Which advocate moderation?

5. Acceptance of the belief in an afterlife is another answer given to the dilemma expressed by Koheleth. How is this concept given different expressions in *The Wisdom of Solomon, Meditations, The City of God,* Donne's *Sermon XIX, Thoughts* of Pascal, *The Vanity of Human Wishes, The Rubáiyát, East Coker* and *The Right Time?*

6. Discuss the Christian interpretation of Ecclesiastes given in Peter Ellis' *Qoheleth.* Does this article help to explain T. S. Eliot's use of Ecclesiastes as a starting point in *East Coker* or Paul Tillich's use of it to explain the "old reality" in *The Right Time?*

7. The young stranger in *The Ambitious Guest* searches for earthly immortality. How is his quest similar to that of Koheleth? Of Gilgamesh? Compare his quest to that described in *The Vanity of Human Wishes* and *The Rubáiyát.*

8. The Hebrews felt it was impious to draw aside the veil which separates God from man. This belief is symbolized by the Holy of Holies in the tabernacle. In what ways is this attitude towards divinity expressed in Ecclesiastes, Proverbs and The Wisdom of Solomon? Do we find the same attitude in *The Rubáiyát?*

9. Discuss the various interpretations of Ecclesiastes, from the *Wisdom of Solomon* (which Plumptre feels is an answer to Koheleth), to *Qoheleth* by Peter Ellis. Which writers seek to superimpose a meaning on the book not supported by the text itself? How does each of these interpretations add to our appreciation of the book today?

10. The essays by O. S. Rankin and Robert Gordis describe the milieu in which Ecclesiastes was written and some information about the author himself. What earlier misconceptions about the book are

dispelled by this information? Discuss the major influences upon Koheleth.

11. The articles by Robert Gordis, Mary Ellen Chase and Peter Ellis mention some reasons for the appeal of Koheleth to modern readers. What parts of the book seem most relevant to twentieth-century man? What parts do T. S. Eliot in *East Coker* and Paul Tillich in *The Right Time* find most relevant?

12. Now that you have studied some of the Related Writings of Part II and the Critical Essays of Part III, reread the book of Ecclesiastes. In the last analysis do you feel that the book is an expression of pessimism or an affirmation of life?

OUTSIDE READINGS

1. Compare Koheleth's search for meaning in life to the quest described in Voltaire's *Candide, or Optimism* (1759). How is the advice of the Turkish farmer at the end of the book, to cultivate one's garden to keep boredom, vice and need at bay, comparable to the conclusions of Koheleth?

2. Samuel Johnson, in *The History of Rasselas, Prince of Abyssinia* (1759), describes the search of Rasselas for happiness. Like Koheleth, the Prince of Abyssinia has the material possessions to make a complete search. Compare the conclusions of Rasselas to those of Koheleth. How are they similar to the conclusions of Johnson's *Vanity of Human Wishes*?

3. The young Indian in Hermann Hesse's *Siddhartha* is unable to accept the conclusions and teachings of others (such as the Buddha) but, like Koheleth, must experience life for himself. He is often bored with the senseless cycle of life, but finally achieves self-fulfillment through renunciation. Siddhartha encounters the same problems as Koheleth; why is he able to achieve the serenity which the writer of Ecclesiastes never really finds?

4. Hemingway uses Ecclesiastes 1:4–7 as the epigraph for his novel *The Sun Also Rises* and even takes his title from verse 5. How is this title more meaningful than *Fiesta*, the original English title of the book? In what way does the title from Ecclesiastes answer the charge of Gertrude Stein (also an epigraph of the novel) "You are all a lost generation"?

5. Meursault in *The Stranger* by Albert Camus is unable to accept the values of his society. How are his reactions similar to Koheleth's "all is vanity"? Compare his reaction to the priest in prison ("I was sure of myself, far surer than he; sure of my present life and of the death that was coming.") to the assertions of Koheleth in Ecclesiastes 9:5ff.

6. In Samuel Beckett's play, *Waiting for Godot*, Vladimir and Estragon wait for something or somebody to act on them. Time is portrayed as arbitrary and hopeless, only to be filled by the antics of the two men. Compare this to Koheleth's attitude towards time as seen in Ecclesiastes 3.

ECCLESIASTES, A SELECTIVE BIBLIOGRAPHY

Barton, George A., *The Book of Ecclesiastes*. Edinburgh: T. & T. Clark, 1908; reprinted, 1959. A volume of the International Critical Commentary which summarizes interpretations of Ecclesiastes until the twentieth century.

The Book of Ecclesiastes and the Canticle of Canticles, commentary by Roland E. Murphy. New York: Paulist Press, 1961. The Confraternity Version text with a succinct interpretation of the book relating Koheleth to the development of Old Testament revelation.

Ecclesiastes, introduction by Irwin Edman. New York: Odyssey Press, 1946. King James Version text with a twenty page essay emphasizing the realism and candor of Koheleth's position.

Forbush, William Byron, *Ecclesiastes in the Metre of Omar*. Boston: Houghton, Mifflin and Co., 1906. A poetical translation with an introduction which points out parallels between Ecclesiastes and *The Rubáiyát*.

Gordis, Robert, *Koheleth—The Man and His World*. New York: Jewish Theological Seminary of America, 1955. Translation of Ecclesiastes and commentary. The long introductory section, "On Reading Koheleth," is an excellent discussion of the major problems of the book and the world of the Hebrew sage.

The Interpreter's Bible, V. Nashville: Abingdon Press, 1956. Parallel texts of King James Version and Revised Standard Version with exegesis and exposition. The introduction discusses the book from a Christian perspective.

Jastrow, Morris, *A Gentle Cynic*. Philadelphia: J. B. Lippincott Co., 1919. A translation of Ecclesiastes omitting parts which the author believed were later additions, and an interpretation emphasizing the difference between Koheleth's skepticism and orthodox Old Testament wisdom writings.

MacDonald, Duncan Black, *The Hebrew Literary Genius*. Princeton: Princeton University Press, 1933. The primary purpose of Koheleth is a self-revelation which involved the development of his experiences, sensations and ideas.

——, *The Hebrew Philosophical Genius*. Princeton: Princeton University Press, 1936. Chapter V on Ecclesiastes emphasizes that the writer was working from already existent bases of Hebrew thought applying to this the skepticism characteristic of the Arab mind.

McNeile, A. H., *An Introduction to Ecclesiastes*. Cambridge: Cambridge University Press, 1904. Ecclesiastes is a natural product of Semitic thought, which resembles Stoicism because Zeno, founder of the Stoics, was a Phoenician born in Cyprus.

Plumptre, E. H., *Ecclesiastes*. Cambridge: Cambridge University Press, 1898. King James Version text with notes and a copious introduction. The appendix compares parts of Ecclesiastes to Shakespeare and Tennyson.

Proverbs, Ecclesiastes, translated with an introduction and notes by R. B. Y. Scott. Garden City, New York: Doubleday & Company, Inc., 1965. A volume of the Anchor Bible which illustrates that Proverbs and Ecclesiastes are instructive in their similarities as well as in their differences.

Rankin, O. S., *Israel's Wisdom Literature*. Edinburgh: T. & T. Clark, 1936. In Ecclesiastes "pessimism dwarfs piety," the pessimism developing from the concept of an omnipotent God before whom man is nothing and feels his nothingness.

Ranston, Harry, *Ecclesiastes and the Early Greek Wisdom Literature*. London: Epworth Press, 1925. Concludes that although Koheleth was not widely acquainted with early Greek literature he drew on Hesiod and Theognis for foreign aphorisms.

Renan, Ernest, *L'Ecclésiaste*. Paris: C. Lévy, 1882. A translation from Hebrew into French. In the introduction Renan anticipates later commentators in his emphasis on the modern tone of Koheleth's skepticism.